D1135390

# SPICE GIRLS

Also by Sean Smith

# The Story of the World's Greatest Girl Band

# SPICE GIRLS

## BY SEAN SMITH

*SUNDAY TIMES* BESTSELLING AUTHOR

HarperCollins*Publishers*

HarperCollins*Publishers*
1 London Bridge Street
London SE1 9GF

www.harpercollins.co.uk

First published by HarperCollins*Publishers* 2019

1 3 5 7 9 10 8 6 4 2

© Sean Smith 2019

Sean Smith asserts the moral right to be
identified as the author of this work

A catalogue record of this book is
available from the British Library

HB ISBN 978-0-00-826756-8
TPB ISBN 978-0-00-826757-5
EB ISBN 978-0-00-826759-9

Printed and bound in Great Britain by
CPI Group (UK) Ltd, Croydon

MIX
Paper from
responsible sources
FSC™ C007454

This book is produced from independently certified FSC™ paper
to ensure responsible forest management.

For more information visit: www.harpercollins.co.uk/green

To Megan

# CONTENTS

PART THREE:
SPICE WOMEN

# PART ONE

## THE WANNABES

# 1

# IRREPRESSIBLE

The five young women who would become the Spice Girls didn't need to be outstanding singers. Nor was proven dancing ability essential. They didn't have to possess supermodel looks or have the wit of a stand-up comedian. They needed to be ordinary girls with a sparkle that could turn them into something extraordinary. They were not easy to find.

Melanie Brown, an irrepressible eighteen-year-old from Leeds, was the first name on the Spice Girls team sheet. She had a spark and exuberance that could poke your eye out. She had no idea that she had the ideal profile to become a member of a new five-piece girl group when she left her parents' house in Kirkstall at the crack of dawn to catch the early coach to London.

She had seen the ad for a 'female pop group' in the *Stage* newspaper – or, at least, her mother Andrea had – but she was just as interested that day in trying out for a spell as a cruise-ship dancer. That job was for the summer months so there would be sun and sea for starters, as well as a regular wage. Still, she had never come across an advertisement for a girl band before so it was worth taking a look at that as well, especially as it was in the same building off Oxford Street.

This was traditionally the time of year when stage-school wannabes would try to secure work for the summer – seaside shows or cruises were the most popular so this was something different. The advertisement didn't mention that one of the places would ideally be filled by a young black girl.

Her colour had seldom been an advantage for Melanie, growing up in some of the tougher areas of Leeds. She was mixed race – not black – an important distinction. The locals were confused by her heritage, not sure whether she was black or white, but that didn't stop her being the innocent target of prejudice and bullying – even being called the N-word. Fortunately, the insults didn't curb her natural high spirits.

While such treatment was upsetting, it didn't signal an unhappy childhood – far from it. She had a loving and supportive family, as well as a best friend, Sherrell Russell, who lived round the corner on the council estate in the Hyde Park area of Leeds where Melanie spent her first few years. The modest family home was a mile from the famous Headingley cricket ground. Sherrell was also mixed race and the two girls became inseparable, forging a lifelong bond. It helped that their mothers were also best friends.

Melanie's parents always encouraged her to fight her own battles, fully aware of the hurdles she would face. Life had been much more difficult for them in facing the full wrath of ignorant discrimination. Her father, Martin Wingrove Brown, was from Nevis, an island in the Caribbean renowned for its beautiful beaches and its reputation as a safe tax haven. As a baby, Martin was left behind to live on a small farm with his grandmother while his parents formed part of the Windrush generation of the 1950s seeking a better life in Britain.

Martin grew up playing cricket on the beach while his parents had to cope with the rampant racism of Britain during the post-war era when a commonplace sign in the windows of guesthouses would read, 'No Irish, No Blacks, No Dogs'. It was a huge cultural change for Martin when his parents decided the time was right for him to join them in the middle of a northern winter. He had just turned nine. His new home was in the depressed and depressing area of Chapeltown in Leeds, where the Yorkshire Ripper committed so many grisly murders in the mid- to late seventies.

Melanie describes her handsome father as a 'cool, charismatic dude'. On a Christmas Eve night out in Chapeltown, Martin, aged nineteen, met seventeen-year-old bubbly blonde Andrea Dixon. The attraction was mutual. She lived in the district of Seacroft, an area on the east side of the city, where the black population was practically non-existent at the time and skinhead gangs were thriving – which Melanie found particularly upsetting as she grew up.

They had been going out for more than two years, as well as taking the daring step of moving in together, before Melanie Janine Brown was born on 29 May 1975 at the Maternity Hospital in Leeds. They married three months later at the city's register office, which was the first time their families had met.

Melanie still recalls being told of bus journeys when, as a baby, she would be handed to Martin to protect him, not her, as he was less likely to attract trouble when he was holding a tiny girl. Fortunately, in time, Martin and baby Melanie were properly accepted by Andrea's family – and she by his, although everyone understood the difficulties they would face.

For much of her childhood, Melanie shared a room with her sister Danielle, who was five years younger. They got on about as well as sisters normally do – Melanie would be mean to her sibling who would run off and tell Dad.

Nobody could fault Martin's work ethic. For most of his adult life he worked as a welder at the Yorkshire Imperial Metals factory in Stourton, a five-mile ride on his bicycle. Melanie proudly declared, 'He worked his backside off to raise his family, never missing a shift.' He would often work double the hours to make sure he could afford the annual summer camping holiday in the seaside resort of Abersoch in west Wales. Many of Melanie's extended family would make the trip, which was the highlight of her year.

Andrea had left school at fifteen and took a number of low-paid jobs to do her bit for the family's finances. She worked at the local C&A clothing store for eighteen years, as well as cleaning in an old people's home. Her earnings would be invaluable when they discovered that their high-spirited daughter had a passion for dancing, which proved to be a good way of channelling her boundless energy. It was the one pursuit guaranteed to tire her out.

Melanie, aged nine, enrolled at the Jean Pearce School of Dance in Horsforth, a ten-minute bus ride up the road from the new family home in Kirkstall, Leeds. Jean was the doyenne of dance in the city. She had set up the school in 1945 and over the years had choreographed many amateur productions and pantos in the north of England.

Jean had also been responsible for the dancing in the popular Yorkshire TV series *Young Showtime*, which helped launch the careers of Joe Longthorne, Bonnie Langford and the *Emmerdale* favourite Malandra Burrows.

She worked wonders with Melanie, barking at her to point her toes and helping her develop the priceless skill for a professional dancer of being able to pick up routines quickly, having been shown the steps just once. She was also anxious to broaden her young pupils' experiences and arranged school trips to see touring productions of *Miss Saigon* and *Cats*. Another valuable contribution Jean made to Melanie's future was in teaching her to do her best at auditions.

At dance classes Melanie made new friends, including a local girl, Charlotte Henderson, who remains her closest friend, despite all the ups and downs of later years. Another was Rebecca Callard, a petite, pretty girl, whose mother is the popular *Coronation Street* actress Beverley Callard, who plays Liz McDonald in the evergreen soap.

The two teenagers saw little of one another at Jean Pearce but became best pals when they started senior school and bumped into each other on the first day. They were the new girls at the Intake High School in the West Leeds district of Bramley. The focus there was less on traditional academic work and more on the arts subjects that interested them – music, drama and dance.

Rebecca, who would go on to become a successful actress, had already appeared on TV, was good fun and introduced Melanie to the delights of smoking Marlboro Lights. She also joined her for sticky-bun binges. The two girls used to spend their lunch money on cakes and pastries and eat the lot in one break. Surprisingly, Melanie never seemed to put on weight. The teenagers were very much partners in crime, even double-dating twin brothers at one time.

Neither girl was considered star material at school. They managed very small roles in a version of the musical *Godspell* but that was about it. The Brown household was not especially musical, and Melanie's love of dance was not matched by an overwhelming desire to become a concert pianist or a professional singer. She didn't have singing lessons until much later, preferring to release her pent-up energy by bashing the drums.

Like most teenagers, she watched *Top of the Pops* every week. Rebecca was a big fan of Bros but Melanie couldn't bear them.

Instead, she preferred two of the biggest female artists of the eighties. Both were strong figures. First was Tracy Chapman, whose multi-million-selling self-titled first album remains a pop classic. She sang 'Fast Car' and 'Talkin' Bout a Revolution' at the seventieth-birthday tribute to Nelson Mandela at Wembley in June 1988 when Melanie was thirteen. They were arguably the highlights of the whole event, especially as she sang them twice, filling in when Stevie Wonder had an equipment problem.

Secondly, Melanie loved Neneh Cherry, who was one of the few mixed-race pop stars at the time. Neneh's father was from Sierra Leone and her mother from Sweden. She had a distinctive style that included large medallions and rugby shirts that Melanie tried earnestly to copy.

Neneh caused a mild sensation when she performed her hit 'Buffalo Stance' on *Top of the Pops* in the autumn of that year. She was the first artist to appear on the show while heavily pregnant, which was not a look normally endorsed by the male-dominated music business. It was a bold move by a young woman who defied convention throughout her career – someone with whom Melanie Brown could readily identify. Nearly ten years later, a pregnant Melanie would follow that particular girl-power lead.

Needless to say, Neneh's 'stance' caused a media storm. One male TV interviewer asked if it was safe for her to go on stage in her condition and received a sharp riposte: 'Of course. I'm not ill.' Neneh later elaborated, 'I didn't feel being pregnant took anything away from my sexuality, who I am, the woman.'

Melanie would stand in front of the mirror in her bedroom at home and pretend to be her favourite star, singing along, just as a million girls would later do when 'Wannabe' by the Spice Girls was an anthem for a young female generation.

Those schooldays were basically happy and uneventful for Melanie, even though she was occasionally chased home from school to her family's house in Kirkstall, a fifteen-minute walk but much faster when you had to run like the wind.

It came as a great shock to everyone, then, when such a vibrant girl tried to take her own life for the first time. Melanie revealed this shocking event in her autobiography *Catch a Fire*, published in 2002 after the Spice Girls had finally split up. Her account is of an unhappy teenager feeling miserable and out of step with a world that didn't understand her. She even fell out with Rebecca over a cruel and thoughtless remark Melanie had made. They didn't speak for seven months.

And then she was nearly expelled from school for her part in composing an obscene poison-pen letter. Life seemed to be going downhill very fast and Melanie started hoarding extra-strong aspirin, building up a stash by taking one or two at a time from the bathroom cabinet. Eventually she had more than enough to overdose, so she wrote a note and took the pills one at a time while she sobbed her heart out.

Luckily her mum had a headache that night and realised what was going on when she went looking for some tablets. Melanie was rushed to hospital where doctors induced her to vomit the undigested pills. Afterwards the suicide attempt became an unspoken secret at home and at school, where nobody discussed it with her.

Looking back, Melanie stressed that nothing was ever so serious that it was worth taking your own life. Her mantra was: 'Never let yourself get like that again, no matter what happens.' It was sound and sensible advice that, sadly, she was unable to follow.

While she would never forget that dramatic event, Melanie resumed normal life as a young teenager. She didn't go out much but went into town to celebrate her fifteenth birthday with

Rebecca, both girls dressed to kill in hot pants. They saw the movie *Ghostbusters II* starring Bill Murray, but their first stop was Pizzaland where, to their surprise, they were able to order drinks, two white wine spritzers. Rebecca recalled, 'Amazingly, I got served that night – the only time ever – and we spent the rest of the night giggling like fools.'

Melanie was restless to achieve. Even though she was not yet sixteen and still at Intake, she wanted to get on with her dancing career, which she saw as a passport to fame. She was in the middle of her GCSE revision when she decided to bunk off school and go for an audition in Blackpool. Her mum covered for her. Martin would have gone ballistic if he had discovered what was happening. He was a great believer in the value of education.

Melanie sailed through the audition and left home for the first time in June 1991, a few weeks after her sixteenth birthday. She spent the summer in Blackpool, dancing in two shows: in the afternoons she dressed in a cheerleader outfit for an open-air rock 'n' roll extravaganza called *The Jump and Jive Show*. For her evening engagement she changed into a catsuit for a pre-show entertainment at the Horseshoe Bar on Pleasure Beach.

The one drawback for Melanie was leaving her home comforts in Leeds to live in digs, although her mum drove over every week to make sure she was eating properly. Her dad was particularly strict with his teenage daughter so it was a relief to have a taste of freedom. Inevitably, his old-fashioned attitude had only fuelled Melanie's rebellious nature.

Back in Leeds she met her first serious boyfriend. She had caught the eye of handsome footballer Steve Mulrain one night when she sneaked out of home to go to the ever-popular Warehouse club in Somers Street. He noticed her straight away: 'She looked sensational. She had on a short tight silver dress with black knee-high boots.'

Melanie pretended not to be bothered, which had the desired effect of grabbing Steve's attention, and by the end of the evening she had agreed to go out on a proper date. He was nearly three years older than her and quite a catch.

Steve had joined Leeds United as an apprentice in the summer of 1991, at a time when the club was one of the top sides in the country. He remained her boyfriend for more than two years and she described him as her first love; a true love. She gushed, 'Our relationship was absolute heaven.'

Originally a Londoner from Lambeth, he never made the jump to the first team, which was a disappointment as Leeds United won the last-ever First Division title in the 1991–2 season. By the end of the following year, he was the only black player on the books of Rochdale in the third division while Leeds were part of the inaugural Premiership.

At the end of her first summer season in Blackpool, Melanie enrolled at the Northern School of Contemporary Dance in Chapeltown Road. The college had been up and running for just six years but already had a growing reputation as the nearest thing to *Fame* in Leeds.

She did not thrive at the college, though, impatient after her spell in Blackpool to get on with her life in show business. She had some money saved from her dancing wages but that soon ran out and she earned some much-needed funds for bus fares and lunches by teaching an aerobics class at the nearby Mandela Community Centre.

She also entered the Miss Leeds Weekly News contest in 1992 and won, much to her surprise, although not to anyone else's because she was a very striking young woman. She was now a Blackpool veteran, a beauty queen and still only seventeen.

Not everything was going so well, however. Like many of her contemporaries, Melanie had to trudge around to auditions,

11

hoping that the next might be *the one*. She soon developed a tough skin when it came to rejections. Her future might have been entirely different if she had won the part of Fiona Middleton, a young hairdresser in *Coronation Street*. Despite getting to the final four, she lost out to another aspiring actress from Leeds, Angela Griffin, who had also been at Intake High. They were never best friends because Angela was in the year below but they once performed a duet in a school production of *Jesus Christ Superstar*.

Angela was also mixed race so, inevitably, she and Melanie often went up for the same part. Usually, neither of them was hired, but on this occasion Angela's success would lead to TV stardom. She started playing Fiona in December 1992 and stayed for six years, appearing in 257 episodes. If Melanie had been successful, there would have been no thoughts of cruise ships, Blackpool or auditions for girl bands. Ironically, Angela impersonated Mel as a Spice Girl in a 1998 celebrity special of *Stars In Their Eyes*.

Melanie, meanwhile, had to be content with some work as an extra. She made several fleeting appearances stacking shelves in Bettabuy's supermarket in *Coronation Street* and had a walk-on role as a policewoman in the locally filmed *A Touch of Frost*.

Closer to home, she took a part-time job in telesales and another as a podium dancer at the Yel Bar in a side street off the city centre. It certainly wasn't a lap-dancing club or anything remotely similar – just a fun night spot where the waiters and waitresses wore swimwear.

Melanie picked up £20 for four hours of dancing on a Friday and Saturday night in front of a mainly male audience. The moment her shift was over, she changed back into an old sweatshirt and jogging bottoms, collected her wages and went home. This was a paid professional job.

Of course, Melanie was very popular with the lads but seemed unmoved by the attention. Lisa Adamczyk, her manager at the club, observed, 'She was a great mover, a very professional dancer, but it was all just an act. At the end of the night she'd be off like a shot to get back to her boyfriend, Steve, who she loved dearly. She'd come across as the wildest girl you'd ever meet but underneath the image was a hard-working girl who was faithful to her boyfriend.'

She was still very much a dancer, never having bothered much with singing, although she started having some lessons to broaden her chances of landing better roles. She danced on *The Bonnie Langford Show* and on *Keith and Orville's Quack Chat Show*, starring the popular ventriloquist and his green baby duck.

Her friend Rebecca had moved to London and Melanie was feeling constrained by Leeds. She was hired for another summer season in Blackpool, this time on *The Billy Pearce Laughter Show* at the Grand Theatre. Billy, the son of Melanie's old dance teacher, was one of the most popular old-school entertainers in the north of England.

This time she would be away from home for four months and so, reluctantly, decided to split up with Steve. She opted for a clean break rather than keep things dragging on when she had ambitions to see the world and be a star – or, at least, a headliner in Blackpool. She did not want to settle for a cosy, settled life in Leeds.

Melanie was very fond of Steven and is nice about him in her memoirs, but she acknowledged that his life took a few wrong turns after his football career was wrecked by injury. He was sent to prison for nine months in 2002. Now working as a decorator, he had been convicted of affray after attacking two men in the street with a machete.

In Blackpool, Melanie enjoyed her new freedom. She was more independent than she had been during her first summer there and enjoyed dating as a single woman, as well as acting as understudy to her show's female star, Claire Cattini. As far as Melanie was concerned, Claire was the epitome of a big star and a role model for the teenager from Leeds, even though she was only a couple of years older.

Melanie fell for another sportsman – this time a professional snooker player from Iceland called Fjölnir Thorgeirsson. Fjöl (pronounced Fee-ol) was very Nordic looking – tall, blond and well built. Melanie fancied him as soon as she saw him in a café on the promenade near the Norbreck Castle Hotel where he was competing in a number of qualifying tournaments for the big professional events.

Blackpool had become an important centre for snooker. The future world champion Ronnie O'Sullivan won an amazing seventy-four out of seventy-six matches at the Norbreck in 1992.

Fjöl wasn't as successful but he did win through to the European Open held in Antwerp in September. He had a walk-over in Round 2 and lost in the next. Melanie knew nothing about snooker but she came to watch him whenever she could get away. She enjoyed a summer of love in a boy-meets-girl sort of way. The chances for any future relationship seemed slim when Fjöl returned to Iceland and promptly suffered a serious motorbike accident, which meant he could not travel.

In fact, it was Melanie who hopped on a plane, as a dancer in a troupe entertaining the armed forces in the Falkland Islands, Bosnia and Northern Ireland. Her last show business job before her life-changing audition was in Lewisham. She had one line in the pantomime *Jack and the Beanstalk* starring Saracen from the hit TV series *Gladiators* – he eventually became a fire-fighter.

Her heart wasn't in it and she was sacked for skipping rehearsals, so it was back to Leeds and scouring the ads again.

Melanie had a habit of landing on her feet but her career to date seemed to be one step forward and one step back. She was still just eighteen but she badly needed something to happen.

# 2

# CASTING THE NET

Imagine you were casting a sit-com. That was what Chris Herbert did. He wanted characters who would appeal to everyone. The series *Friends* wouldn't start until later in 1994 but his idea of throwing together a group of young people with different personalities, characteristics and quirks was very similar to the thinking behind the classic comedy.

He wanted to cover all bases: 'I approached it as if I was a casting director, finding characters that appealed to every colour in the rainbow – finding a gang of girls everyone could relate to. We were looking to create a lifestyle act.'

In the early nineties there was no *The X Factor, The Voice* or *Britain's Got Talent.* The new millennium celebrations would come and go before *Pop Idol* heralded a new era of Saturday night TV in 2001. There was no quick fix to becoming a pop star. None of the young women who became the Spice Girls was likely to thrive in those competitions.

The era of the Spice Girls was closer to *Opportunity Knocks* than one of the new reality talent shows. The old favourite, originally hosted by Hughie Green, left our screens for good in 1990.

Instead, young hopefuls would rush to buy the *Stage* newspaper every week. Chris Herbert, too, would go to auditions, not to grab a spot on a cruise ship but to hand out flyers about his new group and see for himself the sort of personalities who were out there seeking work.

He decided not to limit his search. He went to pubs, clubs, open-mic nights, dance studios – anywhere he could get his message out: 'My number-one focus wasn't looking for singers. I was looking for young girls seeking opportunities within entertainment. I was trying to cast the net as wide as possible.' He even went to Butlins and Blackpool in his search for five stars. He was unlucky not to have come across Melanie before the big audition day.

Chris might have been a young man, filled with enthusiasm and energy for a great new idea, but he wasn't a novice in the music business. He had grown up in that world and was at ease within it, well used to coming home from school and finding pop stars sitting on the sofa enjoying a cuppa.

His father, Bob Herbert, was a millionaire accountant, drove a Rolls-Royce and had a penchant for wearing white suits. Geri Halliwell memorably described him as looking like an extra from *Miami Vice*, the American cop show from the eighties that perfectly captured an era obsessed with designer fashion.

More pertinently from the point of view of the future Spice Girls, he had experience of nurturing young talent. He spotted the potential of two of his son's teenage friends at the Collingwood College in Camberley, Surrey. They were twin brothers, Matt and Luke Goss. At the time they were only fifteen but Bob could see they had the looks to engage a strong female following.

Bob was of the music school that was always seeking to copy a successful formula. He saw the twins as a late eighties version of the Bay City Rollers, the teen heartthrobs of the previous decade. When the brothers formed a band called Gloss, with young bassist Craig Logan (Goss with an L for Logan), Bob stepped in to offer them advice and, more importantly, space to rehearse in his summerhouse. He helped to plot their futures, introduced them to songwriters and financed their demo tapes but, because of their age, could not sign them to a binding legal contract until they were eighteen. When they came of age they were snapped up by Tom Watkins, former manager of the Pet Shop Boys, who secured them a deal with CBS.

The whole nightmare sequence of events would come back to haunt Bob with the Spice Girls. Under the new name of Bros, the boys released their first single, ironically titled 'I Owe You Nothing', which, when re-released in 1988, would be their only UK number one. At this time, a very large poster of Matt Goss was adorning the bedroom wall of an ambitious teenager called Victoria Adams.

Undaunted, Bob decided to have another go at finding an all-conquering band. After his son left college, they went into partnership, forming a management company called Heart, with offices in the Surrey town of Lightwater. Bob was keen to develop a project for his son to take on but, like all good accountants, he preferred to find someone else to absorb the financial risk. He immediately thought of his old music compadre, Chic Murphy.

Tall and silver-haired, Chic had a tiny cross tattooed on his earlobe and spoke in an *EastEnders* Cockney accent, but he frequented the upmarket Surrey haunts more usually associated with stockbrokers and golfers. Chris Herbert describes Chic as 'old school', which in music-business terms means he played it tough and preferred an environment in which the artists had very little control over their destiny.

He had made his first fortune importing big American cars into the UK. Subsequently, he had seen the business possibilities of bringing US pop acts across the Atlantic. In the eighties he signed up chart regulars like the Drifters, who were plying their trade in Las Vegas, and brought them over to the blossoming cabaret club scene where venues like Caesar's Palace in Dunstable or Blazers in Windsor could pack in a thousand people a night. It was very lucrative.

From the point of view of the future Spice Girls, his most important involvement was with the Three Degrees, the popular UK girl group of the seventies. The trio, modelled more or less on the Supremes, were originally part of the Philadelphia stable, a rival of Motown in the US. They had their biggest hit in the UK, however, in 1974 topping the charts with the disco favourite 'When Will I See You Again' before Melanie Brown and Emma Bunton were born.

The public profile of the Three Degrees increased greatly when the media decided they were the favourite group of Prince Charles. This might not have done wonders for their musical credibility but took them off the pages of *NME* and *Melody Maker* and into the columns of the national newspapers. They became much more famous. Prince Charles invited them to perform at his thirtieth birthday party at Buckingham Palace in 1978, and they were subsequently guests at his wedding to Lady Diana Spencer three years later. It would not be the last time the Prince gave an all-girl group the oxygen of priceless publicity.

By the end of the seventies the Three Degrees were moving inevitably towards the cabaret circuit. They were still very popular, though – the sort of act that always gets work – and throughout the eighties Chic Murphy had been a familiar figure at their gigs. Bob Herbert, who did all the accounts for the nightclubs, became part of the group's management team and forged a long-standing alliance with Chic.

If Bob and Chic had decided things, the new band would have been the Spice Boys. The initial conversation in the offices of Heart Management was about putting a boy band together. In late 1993 Take That were everywhere, with three number-one singles in a row and the platinum-selling album *Everything Changes*. The entire music world was looking to jump on the bandwagon of their popularity.

Fortunately, for five ambitious young women, Chris Herbert had a better idea: 'A boy band seemed like the obvious route into the market but I wasn't that keen on it because I thought we were sort of late to the party. There were loads of them.' As well as Take That, there was East 17, Bad Boys Inc and Worlds Apart, with the prospect of another arriving any minute, like a double-decker bus in Piccadilly. Chris explained, 'My feeling was that boy bands of the time were only really appealing to 50 per cent of the market – a female audience. I wanted to put a girl band together that was a bit feisty, sexy and sassy so that they could appeal to both a female and male audience. The girls could relate to them and aspire to be them. The guys would just adore them.'

Bob and, in particular, Chic took a lot of convincing that a girl band was the way forward. Chris observed, 'They were kind of following the market and it just seemed fairly radical that we should be doing the absolute opposite of that.' The first thing they wanted to know was the strength of the opposition. It was anything but strong. An all-girl group called Milan were signed to Polydor in 1992 and looked promising for a couple of years, featuring a teenage Martine McCutcheon before she found stardom playing Tiffany in *EastEnders*. They opened for East 17 on tour but a few singles failed to set the charts alight and they folded in 1994.

Eternal represented more serious opposition. They had already achieved a couple of top-ten singles and their first album *Always and Forever* peaked at number two. Chris, however, did not see them as direct competition. Despite being very glamorous and including the lads-mag favourite Louise Nurding, they were basically a soulful vocal group specialising in R&B. 'They were pretty slick and smooth,' observed Chris. 'I felt we needed more character.'

Eventually he got his way. 'My dad was probably the first to come round to the idea, Chic less so. His approach was "Well, OK, go out and see what you can find and we'll reassess it." Actually, Chic was like that all the way through. He kind of let me out on a rein to go and do it and then was slightly cynical but I suppose he was prepared to see what turned up.'

At first, it seemed as if it was going to be a hard slog – until he paid £174 to place his own advertisement in the *Stage*. The now famous ad that would eventually lead to the formation of the Spice Girls appeared on 24 February 1994. It read:

R.U. 18–23 WITH THE ABILITY
TO SING/DANCE
R.U. STREETWISE, OUTGOING,
AMBITIOUS & DEDICATED

HEART MANAGEMENT LTD
are a widely successful
Music Industry Management Consortium
currently forming a choreographed, Singing/Dancing,
all Female Pop Act for a Record Recording Deal.

OPEN AUDITION
DANCE WORKS, 16 Balderton Street,
FRIDAY 4TH MARCH
11.00 a.m.–5.30 p.m.

PLEASE BRING SHEET MUSIC
OR BACKING CASSETTE

On the day, more than four hundred young hopefuls queued on the stairs of the studio off Oxford Street to impress the 'panel', consisting of Bob, Chris and his fiancée Shelley, who was a stylist. The girls were divided into groups of ten and put through their dancing paces to the sound of Eternal's début hit 'Stay'. The numbers were reduced to fifty before they were asked to do an individual song.

The panel kept rudimentary scorecards that would judge the girls on four categories: singing, dancing, looks and personality. It was the best and quickest way to whittle down the possibles into a short list. Melanie Brown performed her now regular audition song, 'The Greatest Love of All' by Whitney Houston. Chris gave her eight out of ten across the board.

She obviously stood out. It wasn't just that she fitted his vision for the make-up of the group. She had a personality and charisma that shone. Chris recalled, 'For me, she was the one who walked in and seemed the full package. She was good but she also just had the look. Her image was on point. She could sing and she had a big personality. On the day, I immediately thought, We have found one.'

Melanie had enjoyed the experience so much that she decided to skip the afternoon audition for the cruise ship, preferring to chat to some of the other girls before making her way back to Victoria station to get the coach home. Chris had told her he would be in touch and Melanie was confident she'd got it. She was right.

# 3

# MEIN HERR

---

Victoria Adams-Wood, as she was calling herself then, carried herself differently from the other hopefuls at the Danceworks audition. She was a curvy nineteen-year old, strikingly dressed all in black, with a crop-top showing off her very tanned midriff.

On his mood board back at the office, Chris Herbert had been toying with the idea that one of the group should appeal to the more mature man. He was looking for a young woman who might turn the head of a male consumer with a dash of discernment. You don't need to be posh to have a touch of class and that was the quality Chris was seeking.

Victoria came from a North London working-class background. Her dad Tony Adams, the son of a factory worker, had been brought up in a two-bedroom house in Edmonton that had no bathroom, an outside toilet and no heating. These were the austere years that followed the end of the Second World War when money was rationed just as much as food had been during the conflict.

In 1957 when Tony was eleven, Prime Minister Harold Macmillan famously said, 'Most of our people have never had it so good,' which was small consolation for the youngster hanging around outside the pub waiting for his father to finish his pint. Sometimes he would be pressed into collecting cigarette butts from the overflowing ashtrays for his dad to smoke. Truly, Edmonton was a place to aspire to leave in order to make something of yourself in the world – and that was what he did.

Despite its drawbacks, Edmonton then had a strong sense of community and families had pride in their modest surroundings. The planners of sixties Britain have much to answer for in retrospect, bulldozing away those strong neighbourhood bonds in favour of anonymous tower blocks. Families there pulled together and survived together. Tony absorbed that spirit and passed it on to his eldest daughter.

Tony left school to train as an electrician but dreamt of being a pop star. He was unlucky. He shone as the lead singer in two groups, first in the Calettos and then in the Soniks, which was mainly a covers band. The biggest gig he played was at the famous Lyceum Ballroom on the Strand in London.

He caught the attention of the legendary impresario and manager Joe Meek, who had been responsible for one of the biggest hits of the sixties, 'Telstar' by the Tornados, the first US number one by a British group. Joe signed Tony to a contract but, unknown to many in the music business, his life was falling apart because of money problems and blackmail relating to his homosexuality. In February 1967 he murdered his landlady, Violet Shenton, then killed himself with a shotgun.

The difficulty for Tony, who had just recorded his first demo, was that he was under contract at the time and subsequent legal red tape prevented him from recording for five years. This huge disappointment meant that he was always extremely careful when it came to business and, in particular, contracts – a trait inherited by his daughter that would prove to be vital in the progress of the future Spice Girls.

Tony picked up his trade again, working as a rep for an electrical company. He already had ambitions to start his own company, supported by his girlfriend Jackie Cannon, a trainee hairdresser from Tottenham, who soon gave that up to join an insurance company in central London.

Jackie's father, George, was a stevedore in the docks, loading and unloading ships. He worked all hours to improve his family's life, an ethic that Tony and Jackie followed over the years, in much the same way as Melanie Brown's parents. Tony and Jackie married in 1970 but waited four years to start a family, building a better future by moving out of London before their daughter Victoria Caroline was born on 17 April 1974 in the Princess Alexandra Hospital in Harlow, which technically made her an Essex girl.

In 1977, when Victoria was three, Tony bought the Old School House in Goff's Oak, Hertfordshire. The place needed a lot of work but he had the skills and the contacts in the building trade to do it up himself. But, perhaps more importantly, it had a large garage, which would become the hub of his new electrical-supply company.

Goff's Oak liked to call itself a village but was quite suburban, if full of people doing rather well for themselves. One ex-teacher at the local school observed witheringly, 'Wait outside the school gates on any given day and you'd wish you had shares in a fake-tan company and one making leather trousers. They are women with too much time on their hands. They have nothing better to do than shop and get their hair and nails done.'

The media would always make much of Victoria being dropped off at school in her dad's Rolls-Royce. That was much later. For now, she was driven in her father's old Hillman, which also doubled as his delivery van. Victoria was a quiet little girl, who struggled with a lack of confidence, particularly in English, and took extra lessons in reading, comprehension and spelling. She was a million miles away from the outspoken woman with the ready wit she would later become.

Tony loved listening to the Beatles and Stevie Wonder, and would dance his little girl around the house to the sound of the great Motown star's hit 'Sir Duke', which Jackie said gave her daughter her love of performing. One teacher, Sue Bailey, recalled, 'She always loved acting and enjoyed our drama lessons. She liked to sing and dance. She shone one year as Frosty the Snowman. She was a very sweet girl.'

Victoria was inspired by the iconic film *Fame*. She envied the energy and the exuberance of the students skipping down the corridors of the High School for the Performing Arts in New York. She wanted to be Coco, the multi-talented character played so memorably by Irene Cara. It's easy to imagine the Spice Girls dancing on the desks and singing in the streets with the rest of the students.

She stuck a poster on her bedroom wall of the dashingly handsome Gene Anthony Ray, who played Leroy in the film and the subsequent TV spin-off. Ironically, Gene became a victim of his own fame, sinking into a life of drink and drugs and dying young, at forty-one.

Victoria was obsessed by the TV show, taping every episode so that she could learn all the songs and the dance routines. She persuaded her mum to take her to see the Kids from *Fame* on tour and subsequently badgered her into finding a 'Fame' school near Goff's Oak. They couldn't find an exact match but the Jason Theatre School a few miles up the road in Broxbourne seemed the best option for a nine-year-old.

Rather like the Jean Pearce School in Leeds, the Jason had been running for more than thirty years, founded in North London by greatly respected local dance teacher Joy Spriggs.

From the first class, Joy identified Victoria as one of her most eager students, prepared to work her tap shoes off to improve: 'At the time, all the children wanted to do jazz dancing, with the ankle warmers and the leotards and the colourful catsuits. There was Hot Gossip on television and they wanted to copy that. It was the style of the time.'

Victoria may not have been the most talented dancer ever to grace the Jason Theatre School but she made a dramatic improvement through hard work, determination and old-fashioned practice. Quite simply, the harder Victoria worked, the better she became. Joy observed, 'She had a certain natural ability and we just channelled it in the right way. Victoria would shine because she was a very pretty little girl, with big dark brown eyes and long dark curly hair, but she was a little bit self-conscious to start with. She didn't hold back but she wasn't quite as confident as some of the others. We had to build that confidence with her.'

Her self-belief was boosted when the Jason Theatre School linked up with the local amateur dramatic society for productions of *Hello Dolly*, *Sleeping Beauty* and *The Wizard of Oz*, in which she played a Munchkin. Her ambition was also fuelled by trips to the West End to see the most popular musicals of the eighties – *Cats*, *Les Misérables*, *Starlight Express* and *Miss Saigon*.

Week after week, dancing provided a welcome escape from real school for Victoria. After the relatively quiet waters of primary school, her parents decided to send her to St Mary's High School in Cheshunt where she stood out like a beacon, unhappily.

By this time Tony's business was thriving and the family had plenty of money. The Old School House was now one of the grandest homes in the village, with a swimming pool in the back garden and the Rolls-Royce, with its personalised number plate, in the driveway. It was his pride and joy, although Victoria maintained she hated it.

She had to say that because it might have alienated a million potential Spice Girls fans to hear tales of Daddy dropping her off in the Rolls-Royce. Victoria has always been careful not to describe any days that began with a ride in the Roller and ended with a dip in the pool.

One of her best friends growing up, Emma Comolli, recalled that, perhaps unwisely, Victoria would talk about how rich her family was and how she was going to be famous one day: 'The other children would turn on her and call her names.'

Another girl said simply, 'Victoria was considered snooty.'

The full extent of the bullying Victoria suffered at school is a grey area. She was certainly verbally abused but her younger sister Louise recalled, 'I don't think she was bullied that badly.'

In the early days at the Old School House the two girls shared a bedroom, but that changed when Tony had finished the remodelling and Victoria had her own pink explosion of a room with giant posters of Bros and Ryan Giggs vying for space with Gene Anthony Ray.

Louise fitted in well at school and found herself having to stick up for her elder sibling. Their different personalities highlight why Victoria had a tough time. Ironically, considering the pack appeal of the Spice Girls, she was never one of the girls. She had a natural shyness that could be exploited by others, but beneath that apparent vulnerability was a girl who was thoroughly determined and as tough as old boots.

Fortunately, there was some enjoyment to be had at school in its lavish dramatic productions. Victoria was one of the best dancers in *Les Misérables* and *Jesus Christ Superstar*. Her passion for dancing was a double-edged sword. It gave her a sense of escape but also meant she seldom socialised with classmates.

Boys were not on the agenda, although she did have a date aged fifteen with an American pupil called Franco McCurio who took her to the movies. The most memorable thing about it was that it marked the first time she had ever been on a bus.

Victoria met her first proper boyfriend in the kitchen of the Old School House when she was sixteen. Mark Wood had come to fit a burglar alarm. He was three years older, six foot two, and the epitome of tall, dark and handsome. They started chatting and she readily agreed when he asked her out on a date.

She didn't have to travel by bus, which was a relief, when they went out for a drink to a wine bar. Instead, he picked her up in his dad's white van, having taken the ladders off the roof for the occasion. Technically, Victoria was too young to be served alcohol but that didn't stop her getting tipsy, although Mark did not take advantage.

Being in a committed relationship with Mark was not necessarily the most important thing in her life that year. She was determined to leave St Mary's to further her chances of a career in show business. She set her heart on going to a stage school. She still regretted not going to a 'Fame' school like the Sylvia Young Theatre School or the Italia Conti.

Victoria did a tour of the leading 'finishing' schools in and around London before deciding to apply to Laine Theatre Arts in Epsom. Joy Spriggs approved: 'Laine is the crème de la crème really.' The audition was itself an ordeal and a good grounding for more nerve-racking battles later on. One fellow student from Victoria's year recalled that Betty Laine had a fiery disposition: 'You wouldn't want to cross her. She and the teachers present managed to convey a sort of good-cop-bad-cop aura. She was the bad cop!'

Not for the last time, Victoria had no idea if she had made a good impression so she was thrilled when she was accepted. Joy

Spriggs and her other mentors at the Jason Theatre School were equally delighted, especially as Victoria was one of three that year considered promising enough to win grants from the local education authority. Joy observed, 'I know her parents would have paid for her to go there but she deserved her place. She'd worked hard for it and it is so competitive. For the school to get three in with scholarships was quite something. They were a talented bunch.'

Victoria's successful application demolishes the opinion that she has no talent or was in some way lucky to achieve any success. Laine accepted only serious, dedicated and talented young people. It had its Premier League reputation to maintain.

Leaving the Jason Theatre School was quite a wrench. It had been her comfort blanket and her inspiration for nine years. She never forgot how much it meant to her and in 2001, as a world-wide superstar, she went back to present the prizes when the school celebrated its fiftieth anniversary. Joy gave her the Jason Anniversary Award – the equivalent of a lifetime achievement award. Victoria told the girls, 'I wanted to come to the school to give back something that they've given me.'

She was not so sorry to leave St Mary's, although she managed five GCSE passes and won a cookery prize. She left school and home at the same age as Melanie Brown but there was a world of difference between the bright lights of Blackpool and the gentle Surrey town of Epsom. It was too far to commute from Goff's Oak so Tony drove her to some lodgings.

Victoria was quite young and protected for her age. One friend from Goff's Oak remembered, 'She was quite naïve when she went to college, not very streetwise at all.' She made sure she went home every weekend. Slow to settle in, she rang Mark in tears. He recalled, 'The teachers told her she was too fat. She had put on a few pounds after going on the pill. She said the other girls were awful and she wanted to come home.'

Even the slimmest of girls would be told to watch their weight at a dancing college. It's the last thing any young woman would want to hear but Victoria was not being singled out. She was a healthy size twelve. By no stretch of the imagination was she fat – but in dancing terms she was not one of the slender visions that glide around in tutus.

Joy Spriggs explained that dance colleges would tell all the female students that they needed to lose weight if they wanted to get work: 'They just want the girls to be slim, particularly if they are doing lift work. The boys won't want to lift them if they're overweight, will they?'

The girls lived in fear of putting on a few pounds. One fellow student explained, 'It was generally accepted that if you put on a little too much weight in the holidays then Betty would have no qualms in telling you that you were too fat and needed to sort it out ASAP. We were constantly fretting about this possibility.'

Victoria liked a McDonald's when she was out – there was a convenient branch on Epsom High Street – and her mum's meals when she was home. She enjoyed cooking for Mark, particularly pasta. And she loved chocolate, so dieting was not an easy prospect. Like many of her peers, she took up smoking cigarettes to try to suppress hunger pangs. It was bad enough having to deal with the teenage nightmare of acne without having to worry about weight too. She was becoming very body-conscious.

Victoria did not stand out among many fine dancers in her year but she did excel in one of the courses at Laine's. She was the star pupil in image classes. Betty Laine explained, 'She was always very conscious of image, which is, of course, paramount to success. If they are going into the pop world, image is very important. She took it extremely seriously. She was always first or second in our image classes.'

Now seventeen, Victoria was beginning to get a better grip on things. Her parents had bought her a Fiat Uno and some driving lessons for her birthday. They also splashed out on a flat in Epsom where she lived with four girls from college. That meant they could visit her regularly and so could Mark.

She was also developing her image and plotting her professional future. She had some photographs taken locally by Geoff Marchant, whom most of the students used for their portfolios. She knew the look she wanted or, more precisely, the one she didn't. Geoff recalled, 'She didn't want to make herself girly and she didn't want to make herself pretty-pretty. She wanted this moody sort of expression, even though it meant there was a lot of shadow, which didn't help her skin at all.'

Eventually Geoff persuaded Victoria that it might be a good idea to smile for a few shots in case an agent down the line asked her for something more cheerful. She insisted on wearing black for almost all of the pictures, though. At the time Geoff thought she was quite a cold young lady, but his view changed: 'I think it may well have been a mixture of shyness and determination.'

Victoria had a very privileged lifestyle. For her eighteenth-birthday treat her parents arranged for her and Mark to go by Eurostar to stay in Paris. For his twenty-first, Victoria organised a surprise dinner at a West End restaurant and invited his closest friends. They spent their summer holiday at Tony and Jackie's villa on the Costa del Sol in southern Spain.

Mark was treated as one of the family. He was now living full time at the Old School House – a big step for an eighteen-year-old girl and an even bigger one for her parents. When they got back from Spain, looking fit and tanned, she took Mark along to see Geoff Marchant for some shots, separate and together. This time round, Victoria was much more relaxed. It seemed she had designs on her boyfriend becoming a male model, although Geoff thought he lacked the extra something to make it in that competitive world.

Victoria needed to think about her own career. Despite the very obvious advantage of having wealthy parents, she retained her own personal ambitions. During her last days at Laine's she started trying out for professional shows and, like her peers, pored over the pages of the *Stage* for likely auditions. She wasn't sure if her future lay in pop or musicals.

One advertisement caught her eye but it seemed a little ambitious. She went to a call for *Bertie*, a new musical starring Anita Harris about the famous music-hall performer Vesta Tilley. Victoria was auditioning to be part of the 'company', one of the all-singing, all-dancing members of the chorus. She had continued to develop her image: she had the look (moody), she had the costume (all black), and she had the perfect song to match ('Mein Herr'). She had decided on the classic song from *Cabaret* as her principal audition piece; it would prove to be an inspired choice in the future. She liked the song particularly because she felt she could put it across well, a legacy of all the drama classes she had taken over the years. As Joy Spriggs shrewdly observed, 'She was always very good at drama. She used to do very, very well in all of her exams. I mean, she's acting all the time, isn't she really? She's acting her persona. Yes, she's role-playing.'

To her delight, she received a phone call at the Old School House saying she had got *Bertie*. She had just turned nineteen and was technically still at Laine's so this was a considerable achievement. She would be going into a real show, not killing time on a cruise ship.

Unlike Melanie Brown, who gave up her boyfriend when ambition and Blackpool beckoned, Victoria decided to get engaged. Mark maintained, 'I knew Toria was the one for me. She was the sweetest girl I had ever met and all I wanted was for her to be my wife.' His proposal was not a surprise because they had already designed a £1500 engagement ring together. He had also asked Tony for his daughter's hand in marriage.

He got down on one knee at a romantic candlelit dinner at a restaurant near Tower Bridge and she accepted. Tony and Jackie threw a champagne pool party so that all their friends could celebrate the good news. Everyone seemed genuinely delighted, except perhaps her sister Louise, who had never warmed to Mark.

In her autobiography *Learning to Fly*, Victoria said, 'I never for one moment thought that I would marry Mark.' The engagement seemed to be an acknowledgement that they were in a strong relationship and was one less thing to think about when her career was moving forward. Even though they were not married, she decided to add his name to hers.

All seemed set fair during *Bertie*'s six-week run at the Alexandra Theatre in Birmingham. Victoria was paid £250 a week, her first real wage, and was looking forward to her West End début. Without warning, the transfer to London was cancelled. It was back to the drawing board, poring over the new issue of the *Stage* and taking some promotional work handing out leaflets or plugging products. She even worked for the *Daily Mirror* on promotional visits to newsagents, wearing a T-shirt two sizes too small for her.

In August 1993 she noticed a small ad seeking a girl singer for a new group. This was six months before Chris Herbert's. She had harboured a secret ambition to break into pop so sent in a CV and a picture of herself dressed in black, naturally, sporting a pair of sunglasses in the manner of her fashion idol Audrey Hepburn. It did the trick and she was called for an audition.

The ad had been placed by Steven Andrews, a professional model from South London, who wanted to be a pop star. Victoria sang 'Mein Herr' as usual and also danced to the club hit 'Let Me Be Your Fantasy' by Baby D. Steven was impressed – even more so when at a call-back she stood out from a dozen other girls performing the crowd-pleasing classic 'Band of Gold' by Freda Payne.

Victoria was hired as lead singer, although, in a precursor for what was to happen later, nothing was signed and there was no immediate prospect of a deal. Twice a week, the new group of three boys and two girls would meet to rehearse. It proved to be an excellent grounding for her future. Steven recalled, 'She was never late or moody. She just got on with it. Everybody pulled together.'

Steven did think that Victoria lacked confidence in front of the microphone. He was more concerned, however, that the only time she seemed to get upset was when Mark was there, sitting in. He put it down to Mark's possessiveness and hated him turning up. A clue to Mark and Victoria's relationship is found in the birthday card she gave him for his twenty-second birthday, which he later revealed to the world. It read, 'I'll still love you when you're old! Lots of love, your Little Pop Star! Victoria xxx'

Considering how Victoria's abilities were questioned by the media in future years, she was the only one of the future superstars who was actually already the singer in a band when Chris Herbert put the group together. That experience did not mean she was feeling positive during the audition.

She had no idea she was making an impact, although she did notice that girls with what she perceived to be far better voices were picking up their bags and melting away into the Oxford Street afternoon. Her 'look' was keeping her in, and the fact that she coped comfortably with the dance steps they were required to do.

After performing 'Mein Herr', she packed up to leave and Chris told her he would be in touch. He meant it. She might not have made as big an impression as Melanie Brown had, but she was not far behind.

# 4

# IN SEARCH OF THE MAGICAL KEY

---

Back at the office in Lightwater, Chris started to sift through his notes and scoresheets to decide on the best twelve contenders for a second audition. The idea was to have a closer look at the probables and possibles and, obviously, come up with a final five. He couldn't help noticing that his secretary, Louise, was still fielding calls from a persistent young woman from Watford. To his surprise, they seemed to be building a nice rapport.

Eventually Chris's curiosity got the better of him and he told her to put the girl through. He soon discovered for himself that Geri Halliwell was a force of nature. She had seen the original advertisement in the *Stage* and had kept in touch to let them know how keen she was, but on the day she was nowhere to be seen.

Several possible explanations for her absence were volunteered. One was that she had been on a skiing trip and suffered sunburn. Another was that she had needed to make a flying visit to her grandmother in Spain. Chris was impressed by her audacity in keeping her foot in the door. He could see from the photos she sent in that she was sexy without being Hollywood glamorous.

'She was very bubbly on the phone and we wanted to see her. It didn't dawn on me at the time but I think she obviously knew she would have failed in an early-round audition and she wanted to bypass that. I think she'd worked that one out and I think that was her strategy.'

Geri almost admitted as much when she said, 'I didn't think I would have got an audition because my vocal technique was not very good then.' If it was her game plan, it paid off because Chris took a chance and invited her to the call-back at Nomis Studios in West London.

Unlike Melanie Brown and Victoria Adams, Geri hadn't spent half her time as a youngster attending dancing classes. She didn't have any trophies and cups on the sideboard or framed photographs of her singing sweetly in a stage musical. But somewhere along the line she had developed an overwhelming desire to be famous. Chris noted, 'She was incredibly hungry for fame.'

Geraldine Halliwell is one of the few women that Kylie Minogue could look in the eye. She is very petite – not much more than an inch or two over five feet. As a child she showed no inclination to grow. Her Spanish-born mother was so concerned at her small offspring that when Geri was nine she took her to see a specialist doctor to find out if she needed medical help. Her Spanish relatives helpfully nicknamed the little girl La Enana which translates as 'the Dwarf'. It wasn't exactly an improvement on her earlier pet name, Cacitas, meaning 'Little Poos'.

Her mother, Ana Maria Hidalgo, was a stunning girl from a village near the historic city of Huesca in north-eastern Spain. She came to London when she was twenty-one to work as an au-pair and fell for the dubious charms of Laurence Halliwell, whom Geri describes as a 'total rogue'. He was a 'car-dealer, entrepreneur, womaniser and chancer'.

He spotted Ana in Oxford Street and decided to chat her up. He was forty-four when they married after just a seven-week courtship. He turned out not to be the successful businessman his new wife thought he was, and throughout Geri's childhood her mother worked as a cleaner to keep the family above the breadline. Laurence had reached the age of fifty when Geraldine Estelle Halliwell was born in the maternity wing of Watford General Hospital on 6 August 1972. They already had a son, Max, five, and a daughter, Natalie, three. The family home throughout Geri's childhood was in Jubilee Road, Watford, a ten-minute walk to the shops in St Albans Road.

The three-bedroom semi-detached house was in a sombre street in a poorer area of the town but there's a world of difference between this part of Watford and the grim and dangerous sink estates of the north of England. Geri was a happy and outgoing child, who, as the youngest, was more than a little spoilt. She was also prone to telling little white lies, something she was still apt to do when drumming up publicity as an ambitious performer. Her one-time claim that her mum had aristocratic ancestry was just one of her good-natured fibs.

She shared a room with her big sister, who, for the most part, acted as a protector, although they were only at junior school together. They weren't alike – Geri was far more extrovert – but they developed a strong bond that completely survived fame. Geri rather sweetly said that she was Natalie's 'little shadow'.

Her mum had been brought up a Catholic but was a Jehovah's Witness throughout most of her daughter's early years, which meant that they didn't celebrate birthdays or Christmas or have Easter eggs. She used to take Geri with her from door to door, much to her daughter's embarrassment. Geri had to listen to her mother cold-calling in the hope of persuading people, in her broken English, to join the faith or that the end was near. At other times she would sit next to her mum at meetings in the local Kingdom Hall and listen to Bible stories. She was delighted when Ana Maria decided it was no longer the belief for her.

Quite often in the school holidays Geri would have to go with her mum to the places she was cleaning because there was no one else to look after her. Even at a very young age she sensed the hardship her mum faced every day, trying to bring up her children properly. She learnt the value of money early, first by helping her sister with her paper round and then by starting her own when she was seven. She had already decided when she was six years old that fame was the best way to a better life for herself and her family. She described it in her book *If Only* as a 'magical key'.

Apparently her inspiration as a little girl was watching Margaret Thatcher at the door of 10 Downing Street on her first day as prime minister. She watched it with her dad, who was a 'true blue Tory'. She loved him dearly, even though he contributed little to the household. He always encouraged his little girl to give everyone a song when they were at home after Sunday lunch.

Occasionally, he would restore an old car and sell it on but he didn't do much after a road accident left him with a bad hip when Geri was a child. He loved old movies, which he would watch on the telly, sometimes with his youngest daughter, while his long-suffering wife was at work. Geri grew up better acquainted with beautiful Hollywood greats, like Marlene Dietrich and Rita Hayworth, than with the latest chart acts. These were the stars she would pretend to be in front of the mirror with a hairbrush. Her favourite film was the romantic blockbuster *Gone with the Wind* starring Clark Gable and Vivien Leigh as Rhett Butler and Scarlett O'Hara. Geri vowed that one day she, too, would own a splendid mansion just like the Tara plantation house.

Laurence was distinctly old-fashioned in his musical tastes, and the house in Jubilee Road was filled with the sounds of Frank Sinatra and Benny Goodman. Geri observed, 'It's probably something to do with having an older father. I've always been different from my age group in liking that kind of music.' He would often be mistaken for her grandfather when they were out and about.

Although she was devoted to her dad, her mum remained her role model, constantly displaying a determination to get things done. She was quite strict with Geri, which led to some mother-daughter tensions while Geri was growing up. Ana Maria didn't support her plan to sign with a child agent, for instance, telling her she needed to think more sensibly about her future and plan a solid career.

Her parents eventually split when Geri was nine and she went to stay with her half-sister, Karen, who was Laurence's grown-up daughter from his first marriage. After everything was sorted, she moved back to Jubilee Road while her dad settled into a grotty flat in a high-rise council block in a rougher area of the town, close to the M1. Once a week, Geri would go round to clean the place and make sure there was some milk in the fridge.

After she and Laurence divorced, Ana Maria found a new long-term boyfriend but she was always there to support Geri, if asked. Over the years she realised that trying to rein in her headstrong daughter was a thankless task. Those who came across her, when Geri had fulfilled her dream of fame, remarked that she had no airs and graces. Her future manager, Jon Fowler, observed, 'Her mum was absolutely terrific. She was very respectful and modest – and always smiling.'

Not all her contemporaries at the Walter de Merton Junior School in Gammon Lane warmed to Geraldine, as her mother always called her, or Jez, as she liked to call herself for a while.

One classmate described her as a 'show-off with a big mouth'. Another threatened to throw her over the railway line until a teacher intervened. Others, though, found her sociable and fun – a natural leader who would bring out the best in everyone.

One of her close friends at the school, Sarah Gorman, recalled that they would go round to each other's houses for tea and used to play kiss-chase with the boys in the playground.

Despite her small stature, Geri was a demon on the netball court and used to play centre because she was so nimble and nippy. She retained a strong affection for her junior school and returned there in 2008 to read to pupils from the first of her Ugenia Lavender books for children: 'I felt more nervous reading than I ever did performing as the Spice Girls.' She even included one of her favourite teachers, Mrs Flitt, as a character in the book.

Even though Walter de Merton had become Beechfield School, it still retained a strong link with its famous former pupil and one of the houses is called Halliwell House.

Before she left junior school, Geri went to her first concert when she joined Natalie to see Wham! on the *Big Tour* at the NEC, Birmingham, in December 1984. George Michael was performing the number-one single 'Freedom' and when he got to the last line, he pointed at Geri and sang, 'Girl, all I want right now is you.' She fell in love and decided on the spot that they were going to get married. Every night she would give a poster of him on her bedroom wall a goodnight kiss before getting into bed. Many of her classmates fancied Andrew Ridgeley and would gather outside his parents' house a couple of miles away in Bushey but Geri's heart always belonged to George.

Her devotion to George also coincided with her discovery of Madonna, whose flamboyant image would be a considerable influence on her. Even as a young teenager she could identify with the artist who had become the most famous woman in pop, even though she was by no means the best singer or dancer. Instead she had a fantastic image.

After Walter de Merton, Geri was expected to follow her brother and sister to the nearby Leggatts Way Secondary Modern but she had other ideas. She asked her mum if she could try for a place at Watford Grammar School for Girls and surprised everyone by being accepted. It was an early indication that Geraldine Halliwell was someone who could make things happen.

The one drawback was that she lost touch with most of her primary-school classmates, but Geri's lack of shyness ensured she made friends easily. The new school also gave her the opportunity to discover drama. Growing up, there had been no money for dance classes or music lessons so the highlight of her performance career to date was pretending to be Sandy from *Grease* and singing 'Summer Nights' in assembly at junior school.

Now, she was being encouraged to appreciate Shakespeare, and a trip to watch *A Midsummer Night's Dream* at the Open Air Theatre in Regent's Park was one of the highlights of her time at Watford Grammar. The school was one of the best in the area: founded in 1704 as a charity school, it had an excellent academic reputation.

Geri passed an impressive eight GCSEs, without particularly applying herself. She had no desire to continue a formal education by going on to study for A-levels, Instead she decided to follow her sister Natalie and go to the local Casio College in Langley Road, Watford, which Andrew Ridgeley had attended a few years before. If she had been a bit older Geri might have seen him and George Michael perform there with their original band, the Executive.

Geri studied a curious mixture of finance, travel and tourism, which didn't suit her. She decided that she was just wasting precious time, promptly left and started dancing. She had no proper training so would just improvise and hope for the best. She had developed a curvaceous figure and was soon noticed around the London clubs. She was paid £40 for dancing on a Saturday night – and Sunday morning – at the Crazy Club and the house-music extravaganzas held at the Astoria in Charing Cross Road.

Geri moved out of Jubilee Road, staying for a while in a terraced house owned by her half-sister Karen and her husband in the Watford suburb of South Oxhey. She had to leave after she had invited everyone in the Game Bird pub to a party at the house. Word got round: two hundred people turned up and wrecked the place. Shamefaced, Geri moved into a squat on a nearby council estate.

Newly independent, Geri had to buy her own food. This was not necessarily a good thing because she was worrying for the first time about her weight. As a result, she did something she later claimed was 'the biggest mistake of my life' – she went on a diet. The trigger had been a throwaway remark by one of her fellow dancers about her being a bit plump. She had been a fussy eater as a child – avoiding vegetables if she could – but at least then her mum, who could be quite strict, could keep an eye on her. Left to her own devices she wasn't eating properly at all.

At least she was saving money. She much preferred to spend what little she had on going out. These were carefree times in the late eighties and Geri became an enthusiastic embracer of the 'Second Summer of Love'. This was the acid-house culture that had sprung up during 1988 and ballooned into the giant illegal rave events around the M25. Watford was the perfect starting point for dressing up, piling into cars and vans and heading off to the next party location. The Game Bird in Hartspring

Lane was close to the M1 and the best kicking-off point in the area – no wonder Geri's party was mobbed.

Geri was sixteen when she went to her first rave and at seventeen was an old hand. But her cavalier outlook on life took a temporary knock when she discovered a small lump in her right breast and needed an emergency operation to have it removed. Fortunately, it was benign but Geri always felt she was one of the lucky ones and, in the future, would strongly encourage young women to be mindful of breast cancer and make sure they checked their breasts regularly.

She found out that she could earn more money abroad so decided to try her luck in the fashionable Mediterranean clubs. At nineteen, she was a dancer at the world-famous BCM Planet Dance club in Magaluf. 'Dancing' is a loose term because in effect she was writhing around in a cage ten feet or so above the dance floor. To begin with, she was given a week's trial by the manager but soon proved to be one of the most popular dancers, dressed in a variety of wigs, bra tops and leather shorts. Geri, it seemed, had mastered the art of flirtation. As one of her close friends observed, 'She was very good at making you feel special.'

Rather like Melanie Brown in Blackpool, Geri seemed to enjoy her freedom away from her home town and, by all accounts, had a wild few months in the Spanish sun. Kelly Smith, another of her friends from those days, recalled, 'She was a party animal and didn't mind showing herself off.'

Aside from dancing in a cage, Geri was doing little more than thousands of teenagers enjoying a month or two in the Spanish sun. It was a rite of passage but, despite the fun, she didn't lose her focus or ambition.

During her time in Mallorca, she shared a flat with another dancer who had some topless pictures taken by a local photographer. Geri decided to do the same. She had visions of becoming a star in the very lucrative world of glamour modelling. Perhaps this would be her passport to the fame she so desperately wanted – she never tired of telling people she was going to achieve it. Kelly remarked, 'We thought it was funny when she went on and on about becoming a big star.'

On her return to England, she signed up with what she called the 'dodgiest agency you could imagine' but secured one or two decent jobs, including a jeans advert. She also did a Page 3 session for the *Sun* but the shots weren't used. Geri found the topless work boring. She told the chat show host Michael Parkinson, 'I found it very dull – standing there with a window open to keep your nipples firm was not good.' She had to navigate a dodgy world of casting agents who for no good reason would ask her to strip at auditions for non–nude parts. On these occasions she would make a rapid exit.

Another drawback was the constant scrutiny of her shape. Apparently a photographer made a casual remark about her weight and that was all it took for Geri once again to believe she was fat. Her sparky, fearless demeanour masked an all-too-familiar story of vulnerability.

She was already displaying a fearsome energy that never seemed to run out. She had been moved out of the squat by the council and needed to earn to pay the rent on her tiny flat in another unappetising part of town. She taught aerobics, waited tables, washed hair, and found time to do a day course in television presenting run by Reuters.

Her modelling shots led to her next opportunity, providing the glamour on a Turkish game show. It was called Sec Bakalim and was a version of the old US show *Let's Make a Deal*. The producer apparently noticed Geri's photographs and offered her a job that involved flying to Istanbul every weekend. He told her that she would not be wearing a swimsuit – or less – but a tasteful evening gown. She would also have to 'love that fridge'. Geri, who was struggling to pay the rent, needed the money so she jumped at the chance to earn a couple of hundred pounds a show.

She wasn't the presenter. She was the attractive young woman in a movie star dress, who smiled in front of the prizes that the contestants were trying to win. An unexpected bonus was that she was asked for her autograph for the very first time. She enjoyed the experience. Spending time in Istanbul was no hardship and she decided she would accept the role again if she was asked back.

She acquired new representation, Talking Heads in Barnes, run by broadcaster and voiceover maestro John Sachs and well-known agent Anthony Blackburn. They readily saw how appealing Geri was. She was still devouring the *Stage* every week and going to auditions. One was for a small part in a West End comedy. It didn't go well but, significantly, the director asked her, 'Geri, what's the last thing you've read? I bet it was *Cosmopolitan*.' And it was.

She resolved to catch up on her education and so, at the age of twenty, enrolled for an English-language course at Watford College in Hempstead Road. She had grown up a lot and, for the first time, felt she 'understood the wealth and power of words'. She studied *Hamlet*, loved *Sons and Lovers* by D. H. Lawrence, and discovered the genius of Oscar Wilde.

She was in class when she received the message from her brother that their dad had died. She had just got back from a weekend in Istanbul where she was working on her second game-show season. She said, 'I was distraught. I felt that he had been snatched away from me.' She has talked openly about her grief and specifically being in denial that he had gone, even though she went to visit his body at the hospital.

Her description of seeing his body is heartbreaking: 'He was lying there and all his nails were black – everything was black. His features were sunk. He looked like the Penguin in the film *Batman II*. It is a horrible memory of my father. It was hideous.'

She dragged herself into college and even joined everyone on a class trip to the West End to see Alan Cumming's outstanding portrayal of Hamlet at the Donmar Warehouse. The actor would go on to become a familiar figure on British television through his starring roles in US series, including *The Good Wife* and *Instinct*. His 1993 Hamlet, however, was arguably the highlight of his career. Geri was enthralled and forgot her own tragedy for a precious hour or two.

After her father's death, she suffered from bouts of both bulimia and anorexia. She was so down. 'I wanted to kill myself. I could not function. It was awful.' She started wearing black, not so much as a gesture of mourning but because she hoped it would make her look thinner. An unnamed family member remembered that Geri at this time would refer to herself as 'Fatso'. She was getting by on cigarettes and black coffee.

Even her agents noticed how thin she was, although both John and Anthony thought it was because she couldn't afford to eat properly, rather than anything more serious. They would try to encourage her to have a sandwich when she came to the office.

Outwardly, Geri appeared her normal bubbly self. She continued to go for auditions that she thought might suit her. She went to one to appear in a backing video for Pink Floyd. At another, she met one of the wannabes who would become a Spice Girl. She joined Victoria at a movie call for *Tank Girl*, loosely based on the comic strip. Once again it was an advertisement in the *Stage* proclaiming that they were looking for 'the star of this futuristic action feature film'. The role had already been earmarked for the established actress Lori Petty, who had starred with Madonna in *A League of Their Own*, so this was little more than a crude publicity exercise for the movie.

Needless to say neither Geri nor Victoria was cast, which was a lucky break as the film 'tanked', only earning a quarter of its $25 million production costs. For her part Geri decided not to go back for another season to Turkey – and also called time on any future topless modelling. Her Page 3 ambitions were at an end.

The problem she faced moving forward was: what could she actually do? She might not have been drinking in the Last Chance saloon but she was certainly in the bar next door. Perhaps this pop group might be something.

# 5

# MELANIE CHISHOLM
# SUPERSTAR

———

The best-laid plans for the call-back were slightly disrupted when Chris was told one of the shortlist couldn't make it. Joan O'Neill had rung from her Merseyside home to tell him that her daughter Melanie Chisholm had tonsillitis. Melanie obviously couldn't speak to him herself because she was under strict orders to rest her voice. Chris had been impressed by her vitality at the first audition and was able to reassure Joan that her daughter was not going to lose this opportunity.

Melanie Chisholm lived and breathed dancing. Growing up, it was her pastime and her passion and she was brilliant at it. But, secretly, she wanted to be a singer like her mum.

Joan was already making a name for herself around the pubs and working men's clubs of Merseyside before her eldest daughter was born. At the end of the sixties, she had joined a band called Petticoat and Vine, which is best described as a folk-rock group in the tradition of the Mamas and the Papas. She was then going by her maiden name of Joan Tuffley – although in those days she was billed professionally as Kathy Ford.

Norman Smeddles, the guitarist and leader of the group, decided they should have two female lead singers. His girlfriend and future wife, Val, was one and Joan became the other. They were blonde, pretty, and excellent singers. Norman recalled, 'Joan was a typical Scouser with a quick wit and was not slow to speak her mind.'

Joan's voice had a touch of Roberta Flack about it, and she adored Motown artists, particularly the cool and melodious Smokey Robinson, whom she called 'Smokey Robbo', much to everyone's amusement. She was so skinny that her friends used to refer to her as Joan the Bone.

They secured a record deal with the Philips label in 1970 and released a début single called 'Riding a Carousel', a pleasant enough song. It led to their TV début in October that year on *The Harry Secombe Show*, alongside other guests Jimmy Tarbuck and the popular Irish singer Clodagh Rogers.

Joan cheekily managed to buttonhole Jimmy and secure an invitation for the group to appear on his own show. All was going well and national stardom beckoned. The one potential difficulty was that Joan had fallen in love with Alan Chisholm, whom she had met one evening at the Cavern Club, arguably the most famous music venue in the country, thanks to the Beatles' performances there.

As Petticoat and Vine became better known, they had to spend more time in London, which didn't suit Joan at all. She wanted to get back up to Liverpool to see Alan as much as possible, which led to some tensions within the band. When the group were offered a tour of Canada, she decided to leave. Ironically, the trip across the Atlantic never happened, but Petticoat and Vine battled on, eventually calling it a day in 1973. Norman and Val went on to achieve greater exposure with a new line-up called Champagne, a light group that was more Eurovision than anything psychedelic. They appeared on *Opportunity Knocks*, *The Morecambe and Wise Show* and *The Jim Davidson Show* but didn't make a chart breakthrough. Val and Norman continued to enjoy a career as Champagne, touring internationally as well as remaining popular on their native Merseyside.

Meanwhile, Joan had married Alan, who worked as a fitter for the Otis Elevator Company in Liverpool, and settled into a neat semi in Kendall Drive, Rainhill, a suburb about ten miles from the city centre. Their daughter Melanie Jayne Chisholm was born at the nearby Whiston Hospital on 12 January 1974. She was always Melanie – never Mel.

Money was tight, especially when Joan and Alan split up when Melanie was three. She had to divide her time between the two and felt something of an outsider in both homes: 'I felt like I was in the way and I had to make my own life and be independent.'

Home was a series of flats on council estates in some of the rougher areas of Runcorn. When they moved a few miles south to Widnes, she went to Fairfield Primary School in Peel House Lane and was able to move further along the road to start senior school at Fairfield County High. Joan found work as a secretary with the local Knowsley borough council but she didn't give up singing or performing. She found new love with a taxi driver, Den O'Neill, who was a bass guitarist, a bit of a rocker and another familiar figure in local music venues. They set up home together in a small terraced house in Widnes.

Den already had two sons, Jad (Jarrod) and Stuart, from his first marriage. He and Joan married while she was pregnant with their son Paul. Melanie's father Alan also married again and his new wife Carole had two boys, Liam and Declan. That meant Melanie was the only girl with five brothers. She didn't know until she was a Spice Girl that she had a secret sister called Emma, Alan's daughter from another relationship, who was brought up quietly in Llandudno, North Wales.

Melanie later admitted that she felt a little isolated when her father remarried and started a second family – caught between two households and feeling, temporarily, that she was 'completely alone'. Looking back as an adult, she thought that even though her parents never bad-mouthed one another and relations were amicable, she started to blame herself for their divorce.

For a while, she might have given her mother a tough time, shrieking, 'I want my dad,' if she wasn't getting her own way, but Joan and Melanie have a strong mother-and-daughter bond. According to Melanie, they are similar because they're both 'dead soft'. Her mum was also a terrific cook and, unusually among their friends in Widnes, she owned a wok. She introduced her daughter to Chinese food, which Melanie loves.

Melanie was also particularly close to her brother Paul, who, with her support, would grow up to be an ace racing driver and engaging TV commentator. They weren't always best buddies, of course. She used to punch him when he farted. He hated her habit of cracking her knuckles constantly, especially if she was anxious about something. There was a mutual respect, however, and he would always tell her to stand up for herself even though he was five years younger.

Joan didn't give up singing. She and Den formed various bands over the years, including Love Potion, with friend Stan Alexander, who had once been a guitarist with do-wop band Darts. They released a single on Polydor in 1977 entitled 'Face, Name, Number', written by Stan. The song was one of the light disco songs of the time that might have been recorded by a seventies group like the Real Thing. It made a few ripples but didn't reach the charts. Joan also sang with the Ken Phillips Country Band, was in a group called T-Junction and yet another, River Deep, which was a tribute to Tina Turner and named after her most famous hit 'River Deep Mountain High'.

From an early age, Melanie was used to musicians popping into the house to catch up and rehearse. She would lie in bed and listen to the bass line throbbing through the floorboards. She used to go to watch her mother perform: 'I'd sit at the front, miming every word she sang. I felt quite special – you know, when you just want to go, "That's my mum!"'

Joan never achieved her ambition of playing Carnegie Hall, although Love Potion did support Harold Melvin and the Blue Notes in 1978 at the Hammersmith Apollo in London. But she's still gigging around her old haunts – in June 2019, when the Spice Girls performed at Wembley Stadium, the Joan O'Neill Band was playing Woodwards wine bar – Woodies – in Formby.

Tina Turner was not one of Melanie's idols while she was growing up. The first record she bought was *The Kids from Fame* album that had also proved such an inspiration to Victoria Adams. But, more significantly, she was a fan of Madonna. She wasn't so keen on the music but loved the image. She was nine when Madonna started having hits with 'Holiday' and 'Borderline' and she would dress up, pretending to be the unmistakable star in front of the mirror at home – just as a million and more young Spice Girls fans would impersonate the girl group in the future. Later she moved on to Stevie Wonder, whose timeless classic 'Sir Duke' remains her favourite song.

Her first crush was on swashbuckling chart topper Adam Ant until she turned her attention to George Michael, just as Geri Halliwell had done. She was also a secret fan of tough guy actor Bruce Willis, whose album *The Return of Bruno* came out as Melanie turned thirteen in 1987. His cover of the old Drifters standard 'Under the Boardwalk' was a big hit that year and Melanie could be heard singing it constantly. The first song she ever performed in public, though, was 'The Greatest Love of All', the Whitney Houston classic that coincidentally Melanie Brown performed at the Danceworks audition.

She didn't much feel like singing when she had to take holiday jobs to help pay for her clothes and dancing. One of the worst was when her dad Alan moved into the tourism industry and found work as a holiday rep in France and Spain. That meant great vacations in the summer but she had to earn her spending money. One particularly unpleasant task when she was fourteen was collecting the dirty sheets from a Spanish apartment block where Alan was working. It was worth it, though, because she loved the continental lifestyle – late dinners and playing in the squares of picturesque villages – all a far cry from Widnes, where not many of her friends went abroad. 'I felt a bit sophisticated,' she admitted.

Her all-time worst job was in a local chippie. She couldn't bear the smell. She had always enjoyed fish-and-chips night on a Friday at home but working in the shop was something completely different. The only consolation was that it helped pay for her dance classes.

Melanie describes herself as a 'fat, plain, tubby, frumpy kid', which sounds suspiciously self-effacing. By the time she had taken up dancing she was clearly a very pretty girl. Unavoidably, Melanie grew up surrounded by music but it was as a dancer that she shone.

Despite her natural shyness and insecurity about her appearance, Melanie was an attractive teenager and had a succession of boyfriends at Fairfield High School, often connected with school drama. She dated a boy in the year above called Ian McKnight, who was very charming and popular with the girls. They connected when Melanie was cast as his mother in a school production of *Blood Brothers*. Willy Russell's hit musical had started out as a school play in Liverpool in the early eighties and quickly became a mainstay of local culture.

Melanie wasn't entirely happy playing Mrs Lyons, the wealthy woman who persuades her cleaner to let her raise one of her twin boys as her own; she would have preferred to be cast as 'the Scouse mum', as she called Mrs Johnstone. The main character had all the best songs and was played over the years by some famous names in musical theatre, including Stephanie Lawrence, Marti Webb and Barbara Dickson. Melanie was determined that one day she would have the starring role and sing the unforgettable 'Tell Me It's Not True'.

The consolation for now was that she saw plenty of Ian, who said, 'We just clicked.' They went out for a few months, remained friends after they split and could often be seen having a catch-up in the years to come at the Ring o' Bells pub in Pit Lane, even when Melanie had moved down south.

More seriously, she went out for two years with another pupil, Ryan Wilson. He was her first love and she was his. Importantly, his mum Gail liked her: 'Melanie was a charming girl – very feminine and very pretty.' They used to walk home together – Ryan lived with his parents in a large five-bedroom house – and talk about their ambitions. Melanie's plans seemed to revolve around dancing. He remembered, 'She once said to me the hardest thing about life is deciding what you want. Getting it is easy.'

Intriguingly, her old schoolmates do not remember Melanie as a tomboy, kicking a ball around with the lads. Ryan recalled she was a quiet girl, the quietest of all the prefects. Another friend, Mark Devany, agreed it was rubbish that she was a tomboy: 'She was always very girly and ballet mad,' he said.

*Blood Brothers* was not the only school production Melanie was in, but she never secured the lead. In fact, for *The Wiz*, she had to make do with playing the part of one of the four crows. She was a girl who wanted fame and fortune away from the mean streets of a Cheshire town, scrawling 'Melanie Chisholm Superstar' on the cover of one of her school books.

Throughout her childhood and into her teenage years, Melanie won many dancing trophies. She kept her dancing world separate from school but two evenings a week and the whole of Saturday were set aside for classes. Originally she wanted to be a ballerina but realised as she got older that she was better suited to being one of the dancers on *Top of the Pops*, which, naturally, she watched every week.

Her dancing training helped with sport at school. She excelled at gymnastics and could execute a mean back flip, was better than average at netball and athletics but less good at football, even though she was a lifelong fan of Liverpool Football Club.

While she preferred to spend her pocket money on her Saturday dancing rather than on trips to Anfield she has never wavered in her support and would watch the games on telly on a Sunday afternoon with the rest of her family, who were also big fans. These were the glory days of the 1980s when Kenny Dalgleish, Ian Rush and Graeme Souness would thrill the Kop. Her favourite player was goalkeeper Bruce Grobbelaar, who always had a great rapport with the home fans: 'I loved it when he used to walk on his hands up and down the pitch.' As an older teenager, she fancied Jamie Redknapp but he didn't join the squad until she was seventeen and already on her way to college.

Melanie knew what she wanted at this point in her life – to leave school at sixteen and go to dance college. She passed nine GCSEs before she left, even though she was more interested in her next dance class than knuckling down to revision. She retained some affection for her old school and was reportedly disappointed when it closed in 2010 and was subsequently demolished to make way for a new housing estate and a cemetery.

She impressed at her audition at the Doreen Bird College of Performing Arts in Sidcup, Kent. This was another such school founded in the post-war years by a strong-minded woman, who became much admired in the dancing world. Melanie's audition notes read, 'Melanie has a nice appeal. She is strong with a flexible body. Her audition piece was very nice. She is very bright and has good potential. Should do well.' When she applied, Melanie had to mention her ambitions in entertainment and wrote, 'I want to play Rumpleteazer in the musical *Cats* – the part Bonnie Langford played – and to record.'

Melanie was still primarily a dancer. The school's artistic director Sue Passmore observed, 'She was a very strong, technical dancer. She was a hard-working and single-minded pupil.' At this stage she still saw her future as a dancer and not as a singer. Her college musical director Pat Izen did not think her voice was that good when she arrived: 'It was gutsy but she had an excellent ear – and she was a real individualist.'

Melanie's breakthrough as a singer, at least as far as having her confidence boosted, occurred when she took part in a college revue and performed 'Chief Cook and Bottle Washer', a show-stopper from the Broadway musical *The Rink*. She was delighted when the audience started whooping: 'In that moment, I knew I wanted to sing.' This was a song that demanded a 'performance'. In the original production in 1984, the peerless musical-theatre star Chita Rivera gave it the full treatment and won a Tony award.

Melanie thrived at the Doreen Bird College. Sidcup was about as far as you could get from Widnes so it was brave of her mother to support her leaving home at sixteen to go down south. Melanie still had to deal with the dilemma all the future Spice Girls faced after leaving college of trying to get work in a crowded profession.

She signed on the dole and started the round of auditions. The closest she came to a breakthrough in 1993 was nearly being hired for the chorus of *Cats* in the West End, which might have set her off on a career in musical theatre. Instead, it was looking increasingly likely that she would end up taking work on a cruise ship. Fortunately, however, she picked up one of Chris Herbert's flyers and decided to try out for his new girl group.

On the day, the dancing proved no problem and she sang the exuberant 'I'm So Excited' by the Pointer Sisters, a hit in the UK in late 1984. Chris was more impressed than his dad Bob, who for some reason didn't rate her dancing but did think she was a much better singer than the other Melanie from Leeds. He wasn't struck by the looks of either girl, giving them both four out of ten on their informal scoresheets.

Melanie hadn't dressed up for the occasion, a simple cut-off lilac T-shirt and black trousers. Her hair was down and not in a ponytail. But, most importantly, she was just a little bit different from Victoria Adams and Melanie Brown – which worked to her advantage when Chris was back in the office making up his shortlist. He wanted contrast.

From that point of view, he noticed a younger teenager called Michelle Stephenson, who did well with a challenging ballad, 'Don't Be a Stranger', then a recent top-ten hit for Dina Carroll. Michelle had only just turned seventeen so was appreciably the youngest of the probables.

Like Victoria, she was brought up in the Home Counties but was more traditionally middle class. Her father George worked for Chubb Security and her brother Simon was an artist and creative director. They lived in Abingdon, a lovely old market town on the Thames, just south of Oxford.

Unlike the others, however, she was much more involved in acting than any serious stage-school dancing. She had work with the Young Vic and the National Youth Theatre on her CV. She revealed, 'I actually wanted to be an actress. I just went along for the audition because I had not been to an open audition before. I just went along for the experience.'

She already had a place to study theatre and English at Goldsmith's College, part of the University of London, so a back-up plan was in place if the audition didn't work out.

Michelle was invited to the first call-back at Nomis Studios. The building in Sinclair Road, Brook Green, had been turned into a studio complex in the late seventies by Simon Napier-Bell, who would later manage Wham!. Nomis is his first name spelt backwards. At any given time during its golden age, you might have caught Tina Turner, Queen, George Michael or the Rolling Stones enjoying bacon and eggs in the canteen there.

Chris and Bob began the recall by chatting to the girls individually, then dividing them into three groups. One group that seemed promising consisted of Melanie Brown, Victoria Adams-Wood, Michelle Stephenson and a Welsh girl from Cowbridge, near Cardiff, called Lianne Morgan. They were given three-quarters of an hour to devise a dance routine to another Eternal hit; this time Chris had chosen 'Just a Step from Heaven', which was in the charts at the time so at least everyone knew it. Not surprisingly, the irrepressible Melanie took the lead and the others were happy to follow her ideas.

Just when they thought they were ready, Chris and Bob threw a spanner in the works by telling them to bring another girl up to speed – Geri Halliwell. She was a riot of colour, wearing a pink jumper, purple hot pants and platform shoes, topped off with her vibrant dyed ginger hair that she had styled into pigtails. Melanie put it succinctly, 'She looked like a mad, eccentric nutter from another planet.' She certainly knew how to be the focus of attention in any room.

By the end of the afternoon this group of five were by far the most promising. They sent each girl away with a tape of 'Signed, Sealed Delivered, I'm Yours' by Stevie Wonder and asked them to return to Nomis in a week's time to be put through their vocal paces to see how they blended together and whether they could harmonise. The media has found some of those disappointed that day but the one who came closest was Lianne. She was in and then she was out.

Chris and Bob had a rethink during the week and decided that Melanie Chisholm would better fit their concept for the girl group. Lianne was coming up to twenty-four while her replacement was twenty. She was hugely disappointed to receive a letter from Chris in which he said she was too old for what he had in mind and perhaps a solo career might suit her better.

Over the years Lianne has been quoted in various interviews commenting on what she saw as an injustice: 'I'm a better singer than all of them,' she maintained. That may well have been the case but singing ability was low on the list of priorities for the new band. She was older than Geri so the average age of the band dropped markedly without her.

Ability to sing or dance was completely irrelevant. In a later confidential memo, Bob Herbert was frank about how Heart Management viewed Geri: 'We included her because she had a very strong personality and her looks seemed to suit the image we were trying to project. Unfortunately she was tone deaf and had awful timing, which meant she was unable to sing in tune or dance in time.'

6

# A MODEL GIRL

---

Typically, Geri was filled with enthusiasm and positive energy at the prospect of being in a girl band and wasted no time telling everyone she knew in Watford. They included a young researcher at the BBC called Matthew Bowers, who drank in the same bars and was keen to make an impression in television.

He was working on a documentary about Muhammad Ali called *Rumble in the Jungle* and mentioned to the film's director, Neil Davies, that he had a friend who was auditioning for a girl band and asked him if he thought it might make something. Neil, an ex-paratrooper, immediately saw the possibilities and the two went to the next instalment of the search – the 'Signed, Sealed, Delivered' workshop day at Nomis.

Most importantly at this stage, Neil had to make sure Chris Herbert was onside. Fortunately the go-ahead young manager could see the advantages of a film. Neil was impressed: 'I thought he'd had a brainwave in trying to form a sort of Backstreet Girls – everybody at the time thought you would never get another girl band going. It was all boy bands – Take That dominated the scene. So I thought, "This guy is a genius". He's twenty-one so I could see this was going to be a great story – even if they never made it. It would be a kind of warning to teenage girls that this is what happens to you in Tin Pan Alley.'

He shook hands with Chris and started filming that day. He needed to obtain the written consent of the girls but the more pressing thing for the five on the day was making a good impression with Heart Management. Bob Herbert was there and Chic Murphy had come to watch for the first time so that he could see for himself where his money was going. Neil amusingly described the two men as observing the 'Marbella Dress Code' – the top three buttons of the shirt undone and a big medallion hanging in the middle of the chest.

As well as being introduced to Chic, the girls had the chance to meet each other properly. In particular, they hadn't noticed Melanie Chisholm at Danceworks and she had missed the next audition so this was an opportunity to chat to her. She obviously had no airs and graces and seemed to fit in easily.

All the girls thought they sounded terrible together – definitely a cat's chorus. To their surprise, Chris, Bob and Chic seemed a little hard of hearing that day, although the purpose of the get-together was to see if they had a future, not how they sounded in the present. As Chris explained, 'We wanted to create a band as a unit so it did not matter so much if, individually, they weren't so strong.' It went well enough for Chris to move on to the next stage.

He booked the five into a bed-and-breakfast in Knaphill, Woking, which was a few miles down the road from the Heart offices. Ostensibly the week was for them to rehearse, but that was only part the plan: 'It was just for them to spend a little time together, and see whether they actually got on and started to bond. Initially we wanted to observe and see if there was something there or if we had to make changes.'

He introduced them to working together in a studio, picking them up from the B&B and dropping them off at Trinity Studios nearby. That sounded grander than it actually was. It was little more than a glorified village hall in urgent need of a lick of paint and a decent central-heating system. The building had once been a dance studio, so at least provided the space for the five girls to hone their dancing skills. Trinity was run day to day by Ian Lee, who remembered that first week: 'They were like five schoolgirls – a bit giggly and a bit insecure.'

After a general discussion, it was decided that for the moment they would be called Touch, a pretty uninspiring name – sounding more like a group who would perform at Eurovision than one that would inspire a generation of female devotees. Chris was keen, though, for the group to have a five-letter name. More significantly, he began putting together a team who could help shape their future during this training period.

Once more the Three Degrees provided the link. He asked their former musical director, Erwin Keiles, to come up with a song or two to get the girls started. The first they had to learn was called 'Take Me Away', a mid-tempo unchallenging number. Chris brought in the gloriously named Pepi Lemer, a coach of considerable experience and a backing singer since the sixties, when she missed out on stardom.

Pepi realised that collectively the girls had a lot of work to do: 'I remember them being quite attractive in their various ways but terribly nervous. They were shaking and, when they sang, their voices were wobbling. It has to be said that they weren't very good.' At the end of the week, Touch gave Chris, Bob and Chic an exclusive performance of that first song. They were dressed in a manner that would, in the future, never work for the Spice Girls – they were colour-coordinated in black and white. They were the Five Degrees.

It was all exciting, though. Apart from Michelle, this was a bunch of seasoned auditionees, thrilled that they were involved in something so new. Even the cosy, old-style guesthouse was stirred by their vitality. Victoria shared a room with Geri, who complained that she was taking up all the space with her two suitcases full of designer clothes. They clicked immediately. 'You must come with me to a car-boot sale,' said Geri – as if that was ever going to happen.

Victoria was the first of the five to give Chris some concern when he found out that she was already in a band called Persuasion. He told her that she needed to make a decision: 'Are you in or are you out?' Victoria was much cannier than people realised. She kept her options open just in case Touch came to nothing. She told Persuasion that she was going away on holiday for a week or two and would have to miss rehearsals.

Chris had to keep his fingers crossed where Victoria was concerned but another potential problem was building within the group. Four of the girls – Geri, Victoria and the two Melanies – were getting on famously but the fifth, Michelle, was becoming more distant. This was not the gelling unit Chris wanted: 'Even when they broke for lunch or a coffee break, the four would be inside having a coffee and Michelle would be outside. She seemed a bit separated from the others. We spotted it and thought there was a problem developing even during that initial week.'

A bigger concern was their lack of progress at Trinity Studios. Clearly they needed much more time to practise and improve. Chic came up with the solution. He happened to have a spare three-bedroom house in Maidenhead. The girls could move in right away. It was basically a drab semi on a grey estate in Boyne Hill Road. Geri had clearly already had enough of sharing and bagged the tiny single room for herself. She was the oldest so there was no argument. Michelle and Victoria bounded up the stairs and managed to grab the twin-bedded room. That left Melanie Brown having to put up with Melanie Chisholm snoring away in one double room. Having two Melanies in the group was slightly problematic especially as they both preferred the longer version of the name. Chris began to call Melanie Brown 'Mel B' to help differentiate between the two.

Relations within Touch continued to slide throughout the first month. The gang of four were exasperated by what they perceived as Michelle's lack of commitment. She wasn't putting in the work to improve her dancing, preferring, they said, to top up her tan at lunchtimes rather than copy Geri's lead and practise hard to try to catch up with the dance-school veterans. Perhaps, tellingly, Michelle still had every intention of going to university in the autumn. She also had a Saturday job in Harrods that she didn't give up.

Melanie Brown, in particular, tried to motivate her but in the end the gang of four felt they had no choice other than to express their misgivings to Chris and Bob, echoing the thoughts the Herberts already had. Bob explained, 'She would never have gelled so we had to let her go.'

Did Michelle go of her own accord? Was she pushed? Or was it a mutual decision? There were two sides to the story. While it was true that the other girls questioned her desire, Michelle, herself, was struggling with a family crisis – her mother Penny had been diagnosed with breast cancer. She was also the youngest of the group – five years younger than Geri. There's a world of difference between just leaving school and hosting a game show on Turkish TV.

Michelle went travelling around Europe before starting her degree. She has had to live with the label of being the Spice Girl who wasn't – although, at the time, Touch was nothing like the

Spice Girls. She didn't enjoy the music they were rehearsing, considering it far too poppy for her taste. She was not a fan of Take That, for instance, much preferring the harder edge of Oasis and the Prodigy. She later told Neil Davies that she became frustrated by the slowness of it all and she 'didn't think the girls would make it'. She added simply, 'I had different plans for my future.'

Of the four who remained, Victoria was by far the rudest about Michelle, describing her voice as 'cruise-ship operatic', her dancing as 'having less rhythm than a cement mixer' and saying that she 'couldn't be arsed to improve'. The normally more outspoken Mel B described her as 'sweet, very upper class and very well turned out'. In fact, Michelle was probably more posh than Victoria, although she didn't have the wardrobe full of designer labels. Michelle remarked, 'Victoria had some beautiful clothes.'

Michelle has made her own way in music. She has recorded her own songs, acted as a backing singer for Ricky Martin and Julio Iglesias and presented for Channel 4. She once said, 'Of course I regret I'm not a multi-millionaire like them. But at the time I left the group I knew I was doing the right thing – and I still think it was the right thing.'

Eight years after she left, Chris and Shelley were in the Pitcher and Piano bar in Richmond when he recognised the waitress. It was Michelle. He recalled, 'We shared a fond welcome and had a good chat.' By that time, they both had cause for some regret. She would continue to be involved in music by hosting club nights before eventually marrying Hugh Gadsden, the manager of Madness.

Michelle's departure created a vacancy. Chris and Bob didn't go back to their original shortlist but decided to try to find someone new. They still wanted a five-piece band but they couldn't face going through a drawn-out audition process again just to find one girl so they asked Pepi Lemer if she could think of anyone. She could – one of her former students, Abigail Kis, a half-Hungarian girl with a stunning, soulful voice.

She proved to be a non-starter. She had a steady boyfriend who, by all accounts, was not that keen on her moving into the house in Maidenhead. She also had a place at university to study performing arts, which seemed a better option for her. With hindsight, she was probably a fraction too young, and putting a boyfriend first was not in keeping with the ethos of the rest of the band. She became another 'fifth' Spice Girl, observing sadly, 'I would have loved to be that famous. Every time I see them I think, "It could have been me."'

While they searched for the right replacement, there was some good news for Chris when Victoria told him she had decided once and for all that her future lay with his all-girl band and not with Persuasion. She had talked things over with her parents and realised that everything was much more professional with the Herberts and she could not keep both going if she was going to continue living in Maidenhead. This was business and she seemed to have no compunction in ditching her former bandmates.

Nothing was etched in stone as far as the make-up of the new group was concerned. It seemed a good idea, however, that the fifth member should be the youngest – thereby lowering the average age of the five. It was back to the drawing board for Pepi, whose next thought was a bubbly blonde girl she had taught three years previously at Barnet College. She remembered that her name was Emma Bunton but, in those pre-Facebook days, had no idea how to contact her. She had to pop into the college to search through old records before eventually coming up with a phone number. Emma's mother, Pauline Bunton, answered and Pepi explained that she wanted to invite her daughter to try out for a new girl group.

Emma was thrilled to be asked. She had the advantage of being another stage-school veteran and had attended many auditions. Chris drove over to North London to meet her and her mum, and they had a pleasant chat over a coffee before going back to Pepi's house where Emma sang 'Right Here', a top-three hit in the UK the previous year for the all-girl American R&B trio SWV (Sisters with Voices). It was a good choice. Chris Herbert thought she was perfect: 'She was very cute, very nice with a sweet voice, a very "pop" voice. I really liked her character a lot. It was one of those light-bulb moments when I realised she was definitely something we didn't have. It was immediate for me.'

Chris had to explain, though, that it all depended on her being accepted by the other four. They would have to look at the dynamic between her and the current residents of the house in Maidenhead. One thing stood in her favour – that she was from a working-class background in North London. When Emma Lee Bunton was born in the Victoria Maternity Hospital, Barnet, on 23 January 1976, her father, Trevor, was a delivery driver. She would be the youngest of Touch but was actually older than Michelle.

Trevor subsequently became a milkman and sometimes took his daughter out on his rounds during the school holidays. Her mother did her bit for the family finances, working as a home help for a well-to-do local woman. Pauline was raised in Barnet but her father – Emma's grandfather – was Irish, Séamus Davitt, from County Wexford. They were Catholic and Emma had a traditional baptism and attended mass growing up. Sadly, she never knew her grandfather, who died before she was born.

She has an older half-brother, Robert Bunton, from Trevor's first marriage and she would go to the park and watch them play football in the local league at weekends. Her younger brother, Paul James, known as PJ, is four years her junior and the two of them are very close. They shared a room until Emma was twelve. Because money was tight they sometimes needed to share their dinner as well.

Emma might have been the baby of the new band but, more relevantly, she had the most extensive CV. She seemed to have been in showbusiness all her life. She was a natural blonde and a very photogenic little girl, who was much in demand as a child model, getting work from the age of two onwards.

Pauline had done some modelling when she was a child so it seemed natural to sign her daughter up with the prestigious Norrie Carr agency, putting aside Emma's earnings so that she would have a nest egg when she was older. In the end the money proved invaluable when she needed fees for theatre school. Over the years Emma featured in so many promotions that it was a rare household that hadn't come across a picture of her cherubic face plugging some product or business, or on the front cover of a magazine in the dentist's surgery.

She was the poster girl for Outspan oranges, the girlfriend of the Milky Bar Kid, smiling sweetly on the tins of Heinz Invaders spaghetti-shapes and standing next to a pretend mum in ads for Mothercare and Argos. She was a cover girl for *Woman's Weekly* and *Womancraft* magazine. She was the face of best-selling games including and, arguably most famously, the timeless favourite Pop Up Pirate. One of the agents at Norrie Carr said, 'She never stopped working and had that special something we were look-ing for. She had a twinkle in her eye and loved the camera.'

Hardly a week would go by when Emma wasn't whisked out of school so that her mum could take her off to a shoot. If it was in the West End, she always made sure to include a trip to the Science or Natural History Museum to make sure her little girl wasn't falling behind in her educational progress. She was at St Theresa's, a Catholic primary school in East End Road, Finchley, close to the North Circular Road.

Emma loved her modelling days, spending time with the other boys and girls or sometimes inviting her own friends along to join her. Occasionally someone at school might be jealous if they saw her picture in a catalogue but mostly she had a very happy childhood. It helped that she developed such a close bond with her mum. Emma said, 'She's got such a soft nature, so unselfish. But she's also a very solid person.' The biggest drama for her parents came when she was hit by a car at the age of four. She needed hospital treatment and still has a scar on her leg as a permanent reminder of a lucky escape.

One huge bonus of modelling was that every year from the age of about six until she was twelve she was one of ten boys and girls chosen to shoot a catalogue abroad for two weeks. Family summer holidays were always spent in a caravan in Clacton-on-Sea so trips to Corsica, Lanzarote and Mallorca were very exciting for a young girl.

Emma's other great love was dancing. She had started ballet classes aged three and had a natural talent. When she was five, her mum had spotted a flyer locally for the Kay School of Dance in Finchley and managed to enrol her daughter even though she was younger than the other children there. She was always far more interested in ballet, tap and disco dancing than in taking part in any sports at school. Her parents could only afford the ballet lessons but the school gave her the other classes for free. Her early ambition to be a professional dancer was dashed at fourteen when she fell and injured her back. By coincidence, when she was eight she came across Victoria

Adams once or twice in dancing competitions in North London.

When she was ten, Emma was accepted by the Sylvia Young Theatre School, which had rapidly become one of the leading performing-arts schools in the country. Sylvia was an East Ender from Whitechapel and had originally become involved with teaching by organising fundraisers for her daughter's primary school in Wanstead. She enjoyed that so much, she moved on to charging 10p a lesson for talented local youngsters. In 1981 she started a Saturday school in Drury Lane but that soon proved so popular that she decided to look for a permanent base. Two years later she took over a disused former Church of England primary school just north of Marylebone station in Rossmore Road.

Sylvia liked to call her pupils her 'babies' or 'young 'uns', which led her to adopt Sylvia Young as her professional name. Legend has it that she expelled her own daughter, Frances Ruffelle, from the school for being 'disruptive', although the award-winning actress and singer was already eighteen when the permanent school was founded. Discipline, however, was an important ingredient of life at Sylvia Young's – not so much abiding by a long list of rules but, more importantly, cultivating an ability to work hard and be a step ahead of the competition in the tough world of entertainment.

Sylvia was always looking for 'someone who has a certain amount of ability but is trainable' – mirroring Chris Herbert's expectations for his girl group. Another mantra from the school also fitted perfectly with his strategy: 'If you fail to prepare, you prepare to fail.'

She also insisted that her students learn everything equally so they could audition for a television soap one day and for a new pop group the next. It's easy to see how Emma would be a perfect candidate for Touch.

By the time Emma joined Sylvia Young in 1985, the school seemed to have a direct conveyor-belt to Central Casting for some of the most popular programmes on television – if you needed a young Londoner for a market stall in Albert Square, Sylvia's establishment was the first place to look. Adam Woodyatt (Ian Beale), Nick Berry (Simon Wickes) and Letitia Dean (Sharon Watts) were just three of the alumni who became household names in *EastEnders*.

You had to be good to be accepted at the school in the first place, passing an audition, an interview and a written test. Her mum waited nervously in the street outside throughout the process and was as pleased as Emma when she was accepted. Parents had to be able to afford the fees, which weren't cheap and were an obvious drain on the Bunton family finances. It didn't help matters when Pauline and Trevor split up a year later, although he still lived locally and, according to Emma, the disruption to her life was minimal. She remained on very good terms with her dad throughout her teenage years. Pauline retrained as a martial-arts teacher and taught her daughter the finer points of Goju-kai karate. Emma might look sweet but you wouldn't want to get on her wrong side.

Apparently much more traumatic than her parents' split was the news that she would have to leave the theatre school because her mum and dad could no longer pay. She was enrolled for a week or two at a local secondary school, which she hated. 'I cried so much,' she later said. All ended well when she was awarded a scholarship back to Sylvia's.

By this time Emma and her mum had moved to a third-floor flat on a small estate in Rogers Walk. There was no garden so Emma and her friends would spend a lot of time in the local park. One of her best friends as a young teenager was Kellie Bright, then another budding actress. They would spend weekends at

Alexandra Palace in North London, roller-skating or messing about in the rowing boats on the lake. Much later Kellie would become one of the best-known faces on British TV playing Linda Carter, landlady of the Queen Vic pub in Albert Square.

Another classmate was star actress Keeley Hawes, the daughter of a London cab driver, who lived in a three-bedroom council flat practically across the road from the school in Marylebone. She and Emma were London girls and became firm friends; Keeley was a welcome guest at the caravan in Clacton. She, too, had won a scholarship to Sylvia Young's. In those days she didn't sound anything like her famous creations, Mrs Durrell in *The Durrells* or the home secretary, Julia Montague, in *Bodyguard*. A series of elocution lessons gave her the cut-glass vowels of one of television's most recognisable voices.

When she left Sylvia Young's, though, she became a model before her breakthrough as an actress, and didn't need to speak. She had been working in the fashion department of *Cosmopolitan* magazine when she was spotted walking down Oxford Street by a scout for the Select model agency and was signed up. She subsequently appeared in classic Britpop videos, including 'She's a Star', by James, and Suede's melancholic 'Beautiful People', for which she had to look sad while eating a bag of chips in Holborn station.

Emma's musical taste was more middle-of-the-road – she liked songs she could dance to more than those with a deeper meaning. As a youngster she loved the party favourite 'Come on Eileen' by Dexys Midnight Runners, and the early hits of Bros. Like Victoria, her first pop pin-up was Matt Goss. And, like Geri, she was a fan of the film *Grease*, doing a very passable imitation of Olivia Newton-John singing 'Hopelessly Devoted to You'. And she was yet another future Spice Girl who was inspired by Madonna.

Most of Emma's socialising was connected to Sylvia Young's. Her first serious boyfriend was a pupil in her year called Carlton Morgan. They started going out when she was fifteen and were together for more than a year, seeing each other every day at school. Carlton fancied himself as a singer and would serenade Emma with their favourite Michael Jackson record, 'I Can't Stop Loving You'. Inevitably, they drifted apart when Carlton had to leave the school as his parents, too, could no longer afford the fees. His acting career was limited to a few appearances as an extra in *EastEnders*.

Before the phone call from Pepi, it looked as if Emma would be just another actor hoping for a break. She enrolled on a drama course at Barnet College where she met the singing coach. In 1993, she had her first role in the ubiquitous *EastEnders*, credited as a 'second girl'. At least she had a credit. When she had the briefest of roles in an episode of *The Bill*, she wasn't mentioned in the cast list. She was hired for a sketch show called *Thatcherworld* that was never commissioned. Finally, she played a prostitute with a fleeting appearance in *To Play the King*, the third part of the *House of Cards* trilogy.

Her hopes for a breakthrough were raised when she auditioned for the role of Bianca Jackson in *EastEnders* but she lost out to Patsy Palmer, despite making the final call-back: 'I loved the show and thought it was perfect for me. It was really upsetting.' It's hard to imagine Emma as Bianca, shouting 'Rickee!' at the top of her voice. But it was a setback and she needed a fresh challenge to raise her spirits, one reason why she was so excited at the prospect of being in a pop group.

Having impressed Chris, she needed to meet the girls. It would be a trial period of a week or so. Geri, the two Melanies and Victoria made the trip to Maidenhead station to welcome Emma off the train from Paddington. She had travelled with

Pauline, and the first sight the girls had of their new bandmate was of her walking down the platform wearing a Donald Duck T-shirt and holding hands with her mum.

She kissed her mum goodbye, a tearful occasion for them both. Pauline told her, 'You can always come home.' Emma seemed very young to the other four. She certainly *looked* young, a petite Geri-sized girl – but they soon realised that looks can be deceiving and Emma was good fun. This would be the first time she had lived away from home so the first evening was a little difficult for her, with Geri comforting her when she had a good cry on her bed. Mel B recalled that she knew Emma was all right when she joined her on the first night for a midnight snack of scrambled eggs. Emma was delighted to find someone in the house who liked to eat and who would join her for her favourite chicken korma.

After a couple of days, they were all getting on so well that Chris wasted no more time: 'I said to the girls, "Look, are you interested in her becoming the fifth member?" And they said, "Absolutely."'

The five Spice Girls were set.

# PART TWO

## HERE COME THE SPICE GIRLS

# 7

# THE STUDENT HOUSE

There was no guarantee that five spirited young women living together in such modest circumstances would get on. The one small bathroom, for instance, became a war zone with each of them fighting for time. Mel B usually won. She liked to take two baths a day and would hold court in the tub while the others would sit about, on the edge or on the floor, and chat.

The rest of the house in Boyne Hill Road was far from luxurious. Nobody seemed to do any washing-up and the kitchen was constantly full of dirty plates and mugs. The living room had an old grey carpet, a couch and a couple of chairs. At least there was enough space for Geri to get some much-needed practice while the others, tired after a day of rehearsing, slobbed out in front of *Home and Away*.

The bedroom the two Melanies shared had pink walls and a red carpet with matching bedding. Mel B put in a red light-bulb too. Geri's room was a cupboard with a mattress in it. Victoria and Emma shared a bigger bedroom, decorated in blue and yellow with a couple of white wardrobes full of Victoria's clothes. She never minded the others borrowing her stuff if she was away in Goff's Oak but had to grit her teeth if she discovered a favourite top tossed on the bed with make-up all over it.

Amusingly, Mel B maintained she always had to clean the toilet. Victoria and Emma, she said, didn't know how to do it 'because their mums always did it for them'. Despite her angelic appearance, Emma was the messiest of the girls – perhaps because she was the one who had never lived away from home. Melanie C did her best to keep everything clean and tidy but it was a losing battle. Geri, who had a touch of the sergeant-major about her, tried drawing up a rota for domestic jobs – a typical student ploy. She stuck it on the fridge but none of the others took any notice, using it instead to scrawl phone messages or reminders that they were out of milk.

As they were settling in, Neil Davies would pop over to film them. He thought the house resembled the anarchic dump from the classic eighties sitcom *The Young Ones*. He observed, 'It was a student house. They were all jumbled together, finding out their relationships with each other.'

To begin with, Emma found it the most difficult, admitting that she missed home. Neil recalled, 'She was like a rabbit in the headlights. She was totally overpowered by the kind of gang mentality.' She soon became used to the weekly routine, however, and looked forward to going home at weekends, seeing her family and her new boyfriend. He was a dental technician called Mark Verghese, whom she had met in her favourite local pub, the Orange Tree in Totteridge.

Victoria probably had to try the hardest to fit in. It didn't help that Mel B insisted on calling her Vicky, which she hated. She also couldn't bear the way the girls always kept the door to the bathroom open when she was having a wee. Neil recalled, 'Victoria would try and close the door but they would open it all the time. They thought it was fine even if she was sitting on the loo but Victoria didn't like that. She wanted a bit of privacy.' He found her the quietest of the bunch: 'She hardly ever talked.

She worried about the spots on her face. She worried about her weight. I would say that she was paranoid about diet.'

While her parents were from working-class families in North London, Victoria was used to having plenty of money – far more than the rest of them. She arrived in Boyne Hill Road in a smart Suzuki Jeep, which was several divisions above the clapped-out green Fiat Uno that Geri drove. She swapped it for a smaller, less ostentatious black Renault Clio because, she said, it was auto-matic, easier to drive and didn't attract attention parked outside in the street.

That was certainly not the case when her dad Tony picked her up one afternoon in the Rolls-Royce, which raised a few eyebrows. One person she unexpectedly found a natural empa-thy with was Chris Herbert, who was there that day and was as surprised as the rest. He, too, came from a working-class family that had made good and had plenty of money. Coincidentally his dad Bob had a Rolls-Royce and so did Chic Murphy –Victoria might have been forgiven for thinking that every household had one.

On Fridays, Victoria would drop Emma off at her home in Rogers Walk, then head on to the more tranquil surroundings of Goff's Oak for a lazy weekend by the pool. The one cloud on this sunny highway was her fiancé Mark. The girls hadn't taken to him when he dropped in to Boyne Hill Road. They had, it seemed, preferred Emma's Mark.

Despite the lack of amenities in Boyne Hill Road, they had the occasional use of a pool when Chic invited them to his house, which backed on to the Thames at Bray, a lovely village well known for its celebrity residents and fashionable restaurants. The drawback was that it gave Chic the opportunity to criticise their weight, which, unintentionally, was just about the worst thing you could say to young women hoping to be in the public eye.

Chic had form for making such comments. According to Michelle Stephenson, he had told her she had legs like tree trunks. He had also ungallantly expressed concern that Emma's legs were too big, which led to a stern rebuke from Pepi, who told him that all young girls had weight problems and they didn't want 'some tall, skinny blonde untouchable'. That didn't stop him suggesting to Victoria and Melanie C that they could lose a few pounds when he saw them in swimsuits.

Pepi described the Girls' eating habits as a 'pot noodle diet'. She observed, 'They were young girls and they used to be starving all the time.' Geri barely ate at all, and when she did, she nibbled some lettuce or opted for a tasty helping of bean sprouts. Melanie C preferred mashed potato and ketchup. Victoria ate crisps, carrots and apples alongside some low-fat dips. Her boyfriend Mark said succinctly, 'She didn't really eat.'

It was easy to put their unusual meals down to lack of funds. They all signed on the dole and claimed housing benefit. In addition, Heart gave them each sixty pounds a week. Neil Davies observed, 'They were on such low incomes that they were eating rubbish food. With all of them, their weight seemed to be up and down ... but they were teenage girls.' Victoria inadvertently revealed the importance of food to their day-to-day well-being. On film, she said, 'I'm feeling in a better mood now cos I've had something to eat, so I'm not going to be as moody. I'm just really fat now. I'm even fatter than before.' Meanwhile Emma declared that her short-term ambition was 'to lose weight off my bum and thighs. That's for all of us, I think.'

In these early days of the nineties, eating disorders were not openly discussed. Anorexia and bulimia carried with them a stigma that forced sufferers to keep their ordeal secret. Chris Herbert thought they existed on 'pretty much a student diet', although he was aware that Geri didn't look as healthy as the other four: 'Her skin was a bit translucent in colour. And she was this tiny, tiny build. But I never associated any of it with an eating disorder.'

Several years would pass before Geri, Victoria and Melanie C all admitted bravely that they were plagued by eating disorders. Victoria seemed to have most trouble losing weight. A friend who visited the house recalled the others teasing her about scoffing a pizza, then bolting to the toilet to be sick.

Mel B and Geri ran the gang. The daily drive to Trinity Studios revealed the hierarchy within the group. They took Geri's car, which was a leap of faith because she was a terrible driver who had never mastered roundabouts and whose car – all dents and scratches – was testimony to her lack of skill behind the wheel. Mel B sat beside her in the passenger seat. Victoria, Melanie C and Emma squeezed into the back. At this early stage Geri was literally the driving force, an almost manic presence creating momentum for all five. Mel B urged her on, a co-driver who always had one eye on the driver's seat. Chris Herbert said, 'They functioned like a couple.'

The other three fastened their seatbelts, especially when the gang leaders raged at one another. Neil Davies became a huge admirer of both young women: 'They were so brave. They would do anything. They would walk into any pub, any restaurant and just take it over. They had the energy, the ideas and the drive. They had a firm vision they were going to make it. They were going to be the best thing ever. Without those two, nothing would have happened. They were living the dream, but if Mel and Geri weren't voicing the dream on a daily basis, then it all began to get very anxious and tense.'

The tension would lead inevitably to disagreements between the two. Neil added, 'Every now and again they disagreed and had a huge blow-up argument, then hugged and kissed after. They fed off each other. The best thing about their arguments was that they got everything out, said exactly what was on their minds. They thought of new things. One would say, "We've got to have combat trousers and boots and show them we're killers or army types," and they would argue that through – and as they argued they would get a few more ideas. So they were re-energising themselves. I thought it was great.'

Chris confirmed that they would fight and be hugging each other the next day. 'They seemed very, very close,' he said. Sometimes the arguments were so intense that they would hurl things at each other in anger and frustration. Even Mel B admitted that it could get really nasty between them. There were many tears. The one person who didn't find the rows so uplifting was Melanie C. She tried to keep the peace, just as Ringo Starr had calmed things between John Lennon and Paul McCartney. 'Why are we always arguing?' she would cry in frustration. Unsurprisingly, she couldn't wait to get away at weekends and visit the quieter waters of Sidcup.

Melanie C found the constant bickering and bitching a strain on her gentler personality: 'Girls can be terrible bullies, worse than blokes,' she later revealed. She was clearly the least tough. She admitted that she could be 'quite vulnerable'. Even at this early stage she seemed to be up and down emotionally. Neil Davies noticed it: 'She would get depressed, then she would be on a high and then she would get depressed about it all again.'

Muff Fitzgerald, the Spice Girls' PR when they first became famous, observed, 'Despite her initial boyish image, in many ways she is probably the softest and warmest of all five girls.'

At least there was Pepi, who would come over two or three times a week for a couple of hours to work with the girls. She became very fond of them and would patiently listen to their problems and tell them not to worry. Neil said, 'She was like a mother hen – a very warm person.'

Pepi's visits were part of a weekly routine that drifted into months. Their days would begin with Geri trying to motivate everyone to get some exercise, either a run or a trip to the gym. At first, they would all go, but eventually only Geri and Melanie C went to the gym while the other three stayed in bed. By 9.30 a.m. they were all just about ready to start the day, although that became later as time went on.

Geri would then drive them the thirty miles to Trinity Studios, where they would continue to rehearse the same four songs, the dance routines that Mel B had devised and the harmonies that Pepi was trying to introduce. It was boring and repetitive and they didn't seem to be improving much. Mel B said, 'We eat, sleep and drink it, really. Wake up in the morning, go to the studio, rehearse all day, come back from the studio and just go to sleep.'

That wasn't strictly true. They did work hard but they weren't nuns. Maidenhead was not exactly at the cutting edge of popular culture. The girls thought it totally dead and most nights the television seemed more exciting. Occasionally Mel B would suggest going for a dance to the town's only club, 5th Avenue, when it was cheap booze night. Chris Herbert promoted a night at Tuskers in Sandhurst and would invite the girls, or sometimes they would pop into Pantiles in Bracknell. Chris recalled, 'They would come out with me and my friends because they didn't really have many friends in the area.'

The most enthusiastic party animal among the five was Emma, who would happily dance all night to her favourite R&B hits. She was used to going out with a wide circle of friends on her home patch in North London. At Boyne Hill Road she would join Melanie C working out Take That dance routines. They would spend hours in the lounge getting one right.

While Victoria and Emma had steady boyfriends at home, Mel B would happily date locally. At first she tried to go back to Leeds for weekends, but that soon proved too expensive so she and Geri would spend Saturday and Sunday at the house. They were inseparable. Mel called Geri her 'best, best friend'. Sometimes they would have enough money to go to a West End club on a Saturday night but mostly stayed in and talked about the future, their desire for fame and how to achieve it. They also shared secrets and Geri confided in Mel, who was the only one she told about her bulimia.

Mel B's current boyfriend might come and stay for a night. The one she liked best was Richard Meyer, the brother of a friend of Geri's. He was a jewellery engraver in St Albans and a sobering influence on her amid all the madness. The others liked him too. From an early stage, though, they all preferred to separate their private affairs from their professional lives. The boyfriends were kept well out of the way if they knew they were going to be filmed that day.

At this stage Neil and Matthew were making the equivalent of a demo to let commissioning agents at the television networks see what the girls looked like and give a hint of their personalities and ambitions. They needed to film for several hours just to get the right five minutes of tape – a sort of showreel. Fortunately, the girls would phone them all the time with ideas, suggesting they take some shots of whatever was happening next. That even included a trip to the far-from-glamorous setting of a service-station café.

Neil's confidence in the saleability of the project turned out to be misplaced. The networks turned him down: 'They said the girls weren't good-looking, they couldn't sing, couldn't dance, and no one would be interested. I told them that the girls had chutzpah and charm and dynamism. I said that, even if it's a car crash, it was still a great story. But every commissioning agent pooh-poohed the idea. I thought they hadn't got a clue.' The people who turned down the very first Spice Girls documentary have kept very quiet about their mistake.

Quietly, though, the project was beginning to look less of a car crash. They were becoming more confident and accomplished. Geri, though, still needed to do a lot of extra work and relied heavily on the patience of the others, in particular Melanie C, who would spend hours coaching her in dance steps.

Bob Herbert kept a low profile, preferring to let his son get on with things, day to day. But he had some forthright views on Geri: 'For weeks her lack of talent was a severe problem for her but with perseverance we found slots for her in the harmonies and the dance routines. Her strength of character started to dominate the other girls in the group but, at first, this was fairly good as it helped her to organise them into a daily routine. Her lack of natural talent was probably the biggest factor in holding the group back while they routined the same four songs over and over again.'

Bob, with his background in accountancy, would have been well aware that the project was costing £1,000 a week, although Chic for the moment was not complaining. By August 1994, Chris Herbert thought the girls were showing enough progress for him to start talking seriously to his partners about giving them a proper contract.

Chic was not keen and Chris thought him pretty cynical about their prospects. Chris explained, 'His way of doing things was to make everyone involved feel kind of insecure – a "Don't bank on it and don't assume this is certain" sort of thing. And by doing that, the girls felt quite insecure in their position. It was his old-school way of managing acts – "Don't give it to them on a plate. Don't spoil them – make them feel that they are replaceable and you will get the best out of them because they will all be constantly fighting for their position."'

At this stage the contract was kept within the office walls at Heart but Chris was becoming more convinced that the project was progressing well: 'The light started to turn on for me. I began to think they were really forming as a band, functioning as a band. This is going to work! I guess around the same sort of time they were starting to think the same.'

Geri's patience was beginning to wear thin as the summer nights shortened. She wanted something to happen. She and Chris would 'knock heads' from time to time. In his opinion she wanted the shortcut route because she was older than the others. He said, 'She had done all sorts of things to get herself famous at whatever cost and she and I knew it. Her frustrations built up over a period of time and we definitely clashed along the way.'

Geri wanted them to get a foot in the door of a record company by any means and Chris would have to repeat his strategy, that this was a long-term plan, a marathon and not a sprint. The girls, though, were much more confident that they had something, and their families agreed. When Victoria's mother, Jackie, and younger sister, Louise, dropped in, they were treated to an impromptu performance of the songs and dances the girls had practised. Louise recalled being very impressed, particularly with their voices: testimony to Pepi's efforts and their own hard work.

Looking back, Chris is convinced that they sang better then than at any time in the future when there were so many distractions and demands on their time. Now they were ready. It was time to reveal Touch to the world.

## 8

# MAKING IT HAPPEN

———————

They were still preparing the same four songs: 'Take Me Away', 'What a Feeling', 'I Want You' and the aptly named 'We're Gonna Make It Happen'. They were a good, safe bet. Even if the girls were fed up with them, they knew they were not going to mess them up. Chris Herbert, meanwhile, had been trying to get a buzz going about the group, not the easiest thing to do with an unsigned band. He wasn't looking for a record deal yet. The next part of the plan was to attract the best writers and producers so that they could eventually approach the top labels with an album ready to go.

Bob helped his son assemble a hundred guests – anyone they thought might take the girls forward. They again chose Nomis as a suitable venue. The girls knew the place from the auditions and it was a regular haunt for anyone in the business wanting to be involved in the next big thing. Nobody knew that was exactly what they going to witness on 7 December 1994. It was a Wednesday and many of those who had accepted the invitation to check out Touch were making their third journey of the week to West London. Marc Fox, a publisher from the BMG group, summed up the negativity that many felt: 'You think, Oh, God, it's got to have to be something special to bowl you over.'

Touch had to perform the same twenty-minute set throughout the day as guests popped in and out, right up until 6 p.m. Pepi observed proudly: 'The buzz was there from the moment they came on stage. They looked brilliant and they started with that energy.' They were dressed for the street, not for a party. Their image at this stage seemed more like the female equivalent of a boy band. Heart had given them a couple of hundred pounds to find some tops to wear and they had picked up some Adidas T-shirts in Camden Market. They each had a different colour, matching them with jeans. Victoria, for instance, wore an eye-catching red top and blue jeans. Emma and Mel B wore berets. They each added a little finishing touch to their outfit but they were far from the individual statements of later years. Even at this early stage, they believed their look should be less co-ordinated. The choreography was very tight and the dancing flawless. Victoria sang particularly well, highlighting her tuneful voice in some solo lines on 'Take Me High', their very first song from all those months ago. Melanie C was already singing the flourishes that would become such a trademark for her later on.

Nomis had a stage area, which gave the girls plenty of space to perform while the guests watched from the seating section. After each set Chris brought them over. He still enjoys the memory: 'It was amazing to watch because they held court. You've got all these multi-million-selling writers and producers and the girls are firing questions at them. They completely turned it – particularly Geri. She's interviewing them: "What skills have you got that we can use?" and "Why do you think you're good enough to write songs for us?", that sort of thing.

'We had been building up to this so there was an air of excitement and anticipation. It couldn't have gone better. They had been in this grotty little studio rehearsing for the best part of the year, and then, all of a sudden, they're exposed to all of these record executives saying how great they are. And you could see Geri's eyes were like "Yeah, OK. This is something else now."'

Neil Davies, who filmed on the day, summed it up, 'In Geri's eyes, she immediately thought, Bye-bye, Chris. I have seen the Promised Land – guys in Armani suits and chauffeured cars – and she thought, Go with the money.'

As far as Chris was concerned it was job done and he could move on to phase two of the master plan, booking studio time with some of the writers who had been so impressed. He needed to do something fairly rapidly about a contract as well. With hindsight, he realised he had made a huge tactical mistake by not having the girls under contract before he showed the world what he had. Many of the guests already knew that and, if they didn't, Geri could be relied upon to tell them.

Bob Herbert had twigged what was going on. He wrote: 'The response we had from the writers and producers went to Geri's head and from that point onwards she became more and more uncontrollable and wanted to take over the running of the group.' It wasn't long before she made a move. A few days after the showcase she arranged to see Marc Fox. He had been one of the most enthusiastic at Nomis and had given Geri his card, in effect bypassing Heart Management. He had recognised that collectively they were bigger than the individual parts: 'They looked like a gang and they acted like a gang.' Marc knew what it was like to be in a group – he had been the drummer with eighties heartthrob band Haircut 100 and had taken over vocals when lead singer Nick Heyward left.

Geri arrived by herself at the BMG offices in Putney. Marc recalled the encounter: 'She was relatively unclothed and she sort of looked like a very lovable Barbara Windsor character. It was a very cold day and she had very little on so, obviously, with the benefit of hindsight, she decided that was the way to get to my heart.'

She quickly steered the conversation towards her being unsatisfied with the speed at which Chris and Bob were taking the band forward. She asked Marc if he might help with introductions to lawyers and other managers. He was happy to assist, understandably keen to join the girls on their 'roller-coaster ride', as he saw it. Geri promised to go back and talk to the others about the future and what he might be able to do for them. She didn't have to go far to get that ball rolling because the two Melanies were sitting in the Fiat Uno, parked nearby.

Nothing significant was going to happen before the New Year, however. While Melanie C, Victoria and Emma went home for Christmas, Geri and Mel B decided to book a cheap package holiday together to Gran Canaria where they could soak up some winter sun and work out what to do in the coming weeks.

On their return there was a serious and unexpected complication. Geri's bulimia returned, worse than ever. Mel B had travelled up to Leeds for New Year, leaving her alone in the house in Boyne Hill Road. Fortunately, Geri realised how ill she was; her half-sister Karen rallied round and went with her to the psychiatric unit at Watford General Hospital where she spent a week recovering, aided by a course of Prozac. Only Mel B knew what had happened. She told the other three that Geri had a family crisis and would be a few days late starting back in January. The world had to wait until the publication of Geri's autobiography in 1999 to learn the truth.

The Herberts never knew. They finally presented the girls with the long-awaited contract, little realising that it was already too late. The terms were fairly standard, although they all thought a management cut of 25 per cent was steep, even if that reduced to 20 per cent after a year. The maths did not appeal as it meant they would only be getting 15 per cent each. Victoria volunteered to show it to her dad Tony, a shrewd businessman, who bitterly regretted signing his own music contract many years before. In her book *Learning to Fly*, Victoria describes his reaction when she took the contract home to Goff's Oak and showed it to him. He advised, 'It's like throwing hundred-pound notes on the fire. Forget it.'

The gang agreed. Back in Boyne Hill Road, they decided that the best course of action was to stall while they waited for Marc to set up some meetings. He took them to see some executives at RCA, Columbia and Parlophone so at least they had an idea of who might be interested if they ditched Bob and Chris.

The girls were now a formidable bunch of attractive young women. Led by Geri, who was the most upfront, they were cheeky and charismatic. It was something Neil Davies had seen develop when he went to Boyne Hill Road: 'They kind of bounced all over you. You would sit on the chair and one of them would sit on top of the chair; one would be sitting crossed legs on the floor and another would be jumping on your knees and tickling you. They were terrific.'

In the very small world of the music business, it didn't take long for word to reach Bob Herbert about what was going on. He was not amused: 'Geri seemed to have taken control of everything and the only way she was going to control the decision-making was to poison the rest of the group against management to such an extent that they were prepared to walk away from their contractual arrangements. She did this by running the management down to everybody she came into contact with and naturally gained their support because they could see a rift develop and they obviously wanted to pick up any action that became available if there was a complete breakdown.'

Bob was in no doubt what had to be done. They had to sack Geri.

Chris, meanwhile, pressed on with his plan of fixing up studio time for the girls with a selection of writers. First of all, he booked them in to work locally with Tim Hawes, a songwriter he was already managing. Although Tim, an accomplished guitarist, kept a small studio at Trinity, it was decided they would learn more with the better facilities at South Hill Park Studios in Bracknell. Tim had first come to the attention of the Herberts in the eighties when he had written some songs for Bros and would have a long association with Chris in the future.

The songwriting sessions were exciting for the girls because they – and particularly Geri – wanted to be involved in every aspect of their career and knew how lucrative publishing could be. Geri kept a book of creative ideas in which she scribbled down an eclectic mix of buzzwords, names, possible ideas for songs and the odd lyric or two. One of them was called 'Club Scene'. 'Club Scene, It's obscene, If you know what I mean …'

Her efforts might not have been enough to give Tim Rice, Bernie Taupin or the other great lyricists of the time sleepless nights, but Chris thought she had something: 'We recognised that she was creative. It was a good starting point because that's how songwriting sessions can turn into something.' He didn't know that the girls were accustomed to sitting round the lounge in Boyne Hill Road, pooling ideas for songs, each shouting out little phrases as they thought of them. It was good practice and they scrambled together their first ever song called, aptly, 'Just One of Those Days'.

Everyone had agreed that it was time to think of a new name. Only Victoria liked Touch. Even Chic was on board and at his house, one afternoon, he suggested Take Five but that was too similar to Take That. High Five was no better and neither was Don't Touch, so it was back to the drawing board. The best option was still to think of a name that had five letters – one for each girl.

Various stories have circulated over the years about how they finally became Spice. One favourite is that Geri had a eureka moment during one of her regular aerobics classes. She literally turned to Melanie C and said, 'I've got it.' Another suggested by the press was that they had next-door neighbours whose dog was a terrier called Spice and they could hear them shouting for him in the back garden.

Chris Herbert, however, is adamant that the inspiration came from a song the girls helped to write. He explained, 'Tim wrote a song with them called "Sugar and Spice". That's where the name came from. I think it's something that should be put right because I don't think the other stories give Tim enough credit.'

It's not clear who had the actual eureka moment on that after-noon. Chris had returned to the studio after the session to hear the new song. In the middle of it there was a 'Spice' rap that apparently triggered the idea for the new name. Everyone, including Bob and Chic, liked it. The new Spice recorded a demo of the track, but it has never been released.

After Tim, they worked with the American guitarist and songwriter Alan Glass, who had a formidable credit list from the eighties including songs with Aretha Franklin, George Benson and Kenny G. More recently he had worked with nineties chart acts Amii Stewart, Junior, and Lighthouse Family. Although none of the songs from the time the girls spent at his studio have made it onto a record, it was another learning step along the way.

The songs with Alan might have been a little too smooth, better suited to Eternal than to the gang of five. They had decided they wanted a 'song with balls' and that was where Matt and Biff came in. With Richard 'Biff' Stannard and Matt Rowe (Matthew Rowbottom), Spice found their songwriting soul-mates. It was a pure accident that Biff heard the girls at the Nomis showcase. He knew Chris Herbert and had worked with one of Heart Management's acts but he was there that day to meet up with Jason Donovan and literally bumped into Mel B in the corridor. He couldn't escape and told *Gay Times*: 'She ran into me – loud and everything – and asked me straight up who I was, what I did, what hits I'd written, was I gay or straight, the complete thing!'

Mel B dragged Biff into the showcase, which was probably the luckiest break he ever had in his music career. He recalled, 'They were just fantastic straight away. It was a bit of love at first sight.' The feeling was mutual. The girls were impressed to learn that he and Matt, who was not around that day, had co-written the East 17 hits 'All Around the World' and 'Steam'.

Matt Rowe was a former chorister and classically-trained musician from Chester. Biff Stannard was an East Ender and had worked as a dancer and fashion stylist. Perhaps his earlier career had given him the common ground to hit it off with the all-dancing, fashion-conscious girls. The other factor was that Geri and Matt clicked. Mel B let slip in her autobiography that she knew what was going on when they started making eyes at one another. Geri fails to mention it in hers, describing Matt as 'tall, slim and a bit preppy' and Biff as 'round and cuddly'. All Biff would say on the subject was that Matt and Geri were close. And all Matt would say is that they indulged in a bit of flirting, noth-ing more.

The personal chemistry obviously helped the songwriting process. The girls piled into Geri's car and drove over to Matt and Biff's Strongroom Studios in Curtain Road, Shoreditch, which was trendier than Maidenhead. During their first sessions they devised a hatful of songs including one, 'Feed Your Love', which was too X-rated for release. They were having fun, though, and during the second session they came up with a catchy little song called 'Wannabe'. It was the second song they wrote that day, squashed together in a small room, and, as often seems to be the case with classics, took about twenty minutes to put together. The inspiration for their most important song, explained Biff, was the 'madness in the room'. They were sitting around talking about the film *Grease* and, in particular, the way John Travolta moved, and the fun, high-school energy he created. If one song is a starting point for the famous Spice Girls' sound then it is probably 'You're the One that I Want', the unforgettable number one for Travolta and Olivia Newton-John.

Much space has been devoted to speculating on the origin of the words 'Zigazig Ha!' which became a catchphrase for a generation of young girl fans. Mel B thought it up but not specifically as a lyric for this song. It was just something silly she started saying one morning that the rest of the girls latched on to until they were shouting it at one another. Generally Matt would develop the musical content of a track while Biff had a great feel for a winning lyric. He heard them saying 'Zigazig Ha' to each other like a 'gang of girls'. He added, 'I just picked up on it. It was nonsensical – we were only messing around. It was all very innocent.' One entertaining theory about the origin of 'Zigazig Ha' was that it was a corruption of 'shit and cigar' which is what everyone used to call an obnoxious songwriter who was in the habit of smoking a cigar while sitting on the toilet.

The only person not over the moon about 'Wannabe' was Victoria. She wasn't at the studio that day. Instead, she had to accompany her boyfriend Mark to a wedding in Devon and made do with hearing the new song down the phone. When she was back with the girls, she discovered that she did not have a solo line to sing – the others had carved it up between themselves. All Victoria ever did on the Spice Girls' most successful hit was pout and sing a few backing vocals.

Victoria is smart enough to realise this very first song coloured how the media and the public viewed her singing. They hadn't been to the showcase and seen her perform so well. It was assumed she didn't have a lyric to herself because she couldn't sing, which was untrue but did nothing for her confidence. Subsequently, she was forever struggling to change that opinion. Chris Herbert has always defended her, stating that she had a good voice, a view echoed by Pepi Lemer who called it a 'pretty little voice'. One can only speculate as to whether the others knew exactly what they were doing. Geri, in particular, was not too happy when Victoria went to the wedding instead of choosing to stay behind and go to the studio. Doing what Mark wanted was not showing female strength. Perhaps it was time for her to become plain Victoria Adams once again.

The need to ditch Heart Management had become more urgent as the Herberts, Bob especially, were putting more pressure on the girls to sign the contract. He was more determined than ever to replace Geri – possibly Mel B as well – and, without his son's knowledge, had lined up their replacements. In his opinion, Geri guessed what was about to happen and started 'a campaign to break away from the existing management'.

The identity of those replacements has never been revealed. Chris didn't know his father had done that but they both were well aware that the group seemed to be imploding in front of their eyes – just when they were within touching distance of success. The girls had become unruly and were arguing more than ever.

Bob thought the situation was caused by a vendetta that Geri and Mel B had been carrying on against Emma and Victoria, who, they thought, was a snob. He was wrong. As Chris now realises, the bust-ups were staged. They were all building up to the Big Fight.

# 9

# THE BIG FIGHT

Chic Murphy was always generous to the girls and decided to treat them to a night on the town. He told them it was an early celebration of Victoria's twenty-first birthday and they would be going to a couple of his favourite places in Knightsbridge. It might or might not have been a last-ditch attempt to keep Spice on side although, according to Chris, Chic wasn't nervous about the contract because he still thought the girls were in a position of weakness.

The occasion had not started well for Victoria because she had a massive row with her fiancé. Mark had objected to her wearing his present, a pair of shoes, well before her actual birthday. He recalled, 'She flew into a rage because she wasn't getting her own way and said I was selfish. She told me not to pick her up later on because I would ruin her night out.'

The evening began in a style to which Victoria was already accustomed – a trip in a Rolls-Royce. Chic drove them into London to an upmarket Chinese restaurant where the meal ended in a birthday-cake fight. Victoria was traumatised when a splodge of cream landed on her smart Karen Millen suit. Beneath the restaurant was a casino and Chic gave each of them £100 in chips to play the roulette tables. Revealingly,

Victoria was the most careful player, coming away with a tidy profit.

This was by far the most glamorous evening yet for the new Spice, although it did not change anything. Within a month, Heart Management was history and so was the house in Boyne Hill Road that had been home for a year. Several different versions of the sequence of events would surface that made it sound more like a piece of bad television fiction than the reality of five young women taking such a momentous step towards their future.

The dénouement occurred at the beginning of March. Fittingly, perhaps, it was at Trinity Studios. Chris couldn't believe what was happening: 'There was a big fight with screaming and shouting and storming out the door. Mel B and Geri went back to Boyne Hill Road and the other three cleared off.'

At the time he was horrified. He was taking the destruction of the group at face value: 'It was so frustrating because I was thinking the wheels were falling off at a point when we were really starting to gain some traction.' But he later confirmed, 'I now know it was all kind of staged, really.' Bob had already told the girls that if Chic was to find out what was happening, he would stop financing the project – a warning that backfired because it made them more determined to leave.

The girls were due to travel to Sheffield after the weekend for a first studio session with acclaimed songwriter Eliot Kennedy. They would catch the train from St Pancras and stay in a flat that artists used when recording in the city. In Chris's version of events, Geri had been pestering him for all of the details, which made him smell a rat: 'I was reluctant to give her this information. They didn't need to know until they were ready to go up there.'

After the row, Chris did not want the girls leaving for Sheffield until everything had been sorted out. He told them he didn't want the humiliation of what was going on between them now continuing in Yorkshire. He called Eliot to pre-empt things by letting him know that that the girls were feeling under the weather and might not make the session.

He finally managed to get hold of Geri and Mel B on the phone and let them know how angry he was at being put in that position. 'I had words with them and the final, final thing before they put the phone down was from Mel B: "See ya, wouldn't want to be ya," were her parting words.'

Chris had no idea that she and Geri had already done a bunk from Boyne Hill Road and were making their own way to Sheffield. They feared the session would be cancelled if they did not sign the contract immediately. By luck, they managed to find Eliot and he agreed to the session. He was won over by their bravado: 'I wasn't in a phone book so I thought that was pretty dedicated.'

On the morning the official session was supposed to begin, Chris phoned Eliot: 'I said, "Look, the girls are not going to make the sessions today because they are all down with the flu. And Eliot was like "OK, fine." And put the phone down. And then about an hour later he rang me back and said, "I've got to be honest with you, they're here."'

His version of events paints a far from attractive picture of duplicity in the five girls. Geri, however, maintained they were merely taking responsibility for their own destiny. She and Mel B had packed their clothes in bin bags, loaded the car and shut the door to the house in Boyne Hill Road behind them. They left a note that read, 'Thank you for all you have done. We can't agree to the terms of the contract.' And that was that. She has never mentioned any staged row or how the others – Melanie C, Emma and Victoria – collected their belongings. In Mel B's version they all left the same night. In Victoria's account they left after Geri had managed to obtain their demo tapes from Heart's office in Lightwater. Chris, however, states categorically that she never pinched the tape, calling that cloak-and-dagger account a 'fabrication'.

Everyone agreed that Geri and Mel B headed off to Sheffield to find Eliot, not knowing if they would be successful. They were as fearless as ever. The other undeniable fact is that they ran out on Bob, Chris and Chic, but there had been plenty of time to sort out a watertight contract and Heart had failed to do that. It might not have been fair, particularly to Chris, but the murky waters of the music business were not exactly renowned for fairness. The author David Sinclair described the girls' behaviour as 'incredibly self-serving and underhand'.

The Sheffield phone calls in effect spelt the end for Chris Herbert and the girls. He recalled, 'I felt gutted about it, more so because I had spent time with the girls and I felt more of a connection with them. We were all friends as well. I felt that it was a real kick in the nuts.'

Chris, though, was an ambitious young man and did not dwell too long on what might have been. He had been surprised by their ruthless approach, particularly from Mel B, with whom he had never fallen out. He prefers to describe their behaviour as 'rebellious', rather than anything harsher.

The early sessions with Eliot proved as fruitful as the ones with Matt and Biff had been. He was a Sheffield lad but his parents had emigrated to Sydney, Australia, when he was four. He grew up in a musical household in which his father and sister sang while he excelled at piano. He was one of those naturally gifted children who could hear a song once and pick out its melody afterwards. He came back to Yorkshire as a teenager, forming a band at Dinnington High School in Rotherham, but realised his future lay as a producer and composer. He gained invaluable experience as a trainee sound engineer – tea boy – in a local studio at weekends while doing shifts at a Wimpy Bar. His first chart success as a producer was on a track called 'Independence', a comeback hit for Lulu at the beginning of 1993. Take That's manager, Nigel Martin-Smith, liked it and brought in Gary Barlow to work with Eliot. They became the best of friends and the result of their first collaboration was the classic 'Everything Changes', which was number one in April 1994, coinciding with his twenty-fifth birthday and just when the girls were getting started.

Eliot lived in the same semi-detached house that his parents had owned and was very relaxed about having five boisterous girls descend on him. He enjoyed having them around, dressed in pyjamas, watching *Star Wars* movies late into the night. He was a great listener. He had a particular affinity with Geri, who loved to talk and was always the last to go to bed, leaving Eliot to sleep on the sofa with his large woolly dog. He called working with the girls the most exciting project he has ever taken on: 'We were young and had lots of fun.'

Songwriting with Eliot was remarkably similar to what they had done with Biff and Matt. He would sing them a chorus or melody with no words and they would all produce pen and paper, bounce ideas around and come up with the lyrics in about ten minutes. 'It was a really quick process,' he recalled, although he would still have to weave his magic to turn it into a coherent song.

Spice were very fortunate that Eliot took an instant liking to them – just as Matt and Biff had done. Their first week with him produced two tracks, 'Say You'll Be There' and 'Love Thing', which were both destined to become Spice Girls classics. They responded well to the relaxed atmosphere away from the tensions that had built up with Heart. The former, which would become their second single, is Mel B's favourite Spice Girls song.

On their return from Sheffield, the fearless five were in a worse position than they had been with Heart. For starters, they had nowhere to live. In the short term Mel B moved in with her boyfriend Richard in St Albans, taking Geri with her to occupy the spare room. Victoria and Emma went home and Melanie C went to Sidcup where she still had her old room. The good news was that nobody had ditched them over their fall-out with Heart. Both Matt and Biff were happy to work with them. Eliot and his manager, Martyn Barter, who had been at the showcase, refused to be influenced by Heart, while Marc Fox was still waiting in the wings with a Filofax full of useful contacts.

Victoria loved being back home. Mark and she had split after the shoes row and he had moved to a small flat in Hertford. Now free and single, she was the first of the girls to have a Hollywood experience. She came across the charismatic movie star Corey Haim at the Strongroom Studios where Matt Rowe was helping him launch his music career with a demo.

The actor was a colourful character, not someone you were likely to meet in Goff's Oak. He was born in Toronto and was the same age as Mark but had been a teenage star in the 1980s. He gained an international following when he starred in the cult horror movie *The Lost Boys* alongside another child star, Corey Feldman, and a young Kiefer Sutherland. His subsequent life read like the script for a descent into a tragic drugs nightmare. He smoked his first joint on *The Lost Boys* and later explained, 'I lived in Los Angeles in the eighties, which was not the place to be.'

When he met Victoria he was not yet at rock bottom. He instantly took a shine to her and the two became inseparable for a week. He was irrepressible and a hurricane of fresh air, as far as she was concerned. He described her as a 'rocking babe'. He thought her 'cool to hang out with' and really intelligent. She might have been a little star-struck as he was enjoying the fame that she and the other girls all craved.

During the time they spent together they saw Buckingham Palace and she drove him home to meet her mum and dad. He loved seeing the 'beautiful English countryside'. On the way, Victoria played him a tape of the early demo of 'Wannabe'. He was impressed and told her, 'That'll be big in the US.' She had a good time with Corey. He was so different from what she was used to – funny and unpredictable. It was a brief interlude and at the end she dropped him at Heathrow for his flight back to LA. He had shown her that there could be life after Mark. About a week of Corey was all she could manage: he seemed never to sleep – perhaps the effect of too many pills.

Corey's addiction to cocaine, crack and prescription drugs escalated as his career declined. Spells in rehab, bankruptcy and a dramatic weight gain marked a period in the wilderness until a temporary revival with the TV reality series *The Two Coreys*, in which he was reunited with Corey Feldman. He had always been frank about his drug problems, which he said had ruined his prospects 'to the point where I wasn't functional to work for anybody, even myself'. He died in 2010, aged thirty-eight, from pneumonia. The obituaries described his life as a 'cautionary tale'. Victoria was said to be 'shocked and upset' at his death.

A short time after his week with Victoria, her ex-fiancé Mark popped round to the house in Goff's Oak to collect some belongings. On the kitchen counter he spotted a photograph of a smiling Victoria and Corey with their arms linked. Her father had taken it in the garden. The picture might or might not have been left out on purpose but it demonstrated clearly that Victoria had moved on.

Spice, as they were still called, needed to progress too. Chatting to Eliot, they realised that they couldn't take on the world entirely by themselves. They all agreed that 'Wannabe' was the best calling card with which to impress potential managers and producers. One thing they did know how to do was rehearse and they worked up a brief showcase of this one song, emphasising the separate strands of their characters – the loudness of Mel B, the sex appeal of Geri, the mystery of Victoria, the innocence of Emma and the athleticism of Melanie C. They strung it all together with their overpowering exuberance and were ready to go.

The men in suits did not stand a chance. Marc would make the appointments and they would jump into Geri's car or, occasionally, Victoria's and head into London. Emma was now driving an ancient Metro, which made Geri's old banger seem luxurious and was so unreliable that they couldn't risk breaking down in it on the way to an important meeting. By this time, the two Melanies and Geri had found a house to share in Cyprus Road, Finchley, which was conveniently just a couple of miles from Emma's home and only a half-hour drive from Victoria's.

Usually Geri's car doubled up as their office, full of scraps of paper where they made notes about who they had seen and what to do next. It was also their changing room if they needed to scramble out of tracksuits into something more elegant. And then, armed with a tape of 'Wannabe', they would charge into the target office and take it over for a few minutes. Victoria and Melanie C would slightly hang back while the other three went into action. Geri and Mel B were Olympic standard bottom pinchers while Emma would put her hair in bunches and wear the shortest skirt. Despite creating a stir, and mostly a favourable response, they couldn't find the right person. Usually Geri would have to phone afterwards and politely say they were looking elsewhere.

The most significant introduction came when Marc told them about a pair of producers known as Absolute, whom he had recently signed to the publishing arm of BMG. They would become the third key component of the Spice Girls' sound after Matt and Biff and Eliot. Absolute were Andy Watkins and Paul Wilson, who met when they were students in Bristol. They were an unlikely combination. Andy played guitar in a band covering classics by the Clash while Paul had been a classically-trained musician, studying at the Royal College of Music. He did, however, moonlight as a drummer in a heavy-metal band. Together they went into partnership, getting a government grant to start their own studios in Bath and building a reputation as go-ahead producers, re-mixers and writers.

By the time they met the girls they had moved to their new studios on Taggs Island, which is in the Thames not far from Hampton Court. That sounded grander than it was. The studios were little more than a glorified shed and it was a real hike to get there. Andy and Paul were not sure they were the right people to work with Spice. They were used to re-mixing smooth soul artists, including Lisa Stansfield and Al Green, so it was a shock to them to encounter the raucous anarchy of Spice, five girls they described as resembling the cast of *Grange Hill*.

Absolute loved modern black music and wanted to work with a girl group producing R&B, which was not Spice. They didn't much like 'Wannabe', and the first few sessions were not encouraging. To their credit, they quickly realised that the problem was trying to impose their music too much on the girls. Instead, they tried starting off with nothing, a blank canvas, and seeing where the session took them.

It proved to be a blinding success and, in no time at all, they had the basis for the future number one 'Who Do You Think You Are'. Andy and Paul also realised that the girls were imagining how the dance routine might go and how the video might look while still thinking of a catchy lyric for the chorus.

With Spice and subsequently the Spice Girls, it was never a case of sticking their name on the song as co-writers and letting the actual writers get on with it. They might not have had much in the way of musical training but they understood their own identity as a group and how to project it. It was concept writing and, inevitably, Geri led the way. More often than not she would come into a session with a catchy line she had thought up and ask their collaborators to turn it into a musical phrase or chorus. Then the others would chip in with their own additions, a harmony or a catchy rap, perhaps. And there was never any question of them not sharing the credit equally between them. It was never going to be a Lennon/McCartney or Jagger/Richard situation. Their unity was their strength.

During those fruitful sessions with Absolute, they also wrote 'Naked', 'Last Time Lover' and 'Something Kinda Funny'. If you added these to the tracks they had worked on with Eliot, and Matt and Biff, they were well on their way to having enough material for their first album. The most pressing problem still remained, though. They didn't have a manager. That was about to change.

# 10

# HANG ON TO YOUR KNICKERS

---

A conversation with Andy and Paul on the dock at Taggs Island near their studio changed things. They explained that their manager, Pete Evans, had recently joined forces with 19 Management, run by a rising star in the music business called Simon Fuller. He had negotiated the deal with BMG Music Publishing on Absolute's behalf. They had already sent him a tape of 'Something Kinda Funny' and he had responded enthusiastically. It was a promising start.

Spice were beginning to run out of candidates, especially if they wanted someone with a proven track record. Simon had yet to be granted a 'Wannabe' performance but he had heard about it. He knew what to expect when they bounced into his offices in Battersea. He was late and kept them waiting, which, if intentional, was a very shrewd move. For once they were on the back foot.

They had to sit about until he chose to appear, a dapper, perma-tanned figure with shiny black hair and a quietly imposing manner. He was thirty-five and had been building a solid reputation for ten years. He was born in Cyprus, where his father was stationed with the RAF, and had enjoyed a nomadic childhood in Germany and Ghana before his family came back to

England and settled on the south coast in Hastings. His father became a primary-school headmaster and Simon was very much a product of a middle-class provincial environment.

From an early age he seemed to appreciate that he could make money from music, managing his school band and leaving school to run discos. He followed a tried and trusted method of gaining a foothold in pop by being hired as an A&R man with Chrysalis Records. He was noticed straight away when he recommended that his company buy up Madonna and her first hit 'Holiday'. In the end, they chose to pick up the song but not the artist.

After a couple of years Simon decided to go it alone and manage Paul Hardcastle, a young keyboard player. They struck gold almost immediately when Paul's anti-Vietnam war song '19' went to number one. Nineteen was the average age of US soldiers serving in that pointless war. The record was number one in fourteen countries and sold more than four million copies. At the age of twenty-five Simon Fuller had made his first million. He called his newly formed company 19 Management and he kept the prefix as it expanded into the 19 Entertainment Group. Paul Hardcastle could never repeat that huge first success, although his track 'The Wizard' was the theme tune for *Top of the Pops* when Spice were teenagers. '19' proved more of a stepping stone for the manager than the artist.

The next two artists Simon took on were Cathy Dennis and Annie Lennox. He spotted Cathy's potential when he saw her sing with her father Alan's band at the Norwood Rooms in Norwich. To her surprise she became the dance-music darling of the early nineties, with a much-copied bob haircut. Her biggest UK hit was 'Touch Me (All Night Long)', which, more significantly, reached number two in the US, where she also had three consecutive number ones in the *Billboard* dance chart. Simon would use the blueprint of her success to move Spice into the American marketplace at the earliest opportunity.

Cathy had a self-deprecating style, which was strikingly similar to the one Victoria Adams would adopt in the future. She once said, 'It never crossed my mind that I could be a pop star because I came from Norwich. Pop stars don't come from Norwich.' Looking at an image of Cathy Dennis from her early chart days is quite an eye-opener: the dark bob, the sultry look upwards at the camera are quintessential Victoria.

Annie Lennox was another excellent credential for 19. Arguably the most successful female singer in Britain – and one of the richest – her connection with Simon improved his prestige in the eyes of Spice. When he took her on, she had already achieved a number-one album, *Diva*, and was about to achieve another, *Medusa*, that included the beautiful 'No More I Love Yous'. That album was number one in the UK charts as the girls were leaving the Herberts and looking to rule the world. Geri always made sure they had done their homework before a meeting so they knew Simon Fuller was an impressive figure even before they met him.

Managing Cathy demonstrated his ability to guide an artist internationally while Annie showed he could handle the affairs of a very successful performer. He didn't need to tell Spice he was going to make them big stars. That would have been stating the obvious. Instead he explained what he thought he could do for them to maximise their impact both at home and internationally, using Cathy as an example.

He also asked them what they wanted to achieve. Victoria blurted out what became one of the Spice Girls' most famous sayings: 'We want to be household names. We want to be bigger than Persil washing powder.'

At the end of the meeting, Simon conceded a rare compliment to the girls: 'I think you're fabulous,' he said, which really meant something coming from him. Here was a man who smoothly oozed success and the girls were of one mind that they wanted him to be their manager. They made the decision on the drive back to North London. On hearing confirmation that they were going with 19, Simon immediately assigned them a personal assistant, Camilla Howarth, who took over the daily running of their chaotic lives. They may have been skint still, but they had a PA.

It wasn't the end of the 'Wannabe' whirlwind. Simon's first job was to secure them a record deal. He had two big advantages. First, Spice already had at least seven songs ready to form the major part of a first album. Secondly, he had the girls, ready and willing to overwhelm any executive with the power of their collective personality. They now had three songs they liked to perform: 'Wannabe', 'Say You'll Be There' and '2 Become 1', another instantly appealing song written with Biff and Matt during their first sessions. Simon sent them around town to do what was by now a well-known act, then sat back and waited for the phone to ring. Major interest came from BMG, London and Virgin. London was an attractive option because it was the label for East 17 and therefore had a link with songwriters Matt and Biff.

Virgin, however, were especially keen because they did not have a major pop act on their books. If the girls signed with them they would be joining a label that had a reputation as cool and hip with a roster of artists that included the Verve, Lenny Kravitz, Massive Attack and Neneh Cherry, a favourite of the two Melanies as teenagers.

The girls wanted care, attention and the feeling that they were important. Virgin declared their serious interest by flying the girls to the US *before* they had signed, which was a generous declaration of intent. They met all the top executives in Los Angeles, including Ken and Nancy Berry, who ran the company in the States and were well known for entertaining music greats at their luxurious Bel Air home. Spice performed an impromptu number or two on the patio with a boombox providing the music. They were treated royally by a company thoroughly determined to win their signatures. They succeeded, partly because the five-album deal included an advance, if all went to plan, of £1 million. Understandably, Simon was delighted to be offered such a figure for an unsigned band.

Behind the scenes he set about reaching an amicable settlement with Bob and Chris Herbert and Chic Murphy. They settled for a one-off payment of £50,000 to cover their time and expenses. That may not seem much for missing out on millions but nothing is ever guaranteed in the music business. They had spent an estimated £20,000 progressing Spice from a group of wannabes so, at the time, it was a tidy profit. In this case the girls were able to sign on to Virgin with no excess baggage. Chris reflected wryly, 'We worked out the financial settlement with them. It didn't take account of 60 million albums.' It would, in fact, be 85 million albums.

Nobody made or manufactured them. They made themselves. Chris Herbert put together the five young women and gave them the time and training to have a chance of success. Without his initial vision the Spice Girls would almost certainly never have found each other. The well-known singing coach Carrie Grant, who later worked with them, remarked, 'Would they have made it individually? No.'

By the time Simon Fuller came on board, they were set with the sound they wanted and, mostly, the image as well. Chris Herbert bore no grudge and generously conceded, 'I couldn't be confident that I would have been able to guide their careers in the way that Simon Fuller did.'

The important thing was that Chris did not burn any bridges in the very small world of music. An intriguing postscript involved Simon Cowell, then a senior A&R man at BMG. In the 1990s the man who would be synonymous with finding and nurturing new talent managed to miss out on both Take That and the Spice Girls. When he first saw Take That, he said, 'I'll sign them without the fat one.' When he realised his mistake a month or two later, he offered a deal but it was too late. He had told Simon Fuller that he wanted to sign Spice but missed out to Ashley Newton and Ray Cooper at Virgin. Instead Simon had to make do with novelty acts including Zig and Zag and Power Rangers.

Despite all the help he had given the girls, Marc Fox was also sidelined. Simon Fuller signed the girls to a publishing deal with Windswept Pacific. Marc left publishing to move into A&R at BMG with an office along the corridor from Simon Cowell, who was keen to meet Chris Herbert, the man who had put Spice together.

At their first meeting, Chris told Simon Cowell that he wanted to put a boy band together that would appeal to male and female – just as he had done with Touch. He explained, 'Take That would give you roses but I wanted a band that would fuck you up against the garage door.' He again placed an ad in the *Stage*, which the media picked up on, calling it 'Spice Boys Wanted'.

Once again the five boys were put up in a house, this time in Camberley; they rehearsed at Trinity Studios before they were launched properly in 1997 after Simon Cowell had officially signed them. They were called 5ive, a much better name than Touch. Before disbanding in 2001, they had a dozen top-ten hits including three number ones as well as topping the album charts. They sold ten million records worldwide, which might not have matched the Spice Girls but was still a great success. In their first year alone they were on twenty-three magazine covers and followed in the girls' footsteps by securing a deal with Pepsi.

Chic Murphy, for whom the Spice Girls always had a soft spot, had retired to enjoy the Mediterranean sun on Mallorca while Bob helped Chris with 5ive. Chris and his fiancée Shelley were due to marry in August 1999. Sadly, on the Monday before the wedding, Bob Herbert was killed in a car crash. He was fifty-seven. The ceremony went ahead as planned on the Saturday and Bob's funeral took place on the following Wednesday. Chris cancelled the honeymoon. Collectively, the Spice Girls paid tribute to Bob during a press call. He never had let on as to whom he had lined up to replace Geri and Mel B.

The date was fixed for signing the contract with Virgin: 13 July 1995. London Records had not given up and, by coincidence, had invited the girls to a party on a boat on the Thames on the same day. Both companies knew what was going on. The girls duly arrived at the boat and happily knocked back glasses of wine, nibbled the food and generally revelled in the attention they were getting. One can only imagine what the executives of Virgin were thinking as they waited back at their offices in Notting Hill for the girls to arrive.

Their nerves were not calmed by a practical joke the girls decided to play on them. Their limo finally arrived but inside, waiting for the welcoming committee, there was no sign of Spice but, instead, five blow-up dolls from the Ann Summers sex shop in Charing Cross Road. The girls had despatched Camilla to buy them and send them on in advance while they continued to enjoy their riverboat party.

When they finally arrived they were each presented with a bouquet of flowers and a goodwill payment of £10,000, which made their collective eyes light up – some money at last. Victoria was quite merry at this stage, a product of drinking on a permanently empty stomach. After signing the million-pound contract, the girls, all in high spirits, were bundled into a taxi bound for the fashionable restaurant Kensington Place, where Simon had booked a table for them all to celebrate. Victoria, by now very tipsy, shrieked, 'Hang on to your knickers!' whereupon the other four pulled hers off and Geri threw them out the cab window.

# 11

# THE POWER OF GIRLS

Even though they signed the contract in July, it was thought to be too close to Christmas to cash in properly in 1995. There was no rush, and Virgin did not want to mess up such a large investment. Behind the scenes, many powerful people were agonising about the girls' image and where to position them in the pop market. A quick blast of publicity and a hit single or two was not the plan.

The choice of the first single was an early problem that needed to be resolved. Geri and Mel B were, as usual, the most vocal. They wanted 'Wannabe' as their début release. They were convinced that it best represented the nature of the group – upfront and sassy. The head of A&R at Virgin, Ashley Newton, who had been so instrumental in bringing them to the label, did not agree and strongly lobbied for 'Say You'll Be There', which had a stronger melody and a mellower feel. Geri, clearly the *de facto* leader of the group, stood her ground. Even Simon was unsure until he was told categorically that 'Wannabe' was the one.

The delay in releasing a record allowed several things to happen that would have a crucial influence on their future success. Simon was already thinking of the bigger picture in terms of international appeal, merchandise and perhaps a movie. They started off by flying to Los Angeles, a bold move that was typical of his forward thinking: they would be getting attention in the world's biggest marketplace before the UK even knew they existed.

They stayed at the Four Seasons Hotel in Beverly Hills and loved the glamour of it all: the Gang of Five go to Hollywood. They shopped, lounged by the pool and went celebrity hunting, as you might if you were a train-spotting anorak. But they were also thoroughly professional about meeting every movie and TV executive that their new US agent had arranged for them to see. They were now with the prestigious William Morris Agency and met, among many others, important men from Disney, Dreamworks and Fox Studios. It always seemed to be men. They were still the whirlwind wannabes but they were also planting the idea of a film harnessing their energy in much the same way as the classic *A Hard Day's Night* had done with the Beatles in 1964.

At this stage they were still called Spice, but not for long. They discovered there was an American rapper called Spice 1. They did not want to be confused with the man who brought the world the notorious albums, *AmeriKKKa's Nightmare* and *1990-Sick*. Simon had noticed that when the girls were in the US they would charge into a room and someone would inevitably say, 'Here come the Spice girls.' He suggested in passing to Geri that Spice Girls might be an even better name. From that moment on they were known as the Spice Girls. At last they had found the right name.

Before flying back to London to finish recording their album, the Girls were allowed a brief holiday in Hawaii where they posed for a rare picture of them all wearing bikinis – something Victoria seldom wore. They stayed on the island of Maui in the five-star Kea Lani Hotel overlooking the Pacific Ocean. Mel B found the time during the six-day break for a brief fling with a local lad. After a touch of Paradise, it was back to a London autumn and the daily grind of finishing their album. They left Cyprus Road: the two Melanies moved into a house in Jubilee Road, Watford, just across from Geri's old family home. She went to live with her half-sister Karen and her family in Chorleywood so she wasn't far away. Victoria and Emma stayed at home. Life wasn't much different from what it had been in Boyne Hill Road, but instead of rehearsing all day they were booked into various studios to record.

At weekends Mel B and Geri were the ones left behind, this time in Watford rather than Maidenhead. They still went out clubbing or stayed in and watched TV. They both declared that they had found a true friend. Geri wrote in her diary that they had been perhaps through more than most people do in relationships that had lasted much longer: 'It has been demanding, intense and hectic, confusing, frustrating but good.'

The climb to the top can often be more rewarding than reaching the pinnacle, particularly in the music business. Geri, who could be quite sentimental, bought five identical gold rings from Ratners when they were all in Sheffield for some extra work with Eliot Kennedy. On the outside of each she had 'Spice one of five' engraved and gave them to the girls as a mark of their collective strength and bond.

They were all frustrated at being given dates for the release of their first single – only to have it postponed repeatedly. The stumbling block was still 'Wannabe'. The problem was not resolved until Simon Fuller sent the song to engineer Mark 'Spike' Stent. He proved to be an inspired choice. Spike, so–called because he had spiky hair, had established a solid reputation for his work with Depeche Mode, Erasure and Massive Attack. At the time he was in Ireland working with U2 on their album *Pop*, but would come back to London for odd weekends to see his family and catch up on business at his studio. During one of those home visits he turned his attention to 'Wannabe'.

The song had been mixed and re-mixed half a dozen times but still nobody was completely happy. The track did not gel in a radio-friendly manner. There was a world of difference between sticking the demo on while the girls danced around the desks and having a record that sounded good on Radio 1. Spike recalled, 'The problem was that the vocal balance hadn't been quite sussed. It's a very quirky pop record, and there's not a lot going on with it, and my work was all about getting the vocals to sound right. It was quite tough to do, even though it only took six hours.' He did the job so well that, finally, Virgin was happy to release 'Wannabe'. It was time to get a Spice Girls buzz going.

The publicity whirl began in the unlikely surroundings of Kempton Park Racecourse where the girls frolicked around a statue of the famous horse Desert Orchid and generally made a nuisance of themselves, running away from security. A few journalists turned up to take advantage of a free day at the races and one was treated to a live performance of 'Wannabe' in the Ladies.

More seriously, they were on show at the Brit Awards in February 1996. The girls were not the talk of the night. That accolade belonged firmly to Jarvis Cocker, who took umbrage at the sight of Michael Jackson appearing Christ-like on stage among a throng of adoring children: he ran up and waggled his bottom at the man who was then the biggest star in the world. The highlight for the Spice Girls was being introduced to Take That, who had been such an important part of life at Boyne Hill Road. Now, less than a year later, here they were saying hi. Simon

Fuller was on a table with Annie Lennox, along with Tony Blair, then leader of the opposition. 'Would you like to be in our video?' Geri asked the future prime minister. He politely declined, but it was another example of her boldness that swept the Spice Girls along.

Something far more significant to the careers of the Spice Girls than the Brit Awards happened later that month – Take That split up. They were the most popular band in the country and their demise even made *News at Ten*. They left a huge gap in the teen and pre-teen market that record companies were falling over themselves to fill. Could an all-girl band take their place?

Virgin were trying to get more media coverage for the Girls. The then head of press, Heather Finlay, asked music journalist Sonia Poulton to interview them at a recording studio in West London. Sonia had been told by her friend, 'People don't get them. They think pop bands need to be all synchronised and dressed in matching outfits. Nobody in the press is interested.'

Sonia could immediately see how different they were. Victoria, for instance, was wearing a pencil skirt and a smartly tailored jacket while Geri was dressed in what appeared to be a teal green piece of Bacofoil. They came across as a ragtag bunch but were endearingly energetic, treating her, of course, to a personal performance of 'Wannabe', which they must have sung a hundred times or more in public before it was released.

Sonia set about trying to identify them as individuals. Her conversation with the girls is fascinating. Mel B she decided was 'feisty and strong with lots of attitude'. She told Geri, 'You're a vamp – seaside saucy meets exotic dancer.' She thought blonde Emma was cute and needed protection. 'I see you as the Baby Doll of the group.' Melanie C was easy: 'Obviously you're the sporty one.' Finally she turned to Victoria, the least talkative of them, and said, 'You are the sophisticated one. You have a snob-bish quality about you.'

These were only her rough ideas but they were helpful. She discussed them with Heather, and the Spice Girls' characters began to take shape. Feisty, Saucy, Baby Doll, Sporty and Snobby were not exactly right but they were a good starting point for promoting their separate identities. They were not personas invented that afternoon but a useful reflection of how the Girls were already projecting themselves in public; images tailored to their personalities.

In the meantime, the official release of 'Wannabe' was finally set for July 1996 and publicity gradually gained momentum. Together they embarked on a punishing schedule of promotion that would take them all over the world during the next year. It began in the far from exotic surroundings of a ploughed field in Hertfordshire. At 6 a.m. photographer Harry Borden, who was working for a teen magazine, was preparing to take their photo before they embarked on a hot-air-balloon flight for *Massive*, a short-lived Saturday-morning youth show hosted by Denise van Outen. None of the girls was in the mood to look cheerful on a freezing cold morning in the middle of nowhere. They were not dressed appropriately for the countryside and Victoria, who had been out the night before, was particularly unhappy at the mud spoiling her Gucci loafers.

Harry was concerned that the picture of Misery Spices was not going to work. Their new press officer, Muff Fitzgerald, had the solution. Standing behind the photographer's shoulder, he dropped his trousers and mooned at the girls. The famous energy was instantly ignited: 'You're mad, you are,' shouted Mel B, as the others fell about laughing. Harry got the shot.

His impression of the girls at this early stage is intriguing. He recognised that the rapport between the five was more than the sum of their parts. Individually, as well as believing Melanie C to be 'sweet and a nice girl', he noticed that Geri was the most independent, Mel B and Emma the most showbiz; he thought Victoria was shy and demure.

They appeared on MTV's *Hanging Out* and did some local radio but, better still, they were booked on *Surprise Surprise*, hosted by Cilla Black and one of the most popular programmes on British television: an audience of 12 million watched that particular edition when a teenage girl, Sally, interviewed them for Key 103 radio station in Manchester as her 'surprise'. She asked them to introduce themselves. Melanie C went first: 'I'm Melanie C and I love football.' Then, 'I'm Melanie B and I'm a northern nutter;' 'I'm Victoria and I like shopping;' 'I'm Geri. I'm a major nutter but there's method in my madness.' Finally, 'I'm Emma and I love doughnuts, chocolate and pink things.' They weren't the finished article by any means but they were progressing their roles. Only Geri's didn't really fit, although hers was probably the most revealing and honest.

One last important component needed to be in place: the video. The idea was to film the Spice Girls running riot through a building, terrorising the people there in much the same way as they had done for months, performing the song in record-company offices all over London. The initial plan was to film in Barcelona but that fell through. Instead, the shoot took place throughout a freezing cold night at the Midland Grand Hotel, the splendid Gothic building next to St Pancras railway station. At the time it was in need of serious restoration and wasn't the five-star Renaissance establishment it is today.

Simon Fuller recommended a little-known Swedish director, Johan Camitz, to take charge. A former sculptor, he had impressed with his commercial videos for Diesel jeans, Nike and Volkswagen. He could help build a brand. He was very keen to film in one take, which made everything suitably chaotic: Geri stumbled into a chair and Mel B's nipples were noticeably erect – a sight too much for some parts of Asia where the video would subsequently be banned.

The whole thing cost £100,000 but hardly any of that went on outfits. They were wearing clothes that you might have picked up in Topshop. Geri wore a showgirl outfit she had found for twenty pounds at a market in Notting Hill. The dedication they had shown at Trinity Studios stayed with them. Nicki Chapman, the television personality who was then the group's plugger, recalled, 'It's cold even in the summer if you're on set at night and they had very few clothes on. But there was not one word of complaint from the Girls. They were so professional, they were so united. They were just focused and on it. This was their opportunity.'

The overall effect was of brooding high-energy anarchy, which was perfect for their image. The last thing they wanted was to appear pretty-pretty lazing by the pool in Club Tropicana. Virgin was not confident, however. Their reaction was summed up by their director of video, Carole Burton-Fairbrother: 'Everybody at Virgin and I were like "Oh, gosh, I'm really not sure about this."' There was even talk of shooting another video.

They were wrong. The video quickly became the most requested on the cable TV channel, the Box, staying at number one on the viewers' chart for thirteen weeks. Six weeks before the designated release of the single, the video was being shown more than ten times a day. It would be voted number forty-one in Channel 4's *100 Greatest Pop Videos* (Michael Jackson's 'Thriller' was number one).

Carole recognised that the video perfectly represented what the Girls were all about: 'It was rehearsed quite a bit but it has the feeling of being just as they came. It was quite reflective of them.'

When 'Wannabe' was finally released on 8 July 1996, everything was in place for a massive hit. Not everybody bought into the Spice Girls, though. Chris Evans, then presenter of the breakfast show on Radio 1, famously told them to 'fuck off back to *Alive and Kicking*'. They were all shocked. Geri went home, binged on cake and then stuck two fingers down her throat so she could throw up. Chris proceeded to be rude about them practically every day, although he did later change his mind and decide he liked them after all. He also became a good friend of Geri's.

To coincide with the launch, they were interviewed for *Top of the Pops* magazine. One of the writers, Jennifer Cawthron, now founder of skincare brand Love Boo, remembered feeling a bit sorry for them when they burst into the office, sang 'Wannabe' and were met with some half-hearted clapping. 'But they were so enthusiastic and friendly we thought we should mention them in the magazine. That's all it was – a mention, not even a page.'

Their individual personas had developed further since their meeting with Sonia Poulton. They were now clearly acting separate roles. Peter Lorraine, the magazine's editor, suggested presenting them as a spice rack. Jennifer explained, 'The girls were already like cartoon characters of themselves so it only took about ten seconds to come up with the nicknames. Victoria was "Posh Spice" because she was wearing a Gucci-style mini dress and seemed pouty and reserved. Emma wore pigtails and sucked a lollipop, so obviously she was "Baby Spice". Mel C spent the whole time leaping around in her tracksuit so we called her "Sporty Spice". I named Mel B "Scary Spice" because she was so shouty. And Geri was "Ginger Spice" simply because of her hair. Not much thought went into that one.'

Geri would have preferred to be Sexy Spice but that was a little too grown-up for the target age group. So it was Posh, Baby,

Sporty, Scary and Ginger. The nicknames completely transformed their careers. They were cartoon characters that rapidly became adopted throughout the playgrounds of the world. The Spice Girls were no longer just appealing to young women with hopes and aspirations in a male-dominated world. They were loved by pre-teens and little girls, as young as three, four or five, who had no idea what they were singing about but could dance to the music and pretend to have a favourite. To them they were five little princesses.

One article in a monthly magazine didn't make that happen. But the tabloid press ran with the nicknames and the Girls became better known by them than by their real ones. They were a headline writer's dream, short and instantly recognisable. They were the roles they were destined to play for years to come, although they never reflected their true characters. Geri observed, 'Pop music is about fantasy.'

'Wannabe' went to number three in the UK charts in the first week of release. Simon Fuller promptly flew the girls to Japan in a canny move to make them appear an international group. The very first time they appeared on *Top of the Pops* – a huge ambition for them all, especially Victoria – they mimed the song by satellite. Instead of celebrating with their friends and family, they were stuck in hotel rooms thousands of miles away. The next week they were number one, knocking Gary Barlow off the top spot with his super-saccharine 'Forever Love', which was expressing the soppy sentiment that the Spice Girls were trying to avoid. Even jaded pop writers had to admit 'Wannabe's' appeal. Columnist Rick Sky observed, 'It really is a beautiful pop song – one of the very best of the decade.' Not everyone was so impressed: the *Independent's* respected critic Andy Gill was disappointed that 'the initial tough gal rap style dissolves into a harmless cutie pie chorus'.

Worldwide, 'Wannabe' went to number one in thirty-five countries and sold more than seven million copies, one and a half million of those in the UK alone. It remains the biggest-selling single in the UK by a girl group. The song would make the Spice Girls rich very quickly, especially because they were co-writers and insisted on 50 per cent of publishing royalties, which they always divided equally between them. In a 2014 online study, it was found to be the catchiest song of the last sixty years; it took people on average just 2.48 seconds to recognise the track.

Celebrity journalist Kate Randall, who was a twelve-year-old schoolgirl at the time, recalled the excitement of 'Wannabe': 'It was a catchy, easy song and all of us wanted to be one of the girls. You could identify with them so easily. I wanted to be Geri because she was the most fun.' Ginger was also the favourite of Adele, who was singing 'Wannabe' in break time with her primary-school friends in Tottenham. The superstar was aged eight when it was released and, like millions around the world, could sing it, word perfect, without having any idea what 'Zigazig Ha' meant. Adele was transfixed by Geri's fire and energy: 'I just remember seeing her and being like "Fuck it, I'm going to do that. I want to be Ginger Spice."'

Adele has never been considered as poppy as the Spice Girls but they were her favourite group and they remain so. She proved the point nearly twenty years later when she sang a spontaneous version of 'Wannabe' with James Corden for his US chat show's 'Carpool Karaoke' feature.

Their foresight in earning from co-writing the songs was also the blueprint for turning Adele into one of the richest women in music. Despite being so young, Adele was also inspired by the last piece of the Spice Girls jigsaw. They had the song, the name, the nicknames, and now they were about to have the slogan for a generation: Girl Power.

The week that 'Wannabe' was released, another record crept into the lower echelons of the charts at number twenty-five. The track 'Girl Power' was by a female duo called Shampoo from Plumstead, Jacqui Blake and Carrie Askew, who had a few minor hits in the nineties. Their best-known song was called 'Trouble', which could also have been adopted by the Spice Girls. They were bolshy and mouthy and liked to shout their lyrics.

'Girl Power', the song, had a post-punk feel to it, stating 'I don't wannabe a boy, I wannabe a girl.' It was also the title track of their third album, which failed to chart.

Geri Halliwell was a cultural magpie, reading and listening to everything she could lay hands on. She is happy to admit that she embraced the phrase Girl Power: 'I saw them and I thought, Oh, my God, that is so good!'

Geri turned it into a slogan and a cause for millions of little girls and those older ones who had enjoyed one lager too many on a good hen night. It might have been simplistic but it was also good fun and contributed hugely to building the Spice Girls brand that Simon Fuller was masterminding. All the girls embraced the concept, realising that it would do wonders for promoting their profile. It remained at the heart of the group's popular appeal.

The *Golden Rules of Girl Power* as defined by the Spice Girls in an MTV video were:

Be Positive!
Be Strong!
Don't let anyone put you down.
Be in control of your own life and your destiny.
Support your girlfriends.
And let them support you, too.
Say what's on your mind.

Approach life with attitude.

Don't let anyone tell you that you can never do
something because you're a girl.

Have Fun!

Slogans and catchphrases clearly work in promotion and market-ing. Individually the Spice Girls had their nicknames. Now 'Girl Power' gave the whole group a strong, collective persona. Just five years later, in 2001, the *Oxford English Dictionary* defined it as: 'Power exercised by girls; specifically, a self-reliant attitude among girls and young women manifested in ambition, asser-tiveness and individualism'.

'Wannabe' was number one for six weeks and during that time the Spice Girls made the trek out to the BBC studios in Elstree three times to appear on *Top of the Pops*. This was the real deal. Emma recalled, 'It freaked me out. Marilyn Manson was watching us and I forgot the words. I've been on countless times but I never got over that feeling of excitement.'

They made a great impression, always flirting with the crew and remembering everyone's name. They were novices and complete professionals at the same time. One of the floor crew observed, 'All the guys thought they were up for a shag with one of the Spice Girls.' Appealing to men as much as women had been the original vision for the group and this throwaway remark showed it had worked, but as time went on the male audience became less important.

Such exposure on *Top of the Pops* guaranteed interest from the paparazzi. The first time any of them experienced being pictured out and about was when Victoria was spotted two weeks after the release of their first record. She was getting her nails done at a salon in Hertford when a local photographer, Nick Stern, followed her one afternoon: 'I thought it would be worth getting the first picture of the girl in this new wonder band. She saw me and said "Hi, are you paparazzi? Where's the picture going and can I get a copy of it?"'

None of the Girls was jaded yet by exposure to the media. It was still so exciting.

# 12

# THE GENIUS OF GERI

Before the Spice Girls could draw breath, the next single was released. This time everyone agreed that 'Say You'll Be There' was a sound choice. Mel B called the track her favourite and thought it had a 'good groove'. Only six weeks had passed since their début had topped the charts and now the follow-up was number one.

The video is one of their most memorable and provided a striking contrast with their first. The director was Vaughan Arnell, another film-maker with a background in commercials. He shot 'Fast Love' for George Michael and 'Back for Good' with Take That so his credentials for the Spice Girls were impeccable. He took them to the Mojave Desert in California where they sweltered in the searing heat.

Geri had the idea that they should all be fictional characters – sort of comic-strip heroines. Mel B was 'Blazin' Bad Zula', Melanie C played 'Katrina Highkick' and Geri transformed into 'Trixie Firecracker', which would have been a good name for a burlesque artist. Emma played 'Kung Fu Candy', which was an apt choice as she was the only one who knew any martial arts and was able to coach the girls. Victoria's alter ego was 'Midnight Miss Suki': she wore a black PVC catsuit and a wig in temperatures reaching 112 degrees Fahrenheit (44°C) so it was a triumph of professionalism that she survived a long day, especially as she thought her costume was 'silly'. Vaughan said, 'She had to stand on the back of that car in the burning sun in that catsuit without moving. She was unbelievable.'

He was also struck by Victoria's somewhat hidden sense of humour but, at the time, he was more concerned with getting their outfits past the censors. He recalled, 'It was pure sex shop but, by some miracle, it really didn't come across like that.' At the end of the video the Girls have tied one man up and carried off another on the roof of their classic blue American Dodge Charger car. It's not X-rated as they had the gift of making anything racy seem acceptable to all ages. If the finished clip hadn't been PG, it wouldn't have been named Best Pop Video at the *Smash Hits* Awards that year.

The video was the first visual example of Girl Power and much was made of that concept when the publicity was launched for the single and for the album a month later. The Girls helped by mentioning the phrase as much as possible in interviews. If there was a lull they could just shout. 'Girl Power!' and fill the gap.

The first album was called *Spice* and featured ten by now familiar tracks written by a combination of the Girls, Richard Stannard and Matt Rowe, Eliot Kennedy and Andy Watkins, and Paul Wilson. The sales were phenomenal and proved the Girls were no one-hit wonder. It shifted 1.8 million copies in just seven weeks and was the fastest-selling album of the year. *Spice* was still number one at Christmas when their third single '2 Become 1' topped the seasonal chart. By this time the interest in Girl Power was reaching some surprising outlets.

Geri was in her element in the unlikely setting of the *Spectator* magazine when they were interviewed by the writer Simon Sebag Montefiore. She led the way: 'We Spice Girls are true Thatcherites. Thatcher was the first Spice Girl, the pioneer of our ideology – Girl Power,' she said, voicing the opinion that would launch a thousand articles about their political views. One headline was a matchless piece of deadpan nonsense: 'Spice Girls Back Sceptics on Europe', which could have been topical front-page news in 2019.

She was scathing about Tony Blair, who had turned down the chance to be in their video: 'The real problem with Blair is that he's never had a real job. In the olden days, a politician could be a coal miner who came to power with ideals. Not Blair. He's just a good marketing man. No ideals!'

Unexpectedly, Geri found an enthusiastic ally in Victoria. She had always been the quietest publicly, playing at being silent and aloof. She was too posh to speak, it seemed, but now she found her voice. She could have been campaigning for Brexit twenty years before the word was invented. She announced, 'The single currency is an outrage. These new passports are revolting, an insult to our kingdom, our independence. We must keep our national individuality.' About the then prime minister, John Major, she said, 'He's a boring pillock. But compared to the rest, he's far better. We'd never vote Labour.'

Melanie C kept quiet, although inside she was bitterly upset. Later she would defiantly state, 'I'm from working-class Liverpool. I think Margaret Thatcher is a complete prick after what she has done to my home town.' Amid all the bravado of the Spice Girls, Melanie was a sensitive young woman. Away from the relentless public gaze, she was struggling. These were early days, although her anger and frustration at the relentless quest for frivolous publicity would increasingly take its toll. She bottled it all up but was especially hurt when a newspaper referred to her as the 'plain' one of the group.

Mel B thought herself more anarchist than socialist but she, too, was from north-country working-class beginnings. Her loudness only told part of the story. Muff Fitzgerald quickly realised that she was an intelligent young woman who needed time to herself for quiet thought. She even had her own meditation chair at home. He observed, 'Her shouty behaviour is sometimes misinterpreted by people as being somewhat foolhardy. Far from it, she should never be underestimated.'

At least the *Spectator* article was different. Much of the coverage of the Spice Girls in the tabloid press seemed fixated on their love lives. Within a year of the release of 'Wannabe' there were, give or take, thirteen kiss-and-tell stories about them. Geri and Mel B in particular were the targets of former boyfriends' tales.

Geri had the additional entry on her CV that was a headline writer's dream – her career as a topless model. Inevitably, pictures of her from those days started circulating. More interesting than the nudge-nudge, innuendo-filled coverage in the press was the reaction within the band. Muff Fitzgerald noted that, while nobody cared about the photographs, there was a feeling within the group that Geri hadn't been entirely frank about the extent of her modelling career.

On a promotional trip to Thailand, they had a big row that never made the papers. For a while they weren't the fab five but four plus one as the others treated Geri coolly. Muff recalled that 'She was a shadow of her former self for a couple of months.'

In the papers it was open season on her love life, true or imagined, simply because she had taken her top off. A small consolation was that the men involved were of no consequence to her. That was not the case with Emma, who was bitterly upset and burst into tears when her three serious teenage boyfriends sold their stories in graphic detail. Her dad gave her some good advice: 'It's chip papers tomorrow, Emma, don't even think about it.' Even Victoria's ex-fiancé Mark would eventually tell all for a reported £60,000. His revelations included a highly personal story about a pregnancy scare while they were on holiday at her parents' villa in Spain.

While Melanie C did not escape some friends from Widnes speaking to the papers, she arguably had to suffer the most upsetting example of press intrusion. Her dad, Alan Chisholm, rang her out of the blue to tell her she had a secret sister. He had fathered a child during a split from her mother and was telling her now so that she wouldn't hear about it first from the *Sun*, who had found out about the sibling, Emma Williams, and were about to run a story.

Simon Fuller was extremely concerned about the raft of negative stories emerging about the Girls, not just for the effect on their personal well-being but also on commercial agreements he might seek in the future. He appointed a top lawyer, Gerrard Tyrrell of the renowned London firm Harbottle & Lewis, to police the activities of the press where the Spice Girls were concerned. He had an impeccable reputation and would work behind the scenes to encourage the right sort of press coverage. As a last resort, he could indicate that a particular newspaper would not have any access to the Spice Girls phenomenon in the future if they stepped too far out of line.

Gerrard has never spoken about his famous clients, which is just as well as he also represented the Queen and members of the Royal Family, including Prince Charles and his sons, William and Harry. He once said, 'Look behind the headlines. Look always at what the facts are. People's reputations are very easily traduced. People spend a lifetime trying to do the best they can, and it can be reduced to nothing in a matter of minutes by misreporting and falsity.'

The Girls' personal anguish and doubts behind the scenes were swept away temporarily when it became clear how much money they were making. At the 19 Management Christmas party in 1996, Simon Fuller ushered the Girls into an office and handed them each an envelope. Inside was a cheque for £200,000. Mel B didn't even have a credit card. They would soon be getting cheques with an extra nought on them but for the moment it was more money than they had ever seen – and they still hadn't toured. Even Victoria's dad Tony didn't receive cheques for that sort of amount.

Their first thought seemed to be to buy decent cars. Victoria had her eye on an Alfa Romeo. Geri pensioned off the faithful Fiat Uno and bought an even older car, a classic 1965 red MG Roadster that cost £15,000. More typically, perhaps, they wanted to include their families in their good fortune. Mel B gave her mum a Volkswagen Golf Cabriolet and her dad an Audi; Victoria gave her brother and sister each a convertible VW Golf. Melanie C made sure her younger brother Paul O'Neill had the latest bicycle costing £500. He was having a tough time as a result of her fame, and left college, sick of people 'taking the piss'. He was sensitive like his sister: 'I'd pretend to laugh it off, but it hurt me. I couldn't take any more.' Melanie eased things by buying him an MGF sports car as soon as he was old enough to drive.

As the money continued to flood in during 1997, the Girls were able to buy their families new homes. Paul could scarcely believe it: 'We moved from our little terraced house to this big detached thing with two garages and a drive. Our own drive! I went to see it while it was being built and said: "This is it. Life is never going to be the same again."'

That comment was even truer for the Girls themselves. After the New Year, they persuaded their mothers to take part in the video for their next single, 'Mama', which would be a double-A side for Comic Relief with 'Who Do You Think You Are'. All five women made their way to a film set in Perivale, West London, where pictures of their daughters growing up were mixed with shots of their glamorous mothers, who'd all had their hair done, in the audience.

Geri went through a stage of being exasperated with her mum because she wouldn't give up her job as a cleaner, but any rift was quickly healed. Mel B had also fallen out temporarily with her mum so it wasn't all sweetness despite the sentimentality of the song, which, apparently moved Emma to tears every time she sang it.

This was the first time the Spice mums had met each other but they seemed to get on well. Emma's mother, Pauline, and Mel B's, Andrea, are still good friends all these years later, forever sharing little notes on social media. The idea behind the song, which the Girls wrote with Matt and Biff, was that your mum would always be your best friend even if you had caused her problems during your unruly teenage years. Not everyone liked it. Looking back at the Spice Girls' recording career, the critic Alexis Petridis of the *Guardian* thought it the least appealing of their early singles: 'Mama was corny, slushy and cravenly released in time for Mother's Day.'

The Girls had to deal with a common dilemma for bands trying to break America – publicising one single there and another here. 'Wannabe' was top of the *Billboard* charts in the US while they were plugging 'Mama' and 'Who Do You Think You Are' in the UK. The latter had been released on New Year's Day and reached number one six weeks later on Valentine's Day. Once more Girl Power was the key promotional strategy, and the endless grind was exhausting – on one morning at the Museum of Television and Radio they ploughed through thirteen radio interviews in three hours. There was not much fun to be had in shouting, 'Good morning, America!' over and over ... and over again.

The album, *Spice*, was released in the States in February. Once more, critics had mixed feelings about the Spice Girls. *Rolling Stone* gave it just 2.5 stars out of 5: 'Spice Girls are five attractive young things, each with a distinct personality à la the Village People, brought together by a manager with a marketing concept.' The magazine was not impressed by them preaching 'Girl Power!' either, adding, 'The girls don't get bogged down by anything deeper than mugging for promo shots and giving out tips on getting boys in bed.' Despite that, the album reached number one and would eventually sell more than seven million copies in the US.

Once more Girl Power was the promotional strategy, made more effective when the media pointed out that the concept had originated in the States. Although Geri had heard about it through a Shampoo record, the phrase owed its origins to an underground feminist punk movement called Riot Grrl that started up in the Pacific North West states of the US in the early nineties.

Later in the month, before the Brit Awards ceremony at Earls Court, the Girls were photographed with pop royalty, Elton John, and Diana Ross, who congratulated them on being number one in her home country. What a difference just one year had made! In 1996 nobody had a clue who the five brash and exuberant girls were. Now, it seemed everybody knew.

Geri turned the Spice Girls into the only talking point of the awards night. Her super-tight Union Jack mini dress was described by *Harper's Bazaar* as one of the most memorable fashion moments of all time. She wasn't supposed to wear it.

Emma Poole, who was in charge of their creative styling and marketing (Simon made sure they had a person for everything), recalled that she was expected to perform in a specially designed little black dress by Gucci but thought it boring. Emma recalled a conversation two nights before the event when Geri told her she had a much better idea: 'I'm going round to my sister's. She's got these great Union Jack tea-towels. I'm going to make a dress.'

That evening, her half-sister Karen stitched a tea towel to the dress. A designer number costing thousands was embellished with something you might buy from a souvenir shop in Piccadilly Circus. Geri's inspiration, which she described as a light-bulb moment, was realising the Brit Awards were meant to be British. Just to make clear that she was not a supporter of the National Front, she stitched the famous CND peace logo on the back. The Spice Girls collected two awards, for best single, 'Wannabe', and best video, 'Say You'll Be There', but the dress made sure they 'won' the most coveted (unofficial) prize, which is not presented on stage. It goes to the act that gains the most coverage in the next day's papers.

The dress became so famous that it was easily forgotten she wore it on stage just once while the Girls performed 'Who Do You Think You Are' with a 'Wannabe' introduction. It came top in a 2010 online poll to establish which were the ten most iconic dresses of the past fifty years. That year the Girls also collected an award for the Most Memorable Performance of the last thirty years at the Brits.

Mel B acknowledged Geri's flair: 'That was the first time I realised how brilliant she was. She had a real sense of what would catch on in the press. But she never really shared her cleverness with the rest of us.'

And, just in case you missed the Union Jack number, Geri changed into a Jessica Rabbit-style, low-cut sequined red ballgown for the rest of the evening and experienced the most famous wardrobe malfunction in the history of the event: while she was holding up the Best Video award for 'Say You'll Be There', her breast momentarily slipped out of her dress.

Melanie C chipped in with some publicity of her own at the ceremony. Liam Gallagher had announced that he wasn't going because if he bumped into the Spice Girls he would smack them. Collecting the Best Single award, Melanie shouted, to much applause, 'Liam, come and have a go if you think you're hard enough.'

After all the noisy exuberance on stage, there was a more touching exchange behind the scenes. Quietly, and with no fuss, Mel B's mum and dad went to her dressing room after the show to tell their daughter how proud they were and how well she had done.

The Spice Girls were preparing to sing live for the first time. They chose the US where they were now gathering more head-lines than any British band since Beatlemania in the sixties. They were booked on the top-rated *Saturday Night Live* and flew to New York in April 1997 for five full days of rehearsal with the show's house band at a Manhattan studio. They were good at rehearsals. They had to fight the perception that they were a completely manufactured band and, therefore, unable to sing or perform to any standard.

They had sung 'Wannabe' and 'Say You'll Be There' so many times that once more would be no problem, even if the TV audience was twenty million. They were, in fact, very nervous. All five were acutely aware that, until then, they had spent six months miming their two most famous hits. The headlines had already been written: 'Can they really, really sing?'

Before they went on, they had a group hug. Hollywood heart-throb Rob Lowe was the host that night. Comedy star Will

Ferrell was one of the resident performers while the Oscar-winning actor Joe Pesci was the principal guest. For once the Girls were not the main talking point: one of the regular cast accidentally said the F-word and became the focus of attention.

Geri thought she'd been a 'bit squeaky' on one line but everybody else declared themselves satisfied and thought they sounded pretty good. This time she wore a figure-hugging flowing white dress with 'POWER GIRL GERI' emblazoned across her chest, just to reinforce the Girl Power message. The timing was good because that month a Spice Girls book entitled *Girl Power* was published.

Geri was again on genius form when the Girls met Prince Charles at the Prince's Trust twenty-first anniversary concert. Apparently he had sent a hand-written letter asking them to take part. They sang live for the second time on stage at the Manchester Opera House, performing 'Say You'll Be There' and 'Mama'. The latter was a little ropy vocally but at least they were brave enough to do it. They looked fabulous and danced impeccably. The vocals of Melanie C and Emma were clearly a touch above those of the others.

Afterwards, Mel B and Geri both planted big lipstick smackers on the Prince's cheeks while Geri patted the heir to the throne's bum before telling him, in her best Watford accent, 'You know, I think you're very sexy. We could spice up your life.' Charles loved it and happily posed for pictures. He would forge a long-standing connection with the Girls, and Geri in particular.

The next time they posed for pictures with the Prince was one of the great highlights of the whole Spice Girls phenomenon.

# 13

# SPICE ALL OVER
# THE WORLD

Considering the publicity storm that surrounded the Spice Girls, Victoria somehow managed to keep David Beckham a secret from the world for a precious couple of months. The week before the 1997 Brit Awards, Simon Fuller, who was a big Manchester United fan, asked Victoria if she would like to accompany him to watch his team play Chelsea at Stamford Bridge. The finer points of the game were lost on Victoria but afterwards she joined Simon in the VIP lounge and was thoroughly bored while everyone talked about the match. The other drawback was that she had forgotten to put in her contact lenses, which she had started wearing as a teenager, and was peering foggily about the room when Simon suddenly introduced her to David.

'It was the moment I was waiting for and I blew it,' David would later recall, claiming that he had lost his bottle. Did Simon Fuller have some sort of cunning plan to pair off Victoria and the most promising footballer in the country? He almost certainly did, although not even he could have foreseen what would evolve from that first meeting. Rick Sky observed, 'Fuller is a very Machiavellian person. I don't think he would see that as a negative thing particularly.'

Victoria thought David was a good-looking bloke, from what she could vaguely see, but was too busy to dwell on their fleeting encounter. Two weeks after the Brits, she met him again when Simon took her and Melanie C to watch United play Sheffield Wednesday at Old Trafford. As a lifelong Liverpool fan, Melanie really did know about football, even if the rivalry between her team and United gave the home supporters the chance to boo her loudly.

After the match David was more forward when he saw Victoria in the Players Lounge. He chatted to her before blurting out an invitation to dinner. At the time, it was too difficult to settle on a date, so Victoria asked for his number, saying she'd call him. David, fearing the brush-off, insisted she give him hers. She did. As she left, she uttered the famous remark that would have been unthinkable coming from the mouth of Victoria Adams before she became a world-famous Spice Girl: 'If you don't ring me, I'm going to kick you in the bollocks the next time I see you.'

David called the following day, and twenty-four hours later they went on their first date. They were both very recognisable so it was impossible to know where to go for a discreet evening, even on a quiet Monday. They met in an Essex pub car park before spending the evening chatting to Melanie C at her flat. The important thing was that the awkward first date had been successfully negotiated, although nothing more happened than a goodnight peck on the cheek. They agreed to talk on the phone while Victoria continued to live the hectic life of a Spice Girl, flying to New York the day after.

David and Victoria clicked immediately. They understood each other. It may be a cliché but they had a huge amount in common. They came from working-class family backgrounds, were single-minded in their ambitions, had overcome a natural shyness, were not rocket scientists but were very smart about their own identities and their place in the world, and they laughed at the same things. All those reasons allowed them to forge a relationship quickly – and they fancied each other.

Victoria did have one problem. David wasn't dating anyone but she had a steady boyfriend, a florist called Stuart Bilton. Technically she had gone out with David behind Stuart's back but she rectified the situation promptly and finished with him. He had been on a skiing trip when she had her first date with David but she was a free agent before they had taken it further.

One reason why so many stars date each other is that they recognise the pressures of being a celebrity and what they have gone through to achieve that status. The boys in the background of the Spice Girls weren't around for long after their girlfriends became so famous. Mel B and Richard Meyer split, as did Emma and Mark Verghese. Geri's romance with Porsche-driving Giovanni Laporta was fleeting and now Victoria and Stuart were over, even though her parents really liked him. At this time, Melanie C seemed not to have a boyfriend.

Perhaps Simon was trying another footballing trick when stories started appearing about Emma with the Liverpool and England striker Robbie Fowler, which soon fizzled out. Over the years more stories would appear about who Emma might or might not be dating than any of the other Girls. Robbie was one of the Liverpool footballers who, around this time, the press labelled 'Spice Boys', which reflected the blossoming celebrity status of a number of players. They featured on the front covers of magazines, endorsed fashion labels and indulged in what the media gleefully portrayed as bad behaviour. Simon quickly caught on to the earning capacity of these impressionable young men and, for a while, took on the management of Steve McManaman, one of the most gifted and photogenic players of the era. Melanie C said he was one of her favourite players.

Recognising the commercial appeal of football may or may not have influenced Simon in aligning the Spice Girls with that world, although he tired of being so close to it: 'I remember thinking, Ooh, that could work,' he said later. 'But it turned out not to be my scene. The people in the football world are not the kind I want to mix with.' That would not stop him forging a lucrative alliance with David Beckham in the years to come.

The Spice Girls, under Simon's guidance, were world leaders when it came to merchandise and sponsorship. The strategy achieved two things. First, it made a lot of money. Secondly, endorsements raised their profile around the world. They were everywhere. The BBC called it a 'marketing blitzkrieg'.

In 1997, their *annus mirabilis*, they were reported to have generated £300 million in commercial deals. Their alliances included Pepsi, Polaroid cameras, British Telecom, Cadbury's, Fabergé, Benetton, Sony, and Chupa Chupa lollipops, which were the biggest thing in Spain. And that was not including merchandise with Spice labels – dolls, skates, satchels, pencil cases, bicycles, sportswear and *Spice* magazine. The Pepsi deal alone was rumoured to be worth a million dollars. The campaign called 'Generation Next' featured 92 million cans of Pepsi world-wide, picturing the Girls individually or as a group. If you collected twenty pink ring pulls from Pepsi cans you would be rewarded with a copy of the limited-edition single 'Step to Me', a leftover from the early Spice sessions involving Eliot Kennedy and Absolute. An estimated half-million copies of the disc were requested. The track, which featured a Mel B rap, was subse-quently on the Japanese edition of their next album.

A very catchy Biff and Matt production called 'Move Over' was used for a series of three commercials. Once more you could send off ring pulls but this time the record would feature subsequently on all versions of their second album. The video even managed to contain some subtle product placement of their new Impulse fragrances. Described as a fresh Oriental range, it had the catchy slogan, 'Wear nothing but Impulse Spice.' Each Girl had her own scent – zesty tangerine (Sporty), lavender and vanilla (Baby), African paduk wood and musk (Scary), warm amber and red pepper (Ginger), and jasmine and lily-of-the-valley (Posh). Mel B, who had a growing reputation for spending money, noted, 'We wanted a fragrance that reflects the personality of the band – feminine, funky and unpredictable, and at a realistic price.'

The simple fact was that Spice Girl products were popular. The opportunities would have dried up quickly if they hadn't been. Pepsi invested a staggering sum: Simon Fuller would later claim the company spent $100 million on the endorsement campaign. Fabergé were happy to spend £1.8 million on advertising for the scents. The Girls were paid a reported fee of half a million pounds to launch Channel 5 with a lively video called 'Power of Five' that reworked the old Manfred Mann hit '5-4-3-2-1' with several references to Girl Power.

They also signed a £1 million deal to be the face of Asda at Christmas. It would coincide with the launch of a number of seasonal products, including the famous Girl Power dolls: Mel B wore leopard print, Emma had her hair in bunches and a pink dress, Victoria was in a little black dress, Melanie C a tracksuit and Geri, predictably, the Union Jack dress. Over the next few years there were eight different Spice sets to collect. They proved so popular that they became the biggest-selling celebrity dolls of all time with sales of 11 million.

Commercially, all age groups were covered from the three-year-olds coveting the dolls to teenage girls spraying liberal amounts of Impulse for the school disco to their mums buying the Spice Girls line of Cadbury's chocolate. And nobody, it seemed, could resist Walkers Crisps: the Girls appeared in a number of ads with Gary Lineker – 'No more Mr Spice Guy.' Apparently what he really, really wanted was a crisp.

This was Brand Spice on a spectacular scale. Geri called it the 'Spice juggernaut'. She added, 'I couldn't walk down the street without seeing my face on a T-shirt or coffee cup.' The cleverness of their commercial campaigning was highlighted by Mel B when she said Impulse was a realistic price. Mostly the products were well within range of a pocket-money budget – although there were so many that fans needed parental loans to buy them all. Some estimates put the total of Spice Girl items at more than two hundred. No wonder Geri's mum Ana-Maria gave up trying to collect them.

The beauty for Simon and the Girls was that everything was acting as an advertisement for the group's own product – the music, the planned first tour and, most timely, the film that had been on Simon's mind right from the start.

The hype for the movie began the day after they had met Prince Charles. It was more memorable for Victoria than anyone realised at the time because she had spent the night with David for the first time. The Girls joined up at daybreak to fly to the Cannes Film Festival and tell the world about *Spice: The Movie*, as it was titled then. They did a famous photo call standing on the canopy at the entrance of the Martinez Hotel on the boulevard de la Croisette. An engineer had to be called first to make sure it could take the weight of the Girls. They looked fabulous, like true Hollywood stars. A screaming crowd of more than five thousand were watching. Those who weren't gathered in the street were hanging out of the windows.

They stayed on a yacht in the harbour and lapped up the glamour of the glittering annual event. The van taking them to a party at Planet Hollywood was practically hijacked by crowds hammering on the doors and rocking it from side to side. A cameraman was punched in the face, and the girls arrived shaken by this aspect of the fame they had so desired. This was no fun. The trip was a commercial triumph, though, because the producers sold the film to every territory. The whole world, it seemed, wanted to see a Spice Girls movie.

The Girls had always wanted to make one. They had talked about it back in Boyne Hill Road when they were being filmed by Neil Davies. Subsequently, they had voiced that ambition early on to Simon. He knew just the man to help – his elder brother, Kim Fuller, who was an experienced television comedy writer. He had been contributing sketches for nearly twenty years to Tracey Ullman and Rory Bremner but was best known for his work with Lenny Henry. A movie would be a major development in his career, while his family connection with Simon kept the project very much 'in house'.

The blueprint for the film was obviously *A Hard Day's Night* that fictionalised a day in the life of the Beatles. The Spice Girls' success was so often being compared to the sixties' icons' that reworking the formula seemed a sensible option. Instead of a day, the idea was to portray a chaotic fictional week in their lives, building up to a concert at the Royal Albert Hall in London. In some ways it was an extension of the original documentary about Touch – just following a group of girls and filming what happened to them.

Once again Geri was the primary mover. She threw herself into the project, and during much of the previous year had made sure she was available by phone or fax to discuss ideas, even when she was on holiday in Bali. Kim found her the most ambitious for the film and the most helpful with the script: 'She would say to me, "Well, actually, Victoria wouldn't say that." So then I would change it round to make sure the lines were ringing true.'

The second screenwriter on the movie, Jamie Curtis, acknowledged, 'Geri was by far the most interested. She was forever coming up and putting in ideas and asking how it worked. She was an inquisitive person, and she was having the time of her life because she was getting to witness a lot more of the world than she had done before.'

On the rare occasions when the Girls were in London, they would go to Kim's house in Notting Hill and tell him tales from their lives and their travels, which he would write into the movie. One story involved them leaping off a double-decker bus and making a run for it. A London bus, driven by Victoria, would feature prominently in the final draft – fortunately Geri wasn't the nominated driver as she would probably have driven into Nelson's Column.

One of Kim's biggest problems was getting the Girls together to approve the script, which was originally called *Five*. He eventually had two hours of their time: he told them to turn off their phones and listen to him read it. When he had finished, they turned their phones back on, said 'Great. Brilliant', and left the room. In Spice-speak that was enough for Simon to reassure his brother that all was well and they loved it.

Casting proved a joy because so many household names queued up for parts, especially if they had young sons or daughters. Richard E. Grant signed up for the key role of the manager, Clifford. Kim left a message on his answerphone, which his eight-year-old daughter Olivia heard. She insisted he take the part. Melanie C recalled, 'His daughter was a huge fan, so he had no choice – he had to do it.'

Meatloaf, Bob Hoskins, Bob Geldof, Stephen Fry, Elvis Costello, Gary Oldman, Hugh Laurie and many more jumped at the chance to be in it. Geri remembers them flicking through pictures of actors and spying one of Alan Cumming, who brought back memories of her trip to the Donmar Warehouse. She declared, 'Let's pick him. I saw him in *Hamlet*.' The Girls had a wish list of people and, as Melanie added, 'People were just saying, "Yeah!"' On his first day on set, the urbane Roger Moore arrived and broke the ice by asking, 'Do I owe anyone money here?' The Girls brought rehearsals to an end one afternoon by asking Jools Holland for his autograph and persuading him to play piano for everyone.

When filming began in June 1997, the locations were kept secret to limit the opportunities for paparazzi grabbing pictures of the Girls on set. Somehow they always found out – two photographers were discovered dressed as a cow grazing in a meadow next to where the Girls were shooting a scene. The Girls waved as the men were escorted off carrying their cameras and a pantomime cow's head. It was a game, and everyone knew they would be back to have another go in the morning.

That was a funny incident, but mostly the Girls found nothing amusing about the paparazzi who, according to Melanie C, were the bane of their lives. She said, 'You wonder when you go to bed at night if there's going to be one hiding under it.'

The crew loved the Girls because they were so refreshingly normal and never thought of themselves as 'stars', even though that was exactly what they were. Anyone popping into their trailer was likely to see them 'pissing themselves laughing'. Jennie Barnor-Roberts, their on-set hairdresser, thought they were the most professional artists she had ever worked with: 'There's nothing fake about them whatsoever. They were never late, they never bitched about each other, they were always in the chair on time.'

The plot of *Spice World*, as it would finally be titled, is more about the undiluted energy of the five Girls but it did feature some of the distractions in their lives – the paparazzi, being trailed by a documentary filmmaker (Alan Cumming) and, most intriguingly, becoming increasingly dissatisfied with a manager who refuses to give them any time off. Victoria and Emma, who had taken so many acting classes growing up, were probably the most professional. Emma even soldiered on after breaking her foot falling off her platform shoes. Janet Maslin in the *New York Times* commented, 'Emma and slinky Victoria come closest to showing signs of life after Spicedom, but the whole group radiates energy, colour and good cheer.' She added, tongue in cheek: 'Nothing about it should disturb its target audience of media-wise, fun-loving eight-year-old girls.' *Variety* magazine called it 'bright and breezy', but thought it would be forgotten in six months.

Critics, in general, found it hard to be too mean-spirited about the film, perhaps because of its finely tuned self-deprecating style. That suited Victoria, who sent herself up in a way she has employed ever since. Her funniest piece of dialogue involved her choosing what to wear. Melanie C chips in, 'It must be so hard for you, Victoria, I mean, having to decide whether to wear the little Gucci dress, the little Gucci dress … or the little Gucci dress.'

'Exactly,' says Posh.

Fortunately Emma has a thought: 'I know – why don't you wear the little Gucci dress?'

Victoria responds, 'Good idea. Thanks, Em.'

Kim Fuller later told author David Sinclair about a conversation with Victoria, which highlighted her good humour about sending herself up. She asked him, 'You know my character in the movie? I'm just a laughing stock really, aren't I?'

*Left* Natural and image-free, Geri, aged eighteen, in sunny Mallorca where she was a dancer in a club.

*Above* Geri wasn't 'Ginger' at the rehearsals for the girl group that eventually became the Spice Girls. She was twenty-one and desperate for fame.

*Above* Prince Charles always loved Geri's company; she took his arm backstage at the Prince's Trust Comedy Gala at the Lyceum Theatre, London, while he was celebrating his 50th birthday in October 1998.

*Right* Happy days: Geri takes a walk in Regent's Park, London, just before Christmas 2006 with her mum Ana Maria and, in her arms, seven-month-old daughter, Bluebell.

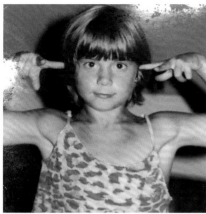

*Left* Melanie C was already practising her Girl Power salute aged seven when on holiday in Cap d'Agde in the Mediterranean.

*Right* Melanie is cheered up by a phone call while on tour with the Girls in May 1998, two weeks before Geri left the group.

*Above* Melanie fulfilled a childhood dream by taking the lead role of a 'Scouse mum' in *Blood Brothers* at the Phoenix Theatre, London, in 2009. She became the hottest ticket in the West End.

*Right* Ditching her sporty image, Melanie was the epitome of grace in a Victoria Beckham-designed dress at the Olivier Awards the following year.

*Right* A shy Prince Harry can't stop grinning as he holds Victoria's hand at a Spice Girls concert in Johannesburg. Twenty years later she would be a guest at his wedding.

*Above* Who says Victoria never smiles? She looks radiant leaving Claridge's hotel, London, in 2004 with her very youthful-looking husband David Beckham.

*Below* Baby Harper finds the world of fashion one big yawn.

*Above* Living her dream: Victoria models one of her own elegant designs at her label's show during Singapore Fashion Week in 2015.

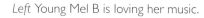
*Left* Young Mel B is loving her music.

*Above* Mel looking fantastic in her forties on the red carpet before a recording of *America's Got Talent* at the Dolby Theatre, Los Angeles, in August 2018.

*Above* Mel models what everyone should wear to go shopping in Beverly Hills.

*Right* Mel poses with her three daughters – Phoenix, Angel and Madison – before boarding the Westfield Christmas Before Christmas bus in London.

*Right* Emma displaying the cute smile that made her so much in demand as a child model.

*Left* Not yet 'Baby', Emma was filmed for a documentary before the world knew about the Spice Girls.

*Right* What to do on a windy day – hold the dress or the hair? Both Emma and Geri opt for the dress at a Buckingham Palace Garden Party in the summer of 2006.

*Left* Emma with Jade Jones, the love of her life. They celebrated twenty-one years together in 2019.

*Right Nous sommes arrivées!* The Spice Girls hit Cannes in 1995 to let the world know they were planning a movie of their crazy life.

*Left* The Girls were very nervous before they performed live for the first time. They sang 'Wannabe' on the top-rated US show *Saturday Night Live* and proved the doubters wrong.

*Above* The Girls turned round during their famous performance at The BRITs in 1997 … Now we all know what was on the back of Geri's iconic Union Jack dress.

*Left* It's a tie between Geri and Mel B in the contest to see who can wear the biggest shoes for a photoshoot in Bali in 1997.

*Right* Stopping the traffic on board their very own double-decker bus, the Girls arrive for a screening in New York of *Spice World*.

*Above* The Return of the Spice Girls: on stage in Vancouver at the first night of their 2007 tour. Only another 96 dates to go.

*Left* Girl Power at London 2012: saluting the crowd in the Olympic Stadium. It was the last time the five Spice Girls performed together.

*Right* Spice Girls: The Next Generation. The Girls always like to include their children – here are six on stage with them in Madison Square Garden, New York. Now, there are twelve.

*Left* On the grid, at the 2015 British Grand Prix – Emma takes a selfie with Melanie C and Geri.

Enough of the dancing: time to sit down and have a breather on tour in Edinburgh, 2019 – what a whirlwind their lives have been!

Kim told her, 'Yes, you are', to which Victoria replied, 'OK, that's fine. As long as I know.'

*Spice World* was not nominated for any Oscars, unlike *A Hard Day's Night*, which won two, but it was honoured at the Razzles, otherwise known as the Golden Raspberry Awards, which was part of the annual Hollywood fun. It was in the running for six awards but 'won' just the one – all five Girls were collectively named Worst Actress. The citation read, 'A five-member girl group with the talent of one bad actress among them.'

Their bank manager wasn't complaining. *Spice World* was a huge success, becoming the second most successful British film in the UK of 1997 with receipts of £8.5 million. Only *Bean* with Rowan Atkinson grossed more. Worldwide, the Girls' movie has made more than $100 million. The film has aged well, a favourite of late-night screenings and fashionable drive-ins. Alice Vincent in the *Daily Telegraph* highlighted its appeal: '… young, fun women in control of their future, kind to one another and devoted to two essential mantras: "Girl Power" and "Friendship Never Ends"'.

The Girls themselves were pleased with their movie début. Geri summed it up: 'We're only human – we have bad days, we have fat days, bad hair days, bad clothes days. And it's all in there. There's one thing we're really glad about and that's that since we entered the public arena we've still always been ourselves. Always! What you see is what you get. Warts and all, you'll see it in the movie. It's just five personalities.'

*Spice World* is undeniably a cult classic with so many lines that seem to have become even funnier over time. When Clifford the manager is on the bus, he announces on the PA system: 'Please refrain from leaving your moisturising cream in the refrigerator as it can be mistaken for mayonnaise. That is all.'

Clifford also delivers the less funny but more poignant line: 'You don't have lives. You have schedules.' For the Spice Girls, their actual daily diary was exceptionally punishing. Somehow they had to fit in writing and recording a new album and preparing for their first 97-date world tour. Bringing together all the aspects of the Spice World encapsulated the commercial philosophy of Simon Fuller. The film, the record, the tour and a private life all at the same time – how could they possibly do it?

## 14

# A SCHEDULE NOT A LIFE

The working day for the Spice Girls began at 6.30 a.m. and ended at 11 p.m. When the cameras stopped rolling at 5.30 p.m. they were whisked off to concentrate on the second album. Hardly any material had been written, so everyone was scribbling lyrics on bits of paper and taking them to the Winnebago where a mobile sound unit had been set up. Some evenings they would be ferried to the famous Abbey Road studios for recording sessions. Broadly speaking, it was the same cast of characters as before, with Matt and Biff, Spike Stent and the Absolute boys. Only Eliot Kennedy had moved on to other projects and was unavailable.

Biff was full of admiration: 'They were just so busy. They'd all come in wearing their film make-up and costumes. I don't know how they physically managed to do it, with the hours and the schedule – especially writing songs, which I know they're really proud of, and doing that while recording and working on the second record. So stressful.' Sometimes Geri would hand him a scrap of paper with one line on it, then disappear for a lie-down.

One particular evening, Biff had a meltdown, clearing everyone out of the studio except the Girls and Matt so that they could all put the film to one side and write a song. He described it as 'just seven friends sitting in a room'. He told them, 'I want to sit down with a guitar and piano. I want to write how we always used to.' And they did, coming up with 'Viva Forever', one of the best-loved of all Spice Girls anthems.

The whole album was an example of the Girls' ability to achieve something in difficult circumstances. 'Spice Up Your Life', for instance, was completed the day before it was due to be used in the film. Simon had reassured everybody that it would be ready on time and, sure enough, it was.

Their fictional manager in *Spice World* was an amusing character but, in real life, Simon Fuller was fast becoming the target for their discontent. None of the Girls was happy about their lack of a private life. He might not have realised it at the time but they simply wanted a day off. Victoria, in particular, was frustrated that she could not see enough of David Beckham, with whom she was falling deeply in love.

Mel B, too, was distracted by the passionate affair she had rekindled with the former Icelandic snooker player Fjölnir Thorgeirsson. He had forged a new career as a male model and was spending more time in the UK. He stayed with Mel at her rented flat in Hampstead, going out for the occasional double date in North London with Victoria and David. Although Mel and he were never that serious about one another, she bought him a diamond-studded Rolex watch – another example of her carefree generosity where money was concerned.

The plans for *Spice World* needed to be altered because of two desperately sad deaths in the summer of 1997. First, fashion designer Versace was shot dead in Miami in mid-July. Then at the end of August the whole nation was plunged into grief when Princess Diana was killed in a Paris car crash.

The appalling tragedy of Diana created a vacancy. The Spice Girls were already a popular subject in the press, but the Princess was entirely different. She was the number-one target of the paparazzi, the top cover girl for every glossy magazine and the front-page dream of all newspapers because she added precious sales. All of the Spice Girls were candidates to fill it, but it soon became clear that Posh and Becks, as they would be known, were the chosen ones – a charismatic partnership that fascinated the whole world, it seemed. Nobody knew at first but the day before Diana died, David had asked Victoria to marry him and she accepted.

The sense that Victoria was beginning to blossom more as an individual away from the group was highlighted when she went by herself to the Versace show in Milan, one of the biggest fashion events of the year, perhaps especially that year because of the death of its figurehead. For the first time she rubbed shoulders with the most famous people in fashion, including Kate Moss and Naomi Campbell. Her introduction to the world that would become so important in her life was made even more special when she was invited to stay at the Versace villa, which made her feel part of everything.

Victoria had almost been to a fashion show before. *Tatler* flew her to Paris for a front-row seat at the Karl Lagerfeld show, but the magazine's photo shoot at the Ritz Hotel lasted eight hours so she had to miss the main event. She had the consolation of being on the cover for the first time. She wore her favourite black but this was nothing like a Spice Girls outfit – her Christian Lacroix crêpe couture dress was topped off with a striking black straw sombrero.

The cover line read 'Posh Spice Goes to Paris – Victoria Adams wears haute-couture'. In an ill-judged article, the writer appeared to mock Victoria's voice 'spraying around her Hertfordshire vowels and her North London syntax with feeling'. She even quoted her: 'When we met Prince Charles we was all really, like, cheeky with him.' It came across as a cheap shot, failing to recognise that millions of ordinary young girls and women, who would never buy a copy of *Tatler*, adored her and the Spice Girls. They were relatable.

In the short term, the deaths of Diana and Versace had some practical effect on the Spice Girls; references to the pair had to be edited out of the final cut of their film. Making movies is an inexact science and Fate can never be factored in – a further four minutes, for instance, ended up on the cutting-room floor when Gary Glitter was arrested on child-pornography charges. They retained their storming performance of 'I'm the Leader of the Gang (I Am!)', his first number one in 1973. The Girls' version would undoubtedly have topped the charts a quarter of a century later.

They performed 'Spice Up Your Life', which would be the lead single from their second album, for the first time on *The National Lottery Show* in late September. These were the days when nine million people stayed in on a Saturday night to watch the 'big-money balls' being drawn. It was part of the TV offensive on both sides of the Atlantic leading up to the UK release of the movie on 6 October 1997. On that day they flew in by helicopter to Granada, southern Spain, for the big official launch where more than two hundred journalists assembled in the gardens of the ancient Palacete del Carmen de los Mártires. They were completely outnumbered by hundreds of young girl fans outside the walls, chanting for their heroes. One reporter thought that many were as young as five and none as old as fifteen: 'You could almost compare it to Beatlemania, except it's girls screaming at other girls.'

The Girls were not just promoting the next single but giving journalists and the adoring fans the opportunity to hear their second album through the loudspeakers. For sheer excitement, it could not have gone better, ending with a spectacular fireworks display that lit up the Spanish night sky. The problem was that Elton John's 'Candle in the Wind 1997', his tribute to Diana, showed no sign of relinquishing its position at the top of the charts. It would be a huge let-down if the much-anticipated 'Spice Up Your Life' did not make number one.

The release was put back a week to ensure it knocked Elton off the top. That was achieved with a sale of 320,000 copies in its first seven days. As usual with the Spice Girls, the critics had mixed feelings. David Wild in *Rolling Stone* said it was 'a global call to arms and legs with a distinct carnival-like flavour and a message of Up with Spice People positivity'. The *Daily Mirror* thought it a 'throwaway Latin-style song'. It was irrefutably catchy and another one to sing in the playground or the shower. It was also a headline writer's dream for years to come.

Simon decided it was sensible for the Girls to spend the following year out of the UK. The tax laws at the time were greatly beneficial if they did this and they would be able to keep far more of the fortune they were earning. Nobody was keen, although they could see the sense of it. In any case, they would be out of the country on tour for most of it.

Reluctantly they left for a month's rehearsal at a luxury villa near Cannes that Simon had rented for them. The new Spice HQ, which cost £10,000 a month, came with high security and a beautiful swimming pool and was a different world from the semi in Boyne Hill Road. They did not have to share bedrooms but, despite the pop-star trimmings, the Girls were not happy. Geri called it 'Spice Kampf'.

The irony of their success was that it threatened to take away Girl Power. Increasingly they felt they were not in charge of their own destiny. They were in danger of losing their precious collective spirit. In her autobiography, Victoria explained sadly, 'None of us were happy but instead of talking about it, like we would have done in the old days, we just kept to our rooms.'

The Girls had not lost their commitment to preparing properly. A marquee was set up in the garden for aerobics and other gym work. A separate venue was found for hours of practice with a band, which was an entirely new experience. They were rehearsing for a landmark in their careers – their first live concerts. Pepsi were sponsoring two nights on 12 and 13 October at the Abdel Ipecki Arena in Istanbul. They were understandably apprehensive, especially Mel B, who had left her lucky charm bracelet back at their hotel. A police car was speedily despatched to retrieve it in time for the first number.

Amazingly, considering this was their very first live show, they were able to talk to cameras before the show, mindful that the evening would be available as a VHS recording. Geri didn't mention her former times in the city – so much had happened to her since her humble TV beginnings on that Turkish game show. All the commercial possibilities of the concert would be fully explored. As well as the video, the concert was scheduled to be shown on Christmas Day on the main ITV channel.

Looking fabulous, the Girls carried off the evening like the group of seasoned professionals they were, even when one of the video screens came loose and almost flattened them. They began with one of the new songs from the second album, 'If You Can't Dance', a collaboration with Matt and Biff that featured a hypnotic repetitive chorus, as well as Mel B and Geri rapping for the first time since 'Wannabe'.

Their first six songs included another new one, 'Saturday Night Divas', in which the lyrics were a dig at ex-lovers who kiss and tell on the famous, a bitter experience for the Girls. After 'Step to Me' they went off stage for a quick costume change, to return and perform 'Naked', a smooth-as-silk number co-written with Absolute for the first album. Sitting astride Arne Jacobsen-designed black chairs, the Girls wore flesh-coloured underwear to give the impression that they were actually naked. The idea was based on the famous photograph of the model Christine Keeler, who, in 1963, was one of the most famous women in the UK because of her role in the Profumo scandal. Everyone assumed she, too, was naked on a fashionable Jacobsen chair, but that was because of photographer Lewis Morley's clever lighting. She was in fact perched on a cheap knock-off he had lying around his Soho studio.

The Spice Girls were sat on the real thing. They had to pretend to be naked for just one song, returning in gold satin outfits to perform the mellow favourite '2 Becomes 1' before launching into two great numbers from the *Spiceworld* album – the Motown-influenced, dance-happy 'Stop' and the sublime ballad 'Too Much', which had already been earmarked as the Christmas single. Emma introduced it as the theme tune from their new movie. For once, Victoria had her own line in a song, and Melanie C demonstrated how her vocals had developed since it had all begun, especially when she sang the unforgettable Spice Girls lyric 'I want a man, not a boy who thinks he can.'

Throughout they looked as if they were enjoying themselves. They appeared to be step perfect in their dance routines. All the hard work had paid off for Geri, dancing faultlessly in enormous red platform boots. Mel B wasn't entirely happy with some of her vocals but only she seemed to be worried about that. The audience, which contained a lot of teenage boys and girls as well as younger fans, didn't notice. And, of course, they ended their encore with 'Wannabe' so everyone went home singing. As they left the stage, knackered, they remembered to shout 'Girl Power!'

The girls flew all around the world as part of the promotion for *Spiceworld*, the album, and *Spice World*, the movie, but they were back in London to launch the Remembrance Day Poppy

Appeal alongside Dame Vera Lynn. The occasion clearly high-lighted how much part of the fabric of British life the Spice Girls had become in such a short time. They were part of an initiative by the Royal British Legion to encourage more young people to buy a poppy to honour the fallen.

There was no larking about. This was a serious event that is as relevant to our armed forces today as it ever has been, and they embraced it in a mature way. Mel B observed, 'It's time to remember and say thanks because many people paid a very high price for freedom and we must never forget them.' Together they read from the poem, 'For the Fallen', written by Lawrence Binyon in late 1914.

The fourth verse, which the girls recited, has become recog-nised over the years as a fitting tribute to those who have lost their lives in military conflict:

> They shall grow not old, as we that are left grow old:
> Age shall not weary them, nor the years condemn.
> At the going down of the sun and in the morning
> We will remember them.

Three days later, at the beginning of November, they flew to Pretoria, the capital of South Africa, for a charity concert and to meet Nelson Mandela at his official residence. The great man was in excellent spirits and was chatting happily to Prince Charles when the Girls arrived, embarrassingly late. It was an informal, relaxed gathering and nobody minded waiting for them. The President brought out some of his grandchildren to greet them, before posing for photographs that would wing their way around the world.

He was in the centre of the group posing for cameras on the steps at the end of a red carpet and couldn't stop grinning as he entered good-naturedly into the spirit of the occasion. Geri sweetly rested her head on his shoulder as he told a small crowd, 'These girls are my heroes. It's one of the greatest moments of my life.'

One of the reporters present asked Charles if it was his greatest moment. The Prince, venturing abroad for the first time since Princess Diana's death, replied, 'Second greatest. The first time I met them was the greatest.' Mel B addressed the President as Nelson, as if they were old buddies but, predictably, it was Geri who turned the occasion into something more memorable.

When another reporter asked Mandela, then seventy-nine, what he thought of the Spice Girls, he answered, 'I think I'm too old for them.'

Geri piped up loudly, 'No, you're not. You're as young as the girl you feel and I'm twenty-five.'

More seriously, she made a touching short speech in which she said the Spice Girls and the President shared the same values: 'I think there's a classic speech that Nelson Mandela made – I can't remember it exactly – but he mentioned never suppress yourself, never make yourself feel small for others' insecurities. And that's what Girl Power is all about – so I think we're on the same level, in that view.' President Mandela's meeting with the Spice Girls was one of the most iconic images of modern times. It was arguably the highlight of the Girls' careers.

That evening they sang three songs at the charity gala: 'Spice Up Your Life', 'Say You'll Be There' and 'Wannabe'. The concert at the Johannesburg Stadium supported the Nation's Trust, founded by Nelson Mandela at the time of the Queen's visit in 1995 to help South African entrepreneurs and small businesses in the post-apartheid era. Prince Charles was there but this time he had brought along a youthful Prince Harry, thirteen, who was on half-term. He looked slightly awkward in a smart dark blue suit and tie, but grinned happily and held Victoria's hand while Geri took a souvenir picture. Both he and his elder brother Prince William were fans, having first met the Girls at Buckingham Palace after the Prince's Trust concert.

While Simon was in New York for an operation on his back, the Girls travelled on to Sun City for a trip to the neighbouring Pilanesberg National Park. Their mums flew in to join them on safari. Geri's mother couldn't make it so her sister, Natalie, came over instead. The jaunt gave the Girls some private time at last and the chance to take stock of their situation.

Geri was fragile and exhausted – a bundle of nervous energy. She put so much into everything and seemingly had to work twice as hard as the others to get every performance just right and, after Istanbul, her bulimia had returned. Away from the gaze of the world, she suffered from chronic insecurity. Victoria was exhausted, missing David, battling her own eating disorder and practically starving herself to maintain her now super-slim figure. Simon had done his best to make sure she ate something, a paternal concern that irritated her. On one occasion in Hong Kong, she had pushed away her food uneaten. Simon reportedly told her, 'You are not going a whole day on just a bowl of rice. Don't be stupid. You have got to eat properly.' Victoria sullenly ate her meal.

Emma was battling away, like the true professional she was, coming to terms with the unwelcome media intrusion into her life and that of her family. She was mortified when a newspaper ran pictures of her mother's karate class. Even Mel B was finding it hard to keep her spirits up, complaining of utter tiredness and becoming more irritated. She was not pleased when Simon had turned down their request for one day off each week and wrote in her diary that, if she didn't stop and take some proper time off, she would soon be mentally and physically exhausted.

Melanie C, the Girl that nobody seemed to notice, was perhaps struggling most of all. She kept it hidden, only finding the courage to speak out many years later: 'I was living on fear and adrenalin. I was with four other girls – some of them very opinionated – and the only way I could cope was by keeping quiet and toeing the party line. Inside I was bottling up so much anger that my body just gave up. The fallout was depression and an eating disorder.'

On their return to England, they sacked Simon. It was a bold move to fire the man who had guided them to superstardom and enormous wealth in such a short time. They were no longer just a pop group with a few number ones – they were a worldwide brand. He seemed to have been a fixture for ever but had been at the helm for only two and a half years. While all five agreed to the split, it was again Geri and Mel B who were most active in making the move. Geri consulted their lawyers to make sure they could actually do it. This was no clandestine flit from Boyne Hill Road; they had grown up and understood that they needed to be careful. Once again, though, they were rebelling against the control of a male figure.

Simon was taken completely by surprise, admitting that it came 'somewhat out of the blue'. He hadn't realised that the Girls had been building up to it: 'My initial reaction was shock and "Fine, OK, sod them. They're missing out on having the best manager in the world."' Arguably, that was probably not an empty boast. What the Girls hadn't realised was that he had been thinking ahead on their behalf and had plans in motion for a second film and third album that would have 'set each of them up with solo careers beautifully'.

He was informed of their decision on the day of the MTV Europe Awards in Rotterdam, at which the Spice Girls performed 'Spice Up Your Life' and won Best Group. They beat a list of nominees that included U2, Radiohead and Oasis. They claimed the top award but failed to win 'Best Newcomer', which went to American teeny-bop favourites Hanson.

The media enjoyed the Simon situation. Here was something newsworthy about the Spice Girls that was entirely different from the conveyor-belt of tiresome ex-boyfriends. Some reports suggested that Simon's dismissal was due partly to his closeness with Emma but this was never confirmed. Another theory was that the Girls had grabbed their calculators and worked out that Simon might actually be earning more than they were – one of their key grievances against Heart Management's contract. If Simon was on 20 per cent commission, that meant the Girls were sharing 80 per cent – a total of 16 per cent each. And they were soon to embark on a 97-date world tour.

Some newspapers seemed determined to chronicle the demise of the group. Victoria observed, 'The media is a very male-dominated industry. Maybe they didn't even realise sometimes what they're doing, but a lot of men, they liked the fact that they thought that a man was behind the Spice Girls. And they don't like the fact that now it's the five girls taking control. We've always been in control anyway, but I think they find the new situation quite hard to accept.' She added ruefully, 'It's a shame that people have to knock you down.'

Simon adjourned to his villa in beautiful Portofino to recuperate from his back operation and to think about what to do next. He was in no rush. One of the people he invited down to the Italian Riviera was Chris Herbert, and the two former managers drank red wine and talked through future possibilities. Chris was keen on starting a group of girls and boys called United Colours – an idea loosely based on the multi-racial advertising campaign 'United Colours of Benetton'. Nothing further came of it, although he did raise an eyebrow when Simon founded S Club 7 the following year, auditioning thousands of hopefuls before finding the perfect combination.

The Girls, meanwhile, had no time to put their feet up. A consequence of sacking Simon was losing most of the 19 staff on their team, so they had to muddle through in the short term. They needed someone to help with the admin and eventually hired Nancy Phillips, better known for managing indie bands, to organise their affairs. In the meantime they had to deal with the release of the *Spiceworld* album. It went straight to number one, which calmed their nerves. The reviews were generally more upbeat this time around, almost all believing it contained better songs than *Spice*.

In the first week, *Spiceworld* sold 192,000 copies in the UK alone. They were clearly not a one-album wonder. Overall, *Spice* sold 22 million copies while the follow-up shifted more than 14 million. If their first album had not been such a sensation, their second would have been regarded as a huge success, finishing in the top ten bestselling albums of the year in both the UK and the US.

They seemed to be working just as hard as when Simon had been at the helm but at least they were making their own decisions. They were guests on *An Audience with ... Elton John*, joining him at the piano to sing his famous hit 'Don't Go Breaking My Heart'. They filmed *An Audience with ... the Spice Girls*, which was 'an evening of Girl Power' watched by nearly 12 million TV viewers. The studio audience was made up exclusively of cheering women, including Barbara Windsor, Twiggy and Jennifer Saunders. Luther Vandross sneaked in to perform disco favourite 'Ain't No Stopping Us Now'. Then they were on stage in front of the Queen for the Royal Command Performance at the London Victoria Palace Theatre.

They mixed with royalty again at the charity première of *Spice World* in aid of the Prince's Trust. More than seven thousand excited and noisy fans crammed into Leicester Square to catch a glimpse of the Girls arriving. Prince Charles, who seemed to be their biggest fan, was guest of honour and arrived with his sons William and Harry for the screening at the Empire cinema.

When the film officially opened in cinemas on Boxing Day they were already celebrating – 'Too Much' had become their second successive Christmas number one, something last achieved by the Beatles in the sixties. At the end of a stupendous year, they could have some proper time off before rehearsing for the start of their first world tour, set to begin at the Point Theatre, Dublin, at the end of February.

The general mood of optimism was made even sunnier when Victoria and David officially announced their engagement. Nobody realised it was a rerun when they posed happily for photographers, showing off their rings at the Rookery Hall Hotel in Cheshire. Hers was a £40,000 solitaire diamond designed by Boodle & Dunthorne. She told the press, 'It's just what I wanted and it was a big surprise' – which, of course, it wasn't.

She had bought David's diamond-encrusted gold band, reportedly costing £50,000, in Rodeo Drive, Beverly Hills, when the girls were on a promotional trip to Los Angeles. On arriving home she had inadvertently walked through the nothing-to-declare channel at Manchester airport and was sent a bill for £3,000 by HM Customs and Excise after the smiling couple showed off their rings at the photo call.

The whole country was happy for them, it seemed – the handsomest young footballer in England was marrying a Spice Girl. It had been a momentous year for all five: true, it had been exhausting, but they had made a hit movie, had a number-one record in the US and the UK, won two Brits and two Ivor Novello Awards, met Nelson Mandela and Prince Charles, and apparently calmed the storm over their sacking of Simon Fuller. 1998 promised to be just as good. What could possibly go wrong?

15

# STOP RIGHT NOW

———————

They sealed off the street in Stoneybatter when the Spice Girls arrived in Dublin to film the video for their next single, 'Stop'. The suburb in the north of the city is quite trendy these days, but in the late nineties it was a perfect location to recreate the feel of fifties working-class Britain. The locals in Carnew Street, which had distinctive stone-built two-up, two-down terraced houses, were given £100 for the inconvenience of the Spice Girls dancing down their street, but nobody minded and it was talked about for many years to come. 'It was a great day,' recalled one resident. 'My aunt is the woman in the scarf with rollers in her hair.' Another reminisced, 'It's against the law to walk up Carnew Street and not mention the Spice Girls.'

It was a cold late-January day in the Irish capital, but a happy one as all five Girls were together, charming everybody with their approachability. One lad who bunked off school for the afternoon got a hug from Ginger Spice. If any of the Girls needed a wee they just knocked on the nearest door and asked if they could pop in and use the toilet. Nobody had a mobile phone and there was no social media to alert fans that the Girls were in town, which would have ruined everything. The next day they travelled on to the small town of Rathdrum in

County Wicklow for some scenes with children at the local fair.

The video, by director James Byrne, oozes joie de vivre. There's pat-a-cake, hopscotch, cat's cradle, hula hoop and Geri on a horse. And in the last scene, in an austere local hall, the older mums and dads start smiling and singing along while the Girls dance on stage in a throwback to the great Motown groups of the past, the Supremes and Martha and the Vandellas. At the end, Geri pokes out her tongue.

Mel B explained that there was no storyboard for the video, which was quite a free-for-all, adding that it was 'complete chaos'. But it worked and the result is perhaps their most natural video and one that has worn well over the years. Surprisingly, though, 'Stop' did not reach number one. For the first time in eight records, the Spice Girls were stuck at number two, behind 'It's Like That' by Run DMC vs Jason Nevins, which was one of the biggest hits of the year.

It made sense to shoot the video in Ireland because the Girls were already there, staying at the magnificent K Club resort in County Kildare while they rehearsed for the opening of their tour. The two nights in Dublin had sold out in two hours. One big difference between their Istanbul gigs and the full tour was the addition of an assigned dancer, a Spice Boy, for each of the girls. The first thing Victoria noticed was that she had known one of them at Laine's, Christian Storm. Back in college days he was known by his real name, Christian Horsfall. She had fancied him from afar but now he seemed to hit it off with Geri, his Spice Girl. She was single after a brief holiday romance with polo player Jamie Morrison, son of the legendary pop manager Bryan Morrison.

By far the most significant new addition to the world of the Spice Girls was a dancer from Amsterdam called Jimmy Gulzar, who was paired with Mel B and bore a striking resemblance to her old teenage boyfriend, Steven Mulrain. The idea was that the men represented the male double of each Girl. Jimmy, who was originally from the former Dutch colony of Surinam, was bald, with tattoos and an imposing dancer's physique. He was happy to have his tongue pierced as Mel B had done.

Although technically she was still seeing Fjöl, he lived in Iceland, and she soon decided that she fancied Jimmy, in an example of what later became known as 'Strictly syndrome' or 'The Curse of Strictly', in which the close physical contact in Strictly Come Dancing led to some serious relationships. She split from Fjöl in March so the coast was clear for what would be a whirlwind romance with Jimmy.

He was with her on stage when the tour opened in Dublin on 24 February 1998. The introduction featured a video screen of a space ship in a pastiche of Star Trek. Instead of 'Space: the Final Frontier', it was 'Spice: the Final Frontier', with the Girls promising to boldly go where no woman had been before. Most of the set was similar to Istanbul's, although the performance of 'Do It' with the male dancers was much steamier.

The encore was 'We Are Family', the disco favourite from Sister Sledge. Geri, however, wasn't exactly feeling that way any more. After just six concerts, she told the others, while they were waiting to go on stage in Milan, that she was planning to leave after the final gigs at Wembley Stadium in September. When Victoria asked her why, she replied, 'I've had enough.' The end of the tour was the ideal time to bring the curtain down on the Spice Girls phenomenon. In the end, she didn't wait that long. The concert at the Hartwell Arena in Helsinki on 26 May 1998 would be her last — just four years after she had burst into their lives at the Nomis audition. Perhaps the other Girls didn't take her seriously, believing that she was merely a bit tired and down and needed to get used to the very different demands of touring.

Mel B was preoccupied, it seemed, by her blossoming relationship with Jimmy. Topless pictures appeared in the media of her with him on a beach in the French Riviera so there was nothing secret about it. He proposed at the über-fashionable Buddha Bar on Faubourg St-Honoré, in Paris, on a night when the inimitable Grace Jones was holding court at the bar. It was not exactly a low-key candle-lit-dinner type of bistro. They ate spring rolls and drank vintage champagne before Jimmy produced a thumb ring for her, which she put on. They had known each other for just ten weeks but she was thrilled.

Her future looked brighter at the end of May than that of the Spice Girls after Geri failed to appear on the Wednesday-night edition of *The National Lottery Show*. Their lawyer had already told the other four earlier in the day that she was leaving. Victoria thought he was joking and needed to be convinced that he wasn't. He confirmed, 'She's had enough.' They went ahead with their TV appearance, brazening it out. Melanie C stares, almost shame-faced, into the camera as she announces, 'Geri's not very well tonight. Get well soon, Geri!' They performed their next single, 'Viva Forever', a song that contained lyrics mainly written by Geri. It begins, 'Do you still remember how we used to be?'

Rumours began to circulate that there was more to it and journalists descended on Oslo for the last concerts of the European leg of the tour on 28 and 29 May, Mel B's twenty-third birthday. A note taped to the doors of the Spektrum arena offered the audience their money back and declared that Geri was ill and would not be performing. Kevin O'Sullivan, showbusiness editor of the *Daily Mirror*, saw it and observed simply, 'It was a barefaced lie.'

Worryingly for the Girls, they had to work out who was going to sing Geri's parts, which at least gave Victoria a line in 'Wannabe' at last. Melanie C sang the shouty bit at the start alongside Mel B and didn't enjoy it one bit but they battled through, although sometimes they completely forgot what to do and would gaze at each other panic-stricken. They managed to sing the lyric from 'Stop' that contains the words 'always be together' without a trace of embarrassment. Melanie C admitted that she kept turning round during the shows and wondering where Geri was.

The Girls kept up the charade about Geri's illness. This time it was Victoria's turn to announce to the eight-thousand-strong crowd: 'We just wanted to say that Geri is poorly and in bed and really she couldn't be with us tonight. But she hopes you are all having a wicked time.' In reality, they didn't have a clue where she was. She was actually in Paris with her elder brother Max, who filmed her in the opulent surroundings of the Hôtel Crillon speaking to camera as if she was compiling a video diary. It hadn't helped that she had been spotted catching a flight to France, undermining the tummy-trouble excuse.

Two days later, everyone was put out of their misery with a series of bland announcements to the press. Geri's statement came first: 'This is a message to the fans. Sadly, I would like to confirm that I have left the Spice Girls. This is because of differences between us. I'm sure the group will continue to be successful and I wish them all the best. I have no immediate plans. I wish to apologise to all the fans and to thank them and everyone who's been there. Lots of love, Geri. PS I'll be back.'

The remaining four responded: 'We are upset and saddened by Geri's departure but we are very supportive in whatever she wants to do. The Spice Girls are here to stay – see you at the stadiums! We are sorry to all our fans having to go through all of this. All our love, Victoria, Emma, Mel C, Mel B. Friendship never ends!'

But it had – at least for the foreseeable future. Publicly, the Girls said all the right things. They had, they said, tried to persuade her to change her mind but with no luck. Victoria expressed the general well-wishing, 'There are no hard feelings. We wish her all the luck in the world. We are totally behind her. We've always said that if anybody was unhappy they should leave. The most important thing is our friendship.'

But there *were* hard feelings. Three years later, in her autobiography, Victoria revealed what she really thought: 'I'd known Geri for four years, we'd shared a room in Windsor, and we'd been through the most extraordinary experiences of our lives together. She was one of my best friends. And now she had walked out without a word. What I felt was first anger at the selfishness of it all, then betrayal. Total betrayal.'

Emma found it very difficult to take in and didn't speak to Geri for many months: 'I was so close to Geri. She was like my elder sister. I didn't think anything other than "I'm going to miss my friend who looks after me." It took me a while to forgive her. We probably didn't speak for about a year.'

At first Melanie C thought Geri might have been seeking to emulate Robbie Williams, who had been the first to leave Take That – although that was closer to a sacking than a voluntary departure. She conceded that Geri had some personal issues and hinted that the volatile relationship between Geri and Mel B might have been an important factor: 'It's no secret that her and Melanie had a very fiery relationship in the past. They are the closest of all the band. They're in each other's pockets or they can fight like cat and dog.' Mel B has returned to the subject many times over the years and admitted that she missed Geri, felt very lonely after she'd gone and experienced 'moments of deep sadness'.

Geri confided that there were lots of reasons why she left the Spice Girls but she stressed that she left on that particular day because of the cancellation of an interview she wanted to give ITN about breast cancer. The *Sun* had run a front-page story about her teenage operation to remove a lump and she was keen to speak about it on television. Apparently, the other Girls vetoed the idea and Geri was not happy. She had always led the way where the press had been concerned and now she was not being allowed to do so. Perhaps breast cancer was too grown-up an issue for the majority of their very young fans. She had, it seemed, lost any position of leadership within the group. She commented, 'I was meant to be an advocate of Girl Power. I felt like a hypocrite.'

Commentators were able to pose the question of whether her departure was the end for the Spice Girls or just the beginning of the end. They had recorded a performance of 'Viva Forever' for *Top of the Pops* earlier in May and this was broadcast on 5 June 1998, the last time the five appeared together on television. Even Prince Charles was concerned and sent Geri a hand-written note: 'The group will not be the same without you. What will I do without your wonderfully friendly greeting?' Charles always appreciated a kiss on the cheek from Geri.

More seriously, he wrote, 'I really wanted you to know how deeply I've appreciated your great generosity to my Prince's Trust and how much I wish you well for whatever the future holds.' He signed the letter 'with lots of love'.

Mel B had more to think about than fretting about Geri. She had invited her parents, Andrea and Martin, to Oslo to get to know better the man she was going to marry. They were both unimpressed, especially on the first day when they went shopping and Jimmy was spending money like it was going out of fashion. Martin said, 'He wasn't just spending a couple of hundred pounds – it was thousands. I thought, "Where does he get all his money from? He's just a dancer."' According to Andrea, Martin wanted to 'knock him out' and she had to persuade him that was not the answer.

Instead, she confronted Jimmy face to face and hit him with a double-whammy: 'I said "Jim, I think you're marrying Melanie for her money – and I think you're gay." She had heard snippets from the other girls that seemed to confirm her worries but there was nothing she could do: 'No one could approach Melanie because she was head over heels in love.' For his part, Jimmy strongly refuted Andrea's opinion of him.

While the Girls could take a short break after Oslo, they had only two weeks to prepare for life after Geri before the first of forty American concerts at the Coral Sky Amphitheatre in West Palm Beach, Florida. The tour proved to be quite a triumph and probably exceeded everyone's expectations.

This was the first time any of them had spent an extended period of time in the US and they loved it, despite the arduous schedule. They did touristy trips, including Disney World in Florida and Niagara Falls in New York State. They revelled in the enthusiasm of the audience and loved the fact that famous people wanted to see them – Stevie Wonder, Prince, Cameron Diaz, Demi Moore and Drew Barrymore were just some of the stars they encountered. Madonna came backstage in New York, bringing her daughter Lourdes, not yet two, to meet the Girls. The superstar asked them for all the gossip about Geri leaving – 'a little girly chat', said Melanie C. The Girls were more interested in making a fuss of Lourdes who, they thought, was beautiful.

The tickets for that Madison Square Garden concert sold out in twelve minutes. In the *New York Times*, Jon Parales noted, 'For a sold-out house filled with little girls, like an elementary assembly with parents invited, the Spice Girls worked the stage like a fashion-show runway. Through nearly a dozen costume changes they touted "girl power", a mandate to enjoy female bonding, push men around, wear snazzy clothes and sell things along the way.'

Vocally, Emma seemed to be gathering more attention, described by Gilbert Garcia in the *Phoenix New Times* as the 'most effortlessly appealing'. She sang solo on the Supremes classic 1964 hit 'Where Did Our Love Go' and it suited her easy style. While acknowledging that the majority of the audience were under ten, Gilbert also pointed out that many of the Spice Girls songs were 'guilty pleasures in a song catalogue that's easy to dismiss but equally hard to get out of your brain'. He added, 'Only a complete curmudgeon could have denied the Motownish charms of "Stop" or the salsa-flavoured "Spice Up Your Life".' Moira McCormick in *Rolling Stone* summed up the appeal of a Spice Girls concert perfectly: 'If you went there with your daughter, it was worth it to see her delighted face.'

While they were away, 'Viva Forever' became their seventh number-one single. The video had been commissioned while Geri was still with the band, which was fortuitous as the five girls were represented by puppets, so she did not appear in person. After the minor disappointment of 'Stop', 'Viva Forever' sold nearly 300,000 copies in its first week. The lady herself was much in evidence during the concerts on pre-shot film and pre-prepared programmes. Every time her image flashed up on screen, it would be greeted by a huge cheer, which must have been galling for the remaining four flogging round the US.

While Mel B and Jimmy were together all the time, Victoria had to make do with calling David every day on the phone. He was in St Étienne near Lyon preparing for a World Cup quarter-final against Argentina when she rang from New York to tell him she was pregnant. David burst into tears of delight. He flew over as soon as he could after the match had finished – he was infamously sent off and England lost. By a weird coincidence, Mel B had taken a positive pregnancy test on the same day as Victoria – two Spice Girls were expecting at exactly the same time. They had to field questions about whether the pregnancies signalled the demise of the group, which prompted Victoria to say, 'I don't want people to read all this negativity.'

When they reached Nashville, they were joined by Matt and Biff, who had flown over to work on some songs with them for a third album. It would be the first time that Geri hadn't been part of the process. The best known of them, 'Goodbye', had already been sketched out while Geri was still with them but was inevitably interpreted as a message to their former bandmate – or, even more upsetting for the fans, a sign that this was really the end of the Spice Girls. Mel B confided, 'It's a very sentimental song and the very first time I heard it I cried.'

The gang of four were clear that while it was in part directed at Geri, it was not over for the Spice Girls. After all, the song ends, 'Goodbye my friend, it's not the end.' Biff explained that it wasn't literally about Geri: 'It was about moving on and saying goodbye to the old Spice Girls.'

In the video, shot at Mentmore, a stately home just north of London, both Mel B and Victoria are showing their pregnancy. They would soon be Spice mums and Spice wives. All of them were thinking about their solo careers. 'Goodbye' might not have been the Spice Girls' farewell but their lives were moving on.

After the American leg of the world tour ended in Dallas in August 1998, there were still four stadium concerts left to perform in the UK the following month, two at the Don Valley Stadium in Sheffield and two at the old Wembley Stadium. In the *Guardian*, Alfred Hickling described the gigs as the 'climax of a year-long round-the-world slog'. The audience did not seem to have grown any older, still pre-teen and still screaming when their heroes proclaimed that friendship never ends and still grinning happily on their way out. The final concert in front of 72,000 fans at Wembley was a triumph, broadcast live on pay-per-view TV. Geri Halliwell watched it on television.

# PART THREE

## SPICE WOMEN

# 16

# NIGHTMARES AND
# FAIRYTALES

---

Geri's final concert on the *Spice World* tour was in Helsinki on 26 May 1998. The next time she would appear in concert with the group was in Vancouver on 2 December 2007, almost ten years later. During that time, between them the Girls had eight solo number one singles in the UK and a further 21 top-ten hits. The problem that each of them knew they would have to face was whether they could sustain the initial curiosity the public had in them as individual performers.

Of all the Girls, Melanie Brown always seemed to be a step ahead – and not always in a good way. She was the first to walk down the aisle, but her marriage to Jimmy Gulzar seemed doomed while the ink was still drying on the register at St John the Baptist Church, in the sleepy Buckinghamshire village of Little Marlow – a world away from the hurly-burly streets of Leeds where she grew up.

Hundreds of well-wishers and bemused local residents came to have a look on her wedding day, but there was little for them to see. Security men in smart dinner jackets made sure there were no unwelcome gatecrashers taking photographs. A white canvas tunnel ran from the church to the manor house next door to ensure that guests weren't seen making their way to the reception in a marquee in the eight–acre garden. Mel had recently bought the property, known locally as the manor, for an estimated £2.5 million. The privacy had a purpose; the rights to the big day had been sold to *OK!* magazine for a sum rumoured to be £350,000.

The day after the wedding on 13 September 1998 – an unlucky thirteen – Mel B became the first Spice Girl to release a solo record. While on tour, she had been contacted by the rapper and producer Missy Elliott, who asked if she would like to collaborate on a single. The resulting track, 'I Want You Back' by Melanie B featuring Missy 'Misdemeanor' Elliott, was a slice of nineties' hip hop and nothing like the songs of *Spiceworld*. Fans accepted it, though, and 'I Want You Back' reached number one in the UK.

Mel G, as she was now calling herself, gave birth to a baby girl a month prematurely at the Portland Clinic in London on 19 February 1999. Jimmy couldn't wait to share the news and bounced outside to tell the press: 'She is wicked.' They had already named the baby Phoenix Chi; he explained that Phoenix meant fire and Chi stood for an aura. Geri wasn't there but Emma and Melanie C arrived together and toasted the new mum with a glass of champagne, while a heavily pregnant Victoria made it the same evening. As she left, Melanie C exclaimed, 'I am very proud – Girl Power!'

Mel decided now was the time to release photographs of herself naked and pregnant to the *Sunday Times*, imitating the famous pictures of Demi Moore in *Vanity Fair* eight years earlier. She also maintained she was toning down her image: 'I'm not as nasty as I was. Two years ago, I was a terribly aggressive person, very defensive. I could be a total cow, but I've learned to control that.'

By May, her marriage was on the rocks when it was revealed that she and Jimmy were living in separate wings of the family mansion. Among other things, they had clashed over Mel's plans to take her three-month-old baby on a short trip to the US when she flew to Minneapolis for recording commitments. Jimmy, who had given up dancing because of a back injury, didn't want their baby to go. Rows over their child were only part of the problem, though, with Mel reportedly becoming more exasperated by her husband's spending sprees. The papers gave him the nickname Jimmy Goldcard, because of the apparent liberal use he made of her credit card. She also didn't take to his old friends from Amsterdam from his days as a star dancer at the iT club, one of the best-known gay discos in Europe, and with whom he still kept in close touch. Jimmy, speaking in 2002, maintained he was spending his own money – his share of the money they received from *OK!*. He blamed Mel's mum Andrea for speaking to the press, causing him to be nicknamed Jimmy Goldcard and raising questions about his sexuality.

They were not as well suited as she had hoped. She wanted a fairytale, but it did not turn out to be the reality. The *Mail on Sunday* observed, 'Like a heroine from a Barbara Taylor Bradford novel, she married with great noise and in haste to a man who could never fit in with her romantic vision of marriage.'

Despite their obvious problems, she was credited as Melanie G when her follow-up single 'Word Up' was released at the end of June. Jimmy had suggested she record the old Cameo disco hit from 1986. Her version only reached number thirteen – unlucky again – in the UK chart.

Mel was struggling to juggle the demands of new motherhood with the schedule of recording her solo album. Trying to balance the two, she confessed, was leaving her 'empty and knackered'. She did find the energy to attend the Los Angeles première of *Austin Powers: The Spy Who Shagged Me*, though, which featured 'Word Up' on the soundtrack, as well as the end-of-tour party for fellow girl group All Saints, which was held closer to home in the Mayfair Club, London.

Mel and Jimmy had their final bust-up at the turn of the millennium, when Mel rushed off to Leeds, taking their daughter with her, where she stayed with her dad Martin. From there she flew with her sister Danielle and ten-month-old Phoenix to the Thai holiday island of Phuket, where she was noticeably quiet and, according to a fellow holidaymaker, 'rather sad'.

Expensive lawyers were needed to sort out custody arrangements and a divorce settlement. Mel offered Jimmy a reported £750,000 cash plus a £500,000 flat. Despite their differences, Mel was adamant that she wanted Phoenix to grow up having two parents and agreed that Jimmy, who doted on his daughter, could look after her at weekends. She acknowledged, 'He is the father of my child and a very good dad.'

She explained to the *Daily Mail* what had happened in a poignant and heartfelt interview: 'I had a relationship where I let my man crush my spirit. He tried to change the things about me that had made him fall in love with me. A lot of men do that. I felt very vulnerable and insecure about myself and I let that happen. I don't blame anyone for that – only myself.'

She was back being Mel B when she started dating actor Max Beesley soon afterwards. The world knew all about this relationship because they went on holiday together to Barbados. Mel had met him at a dinner arranged by Emma Bunton. At the time he was a relatively new star name, gaining public attention in the title role of the BBC costume drama *Tom Jones*. Like Mel, he came from a working-class background in the north of England, raised in Manchester by his mother, Chris Marlowe, who was a well-known jazz singer. Max had more of a musical background than a theatrical one, having been a session musician with Take That and George Michael, as well as being a great friend of Robbie Williams. He also had a reputation as a man who enjoyed the company of beautiful women, numbering television presenters Melanie Sykes and Dani Behr, as well as the acclaimed actress and singer Carmen Ejogo, among his former girlfriends.

Despite Mel and Max quickly becoming an established couple, she felt isolated in her mansion, although it helped when Danielle came to live in a flat in the grounds. The house itself was quite low-key and homely for a pop star, although her bedroom was more boudoir than mumsy, with mirrors mounted on a low ceiling. Her dad took one look at it, sighed, 'Oh Melanie', and quietly shut the door. Perhaps the least conventional feature was two toilets facing each other in the downstairs bathroom because, as she delicately put it, 'Girls always go to the toilet together.' Victoria would have hated it.

Mel finally bumped into Geri for the first time in two years at a local health club in the summer of 2000. They exchanged a cordial hello but nothing more. Ironically, they had more to say about one another in interviews than in person. Mel corrected the views of many: 'When people say we're big enemies, they forget that we used to be so close.' She recalled that they spent not just one Christmas together in the sun, but two more which went unreported. She acknowledged, 'Sadly, our friendship did fizzle out a bit when Geri went off to do her own thing.'

For the most part, Jimmy Gulzar has kept a low profile since his relationship with Mel ended, but he did give a television interview in 2002 in which he said, 'Melanie and Geri had a relationship with each other which goes deeper than a lot of people think.' He claimed that it was more than just being members of the same group. He observed, 'I don't think that if any other member of the group left, Melanie would have been so negative towards them. But Melanie was just hurt that Geri left the group because they were really, really close.'

The *Daily Mirror* described the revelations from Jimmy as pointing towards a 'not so platonic' relationship between the two women. At the time, neither of them commented, although in one completely unrelated interview Geri revealed she had tried lesbian sex with a famous woman but didn't say who it was. At the time nobody tried to connect the dots with Mel B.

They didn't keep in touch after their brief hello at the gym, and when Geri was number one with 'It's Raining Men', Mel said she preferred the original version. She added the back-handed compliment: 'Geri's brilliant at the whole publicity game and I wish her well. She's a clever lady.'

While Geri managed four number one singles, Mel couldn't repeat the success of 'I Want You Back'. She waited two years to release another record, and by then the momentum had been lost. 'Tell Me' did attract attention because of its lyrics, which were aimed unsubtly at Jimmy. She sings, 'All you loved was Mel B's money.' Writing about one's exes is a trusted formula for getting a track some publicity.

'Tell Me' reached number four in the singles charts, but her solo album, *Hot*, was a disaster. The reviews of what was essentially an American R&B album were very mixed. The *Daily Mail* thought her style was 'energetic and surprisingly effective' but *NME* was damning: 'It's hard to overstate just how bad this record is.'

The public were unimpressed and the record peaked at number twenty-eight in the album charts, selling little more than 50,000 copies. It all seemed a bit rushed. The third Spice Girls album, and the first without Geri, was due to be released in a matter of weeks, so nobody cared much about Mel's offering.

Max was still on the scene and was listed as sole writer and co-producer on one track from her album, 'Step Inside'. Only Biff Stannard from the great days of the Spice Girls had a credit and that was just as a co-writer on a track called 'Lullaby', a sentimental tribute to her baby. At least Phoenix seemed to appreciate her music. Whenever one of her records was played on the radio, she would shout out, 'My Mummy!'

Victoria was in a much happier place with her man. One of the most endearing images of the soon-to-be Mr and Mrs Beckham is of David tenderly kissing his pregnant fiancée's stomach as they lounged on a beach in Marbella, Spain. While they were there, they chose the name Brooklyn for their unborn son. One of the many urban myths about the couple is that they were acknowledging the place where he was conceived. It's a good story, but if that had been the case, Brooklyn Joseph Beckham would probably have been called Copenhagen.

More mundanely, Victoria had always liked the name Brooke for a girl, so her train of thought went from there to Brooklyn and, by chance, she had been in New York when she found out she was pregnant. She was due to be the first Spice mum but their plan to have the baby induced at the Portland was delayed, so Mel B was able to slip into the hospital and give birth while Victoria was stuck at the starting gate. Someone suggested curry and raspberry tea might help. Victoria laughed, 'As soon as David heard that, he was dragging me out to a curry house every night and force-feeding me raspberry tea. It was ridiculous.'

Brooklyn was finally born by emergency Caesarian on 4 March, two weeks after Phoenix. David Beckham came of age as a modern-day icon when he became a father. Until his son arrived, David was a good-looking, talented footballer who dated a pop star. He was living the life many young men could only dream of but it took something universal to give him fulfilment. He was completely besotted with his child from the first moment he held him in his arms.

While Victoria seemed beset by insecurities as a young mother, Becks, just twenty-three, approached being a dad with a masculine confidence and an almost feminine affection. It was entirely genuine. Victoria echoed the views of millions of women up and down the country when she said there was 'nothing nicer than seeing a man who was good with a baby'. When Brooklyn came along, Brand Beckham was born.

The essential difference between Victoria and David after the birth of their eldest son was the classic one that can affect a man and a woman in this situation. David barely broke stride in his life; he was still the charismatic footballer, kissing his partner and baby goodbye before jumping into his Ferrari – a gift from Victoria – and going off to the training ground each day. David was still Becks but Victoria was living a life that was not remotely Posh Spice.

Victoria didn't enjoy being stuck in David's penthouse flat in Alderley Edge, Cheshire. She felt completely isolated, especially when David had to travel away for a match. Her mum Jackie would drive up from Hertfordshire when they needed her, but there were many days spent staring out of the window and sobbing for no reason. She explained, 'It's hard going from Spice Girl to a flat on your own with a baby, no friends, no family, no nothing.'

At least she had a wedding to plan, although much of that was done by their exclusive party organiser, Peregrine Armstrong-Jones, the half brother of Princess Margaret's ex-husband, Lord Snowden. This time, *OK!* magazine agreed to pay £1 million for exclusive rights to pictures and text to what promised to be the wedding of the decade. It was an obscene amount of money and dismayed those who thought it demeaned the ceremony. Victoria sought to justify it by claiming that it gave them complete control over media interest on the day. She had a point – anarchic chaos would have been the result of a photographic free-for-all. Control was something Victoria valued very highly. Her natural desire to keep her hands on the reins was developed in those early days of the Spice Girls when she absorbed the skills of Simon Fuller.

Peregrine had thought Luttrellstown Castle, near Dublin, might be an enchanting venue, so while she was pregnant Victoria had flown out to take a look on a cold and miserable January day. She instantly fell in love with the place. It would have been a superb choice for a Spice Girls video. The fifteenth-century building had a magical feel to it and, best of all, was very private. She explained, 'I wanted somewhere that had a big wall around it so I wouldn't feel paranoid every time I walked past a window.'

The wedding itself cost an estimated £500,000 to stage, so the *OK!* money was useful. Her champagne-coloured Vera Wang dress alone cost £50,000, and the jewellery that was on show could have stocked a small shop in Hatton Garden. The wedding rings were made in London by Asprey & Garrard. Victoria's was dominated by a huge diamond supported by a host of baguette diamonds set in 18-carat gold. David's was an eternity-style ring with twenty-four baguette diamonds and twenty-four smaller ones, again set in 18-carat gold. The present for the best man, Gary Neville, was a £12,000 Cartier watch; Victoria's brother, Christian, was given a £12,000 gold and silver Rolex watch for doing a spot of ushering.

Victoria's wedding dress was to travel over from London in the same private plane as the bride and groom and her family. At the last minute the dress in its travelling case proved too bulky for the small hold, so it had to be unpacked rapidly and hung in the toilet. Nobody was allowed to use the loo during the flight and David was firmly told to keep his eyes shut while the dress disembarked so that he could avoid the traditional bad luck of seeing the bride's gown before the big event.

On the day of the wedding, the fourth of July, the star guest, Elton John, fell ill. His partner David Furnish rang to say he had been rushed to hospital. Victoria was very worried about her friend, notwithstanding that he had promised to sing at the big event. Fears that it was a heart scare were misplaced and he turned out to have an ear infection.

Victoria decided against walking down the aisle to a Spice Girls song, instead making her entrance on her dad's arm to Wagner's wedding march from the opera *Lohengrin*. Emma Bunton burst into tears. The two Melanies were also there and all three of these Spice Girls brought their mums with them. Mel B carried Phoenix in her arms. Geri's absence was, according to Victoria, the saddest thing about the day. She said she could not invite her former bandmate because it was 'too public', which presumably meant that it would have attracted too much publicity and taken some of the attention away from the bride and groom. Geri, who had not met Brooklyn, sent her a handwritten poem.

In his best man's speech, Gary Neville couldn't resist a risqué joke about the Spice Girls. Referring to why the Girls wanted the Bayern Munich football team to be there after their injury time loss to Manchester United in the Champions League final in May, he said, 'They wanted to meet any man who could stay on top for ninety minutes and still come second.'

The whole occasion, which for some never-explained reason had a Robin Hood theme, was like a fairytale. Millions of little girls who adored the Spice Girls might have dreamed of this day – marrying a handsome prince in a castle.

The honeymoon plans were spoiled by the rotten king or, in this case, by United's manager, Alex Ferguson. He did not like the celebrity culture of the Beckhams, so David was only allowed four days away before having to resume pre-season training. At the last minute, with no honeymoon in place, they were helped out by Andrew Lloyd Webber's wife, Madeleine, who said the newly-weds could stay at their villa in the South of France — which was not that much of a hardship. Victoria, though, increasingly resented the control the manager had over her new husband. Something would have to change in the future. Their dislike appeared to be mutual.

The grandiose marriage provided Victoria with the opportunity to make another very smart move. She took the name Beckham. For the first twenty-four years of her life she had been Victoria Adams (except for her brief flirtation with Victoria Adams-Woods). She had achieved worldwide fame as Victoria Adams but she was prepared to drop it immediately and take her husband's name. Now, 'Victoria Beckham', is so etched into public consciousness that it's easy to forget that she has only used it for under one half of her life. The genius of the Beckhams is that they are a joint brand. Andy Milligan, in his fascinating study *Brand it Like Beckham*, puts it simply, 'Think of Posh and you think of Becks. Think of Becks and you think of Posh.'

From now on, if there was a picture of Victoria on the front page, it was far more likely to be in connection with David — and vice versa — than anything to do with the Spice Girls. She set up a company, Yandella Limited, which for the next five years would be the Beckhams' family business, banking £2.5 million in deals in the run-up to the wedding alone, which was a bright start.

The couple paid that same amount for Rowneybury House, in the small Hertfordshire town of Sawbridgeworth, about twenty minutes in the car from her parents' house. Prising David away from his Manchester environment was not difficult. He loved the celebrity lifestyle of London, where he and Victoria could indulge their shared interest in fashion; and they both wanted to create a proper home for their family.

It took two years to install all the 'homely' features Victoria wanted, including an indoor swimming pool, recording studio, snooker room, gym and floodlit tennis courts. They spent £20,000 on hundreds of fibre-optic lights to create a night sky in Brooklyn's bedroom. Victoria designed a bathroom devoted to her fashion hero, Audrey Hepburn; and there was a room that wouldn't have been out of place in Mel B's house – covered in leopard print with a mirrored ceiling. The media wasted little time in renaming the house Beckingham Palace. The over-the-top project, however, was not money wasted. When they eventually sold the property in 2013 they collected £12 million.

It was time, however, for Victoria to resume the day job, even if her heart wasn't in it. The four remaining Spice Girls were planning their second tour – although this time *Christmas in Spiceworld* would be eight nights only at two venues in the UK. It was the chance to introduce a couple of new songs that they had been working on for the next album as well as reacquaint everyone with their best-loved hits.

The most intriguing new number was called 'W.O.M.A.N.', which Victoria put her heart into. The track was like a grown-up version of a Spice Girls song with all their trademark exuberance, but a lyric that confirmed 'No longer are we teenagers'. Instead of shouting Girl Power, they declared 'Be Independent like a woman'. Two other new songs, 'Right Back At Ya' and 'Holler', suggested a then more fashionable R&B sound was on the cards for the next album. 'W.O.M.A.N.' didn't make the final selection.

The concerts, four at the MEN Arena in Manchester and another four at Earls Court, London, were a personal triumph for Victoria. Mel B did confide one night that the two of them were in bad moods backstage but that certainly wasn't the case on stage. There was no pouting or looking serious; Victoria came out of her shell, especially during the Christmas encore, when all the Girls, dressed in Santa red, belted out the Slade favourite

'Merry Xmas Everybody'. Victoria then sang lead on another classic, Wizzard's 'I Wish it Could Be Christmas Everyday', which was just as well because Mel B had no idea what the words were.

Victoria, it seemed, could not have been happier to cast off the responsibilities of motherhood and marriage, but that was not the case before the Brit Awards, at which the Spice Girls were given the Outstanding Contribution to Music award. She was upset and on edge all evening. She called the other Girls together before they were due to go on stage and told them, 'I've had death threats.' She proceeded to fill them in on how she had received bullets in the post and threatening letters and how she was worried that there were plans to kidnap Brooklyn.

The letter that had triggered her anguish had arrived two days earlier. Inside was a newspaper photograph of Victoria that had been tampered with to show blood spurting from a bullet hole in her head and the warning 'You are going to die', with the date 3 March 2000, the day of the Brits. She called the police immediately.

Victoria spent the day of the awards with a bodyguard glued to her side. The worst moment came when she walked off stage following the afternoon rehearsal and saw a red laser light shining on her chest. It was like something from a Clint Eastwood movie. Victoria was terrified. Police dashed up the gantry but whoever had been there had made their escape.

That night, Geri performed earlier in the show, but she had left the arena before the Girls went on to sing 'Spice Up Your Life'. During their last song, 'Goodbye', Victoria appeared to be too upset to continue singing. In reality she thought she had been shot. In her anxiety, she had mistaken the bursting of balloons for gunshots. She broke down in tears, which the world's media thought was because she was overcome with emotion. They were, in fact, tears of joy that she was still alive.

# 17

# DARK CLOUDS

―――――――

After the Brits, the Girls threw a party at the Sugar Reef restaurant in Soho. Melanie C was in high spirits and marched up to the lead singer of 5ive, Jason Brown, to have a stern word about an interview he had given in which he had allegedly described her as 'ugly'. To everyone's surprise the two of them got on really well. This was not the most discreet occasion to start a new relationship, because all the well-known pop columnists were there and they all saw them having a snog before they left.

It's easy to see how they might strike up a friendship. The very handsome J, as he was called, had been brought up in Warrington, just down the road from Widnes where Melanie spent her early years. He too had been discovered by Chris Herbert and had rehearsed in Trinity Studios in Knaphill. Melanie was someone who clearly understood what had to be done to make it in the pop business.

Soon afterwards she was asked if she had a new man in her life and she was coy about naming J. She did laughingly suggest that she might go and see 5ive in concert. J was less guarded and very complimentary about Melanie: 'It's nice to meet someone who I can sit down with and talk to about normal things; someone who wants to chat and isn't away with the fairies. We've met each other a few times and we get on and we're just seeing what happens. We won't be conveniently photographed. Hopefully she'll come to one of our shows.'

That was exactly what she did, more than once. The group were touring and Melanie would slip along unannounced. It was all kept top secret so that the tabloids and the paparazzi weren't camped at their door. It didn't amount to anything more serious, mainly because of their busy schedules, and it eventually fizzled into more of a phone friendship.

Professionally, Melanie had instant solo success. Three weeks after the Brits, she had her first number one – 'Never Be the Same Again' that featured a rap by Lisa 'Left Eye' Lopes, who had great credibility in the R&B world as a member of TLC. Melanie was keen to prove herself without the security blanket of the Spice Girls. She wanted her solo music to be taken seriously and not to be successful just because she was famous. She didn't care for being in the spotlight, though.

Melanie had actually been close behind Mel B in releasing a record away from the Spice Girls. She was the featured artist on Bryan Adams's enduring classic 'When You're Gone'. The song may not have quite reached the top but it remains a karaoke favourite for couples singing badly in the pub. Melanie was not the first choice for the duet, though. Bryan revealed that he approached the American singer Sheryl Crow, but didn't hear back from her. By chance he was in a hotel lift in Los Angeles when Melanie walked in. Having said hi, he suggested, 'We should sing something together.' She said she'd love to and Bryan quickly answered, 'I've got one for you.'

In the small world of music, 'When You're Gone' was a song he had written with Eliot Kennedy, who would become a close friend of his. Originally Eliot had been shopping in his local Sheffield supermarket when Bryan, who had been performing a concert in the city the previous night, rang and suggested a songwriting session. 'When You're Gone' was the result. It was one of Bryan's trademark easy-listening soft-rock tracks that stuck in your head for days. He and Melanie also became good friends; he appreciated her energy and down to earth character.

While Mel B, Geri and Victoria would all initially opt to live in big mansions in the country, Melanie chose a million-pound penthouse flat in a converted Victorian hospital close to Hampstead Heath. Although there was nobody special in her life, at least she had Emma living in the same block.

Melanie then decided to spend several months in Los Angeles, working on her solo album. A little like Geri, she started talking in interviews about all the healthy food she was eating and the yoga, gym and running she was doing to get her body in shape. Mel B accused her sarcastically of 'going all LA'. She hung out in the famous Viper Room on Sunset Strip with former Sex Pistol Steve Jones and John Taylor of Duran Duran. On one evening she joined them to sing the punk anthem 'Pretty Vacant' and declared, 'They were fucking rocking.' On a trip to New York, she had dinner with Madonna, her childhood hero.

Melanie wanted to cast off her Spice Girls persona, which was certainly the most boring of the five. She was the one nobody paid much attention to, often stationed at the back in photographs while the others – and Geri in particular – took the lions' share of the limelight. Now she had more to say; she observed acidly, 'Geri only got all the attention because she got her baps out.'

Her outspokenness in general seemed to be a concerted effort to present a new, tougher, punk rocker image that was nothing like the nice, soft young woman with a ready smile who hated arguments. Now she seemed ready to start a few. Her harder edge was complimented by a well-muscled physique and a fondness for tattoos. The most recent inking was a sweeping painting on her back depicting a phoenix rising from the flames, a symbol of her desire to create a new identity from her past Sporty Spice image.

Melanie's new style meant she had to deal with a huge amount of innuendo that she was a lesbian, when the only 'evidence' in the minds of narrow-minded observers was that she looked like one. She could not have been clearer: 'How can you look like a lesbian? I find it very rude and extremely offensive to gay people to call me a lesbian because of the way I look.' It was galling that speculation about her sexuality was gathering more interest than her music. She stressed, 'At first I thought it was funny and quite comical because I've got no homosexual tendencies at all – and I never have had.'

Melanie had the dilemma of wanting to keep her private life away from the media but having to face a lot of half-baked stories as a result. She hadn't had a serious boyfriend during the Spice Girls' reign at the top. She had become close to Robbie Williams, who once boasted with bravado on a radio show that he had been in four of the five Spice Girls. That brag didn't go down well with the Girls. He emailed them to apologise saying, 'Sometimes I think I'm being funny.' Emma told him, 'You are funny and we adore you but stop saying it now. We forgive you if you never say it again.'

Melanie was constantly asked about her relationship with him. Eventually she admitted that it was nothing serious but that they did go on a couple of dates together. 'It didn't really work out,' she said. 'It was a chemistry thing really, sometimes there's not a major reason. He was busy travelling all over the world and so was I.'

Potentially more interesting was her friendship with Anthony Kiedis, the charismatic lead singer with revered American rock band, Red Hot Chili Peppers. He had previously dated Madonna and had a reputation for being a bit of a wild character, once performing naked on stage with just a sock covering his privates. He was seen having lunch with Melanie, which inevitably led to speculation that they were an item. The reality was slightly different.

He realised that the Spice Girls were a 'raging phenomenon' and was happy to help when the boss of Virgin in the US, Nancy Berry, rang and asked if he could take both Melanies out to a tattoo parlour while the Girls were in Los Angeles. He was happy to do that, especially as Clara, the nine-year-old daughter of the Peppers' bass guitarist, Flea, was a devoted fan. She and her friends knew all the songs and the dance moves that went with them. Anthony was able to take her backstage and watch her delighted face as she met 'these incredible characters she'd been worshipping'.

Anthony hit it off with Melanie C and the two kept in touch by phone when the *Spiceworld* tour moved on. Melanie poured cold water on the prospect of any love affair with the singer, who was eleven years older than her, but he did write a song for her called 'Emit Remmus', which spelt summertime backwards. She described it as the most romantic thing anyone had ever done for her and was delighted when it featured on the Chili Peppers' acclaimed 1999 album, *Californication*. The song is about an English woman and an American man living apart in their separate countries. Perhaps the most intriguing line is 'Felony sends me all the gold in your smile.' Melanie famously sported a gold tooth at this time. If you're going to have a song written about you, it's especially satisfying if it appears on an album that sold 15 million copies worldwide.

Closer to home, Melanie dated the record producer Jake Davies, who she originally met in a Dublin recording studio. He was a familiar face around the Spice Girls. He was the sound engineer on the *Spiceworld* album and the single 'Goodbye'. He worked with the Girls on their third album, *Forever*, and later on Melanie's second solo album, *Reason*. She didn't keep him a secret and the pair enjoyed cosy dinners and not-so-relaxing workouts in the gym near her flat. Melanie had to accept the fact that every time she was seen with somebody, the papers would be marrying her off the next day. That was why she tried to keep her fling with J Brown as private as possible. In any case, she still thought of herself as 'young, free and single'. And she wanted to progress her career.

Melanie's first solo gigs received a mixed reaction. At the V99 festival, held in Weston Park, Staffordshire, she was cheered by some while others jeered and pelted the stage with plastic water bottles and cans. She performed the Sex Pistols' notorious punk classic 'Anarchy in the UK', which was about as far from 'Spice Up Your Life' as you could get. It was entertaining, especially when she sang 'I am the Anti-Christ, I am Sporty Spice.' At least she was getting out there and doing it. She followed up with her first tour, called *From Liverpool to Leicester Square*, which began in her home town in September 1999. She played fourteen dates from New York to Tokyo, Munich and Paris, before ending up at G-A-Y at the London Astoria.

Her début solo album, *Northern Star*, was better received than her initial live work. She had attracted some of the best-known names in the music business to work with her, including Rick Rubin, William Orbit and Rick Nowels. Rick Rubin was a character you couldn't miss in a crowd – his long flowing hair and beard made him stand out as a throwback to the great rock groups of the seventies. He had produced most of the Red Hot Chili Peppers' albums, including *Californication* – another link between Melanie and Anthony Kiedis. William Orbit had been responsible for much of the production on Madonna's masterful *Ray of Light* album, while Rick Nowels would tackle Geri Halliwell's *Scream If You Wanna Go Faster* in the same year as helping with *Northern Star*. Melanie wanted the album to have a rocky sound: 'I wanted to be a bit of a head-banger. I thought, "Oh no! I can't head-bang because I've got no hair."'

*Rolling Stone* was impressed enough to declare, 'Give it up for Gifted Spice.' It turned out to be a mixture of rock, punk and ballads, including the title track which highlighted what the majority of critics thought – Melanie had the best voice of any of the Girls. The most exuberant track, 'Suddenly Monday', was, by coincidence, the only one that featured a contribution from Matt and Biff.

*Northern Star* was one of those records that kept being boosted by the release of its tracks as singles. The album didn't reach its peak position of number four until a year after first coming out and shortly after 'I Turn To You', her fourth solo single, was number one in the charts, selling 120,000 copies in its first week.

Melanie hated the personal attention she was attracting from the media. She had to face yet more lesbian rumours after going on holiday to Barbados, her preferred destination abroad. Her trusted personal assistant, Ying, went with her. She was half Chinese, brought up in North Wales, where her dad ran a restaurant in Llandudno. She had broken into the pop world in Manchester when she worked for Nigel Martin-Smith, the manager of Take That. Simon Fuller had taken her on to work with the Spice Girls but she now worked exclusively for Melanie.

Even more upsetting than the suggestive remarks about two women relaxing in the sun were the snide comments about Melanie's weight gain. Beefy Spice, Sumo Spice and 'thunder thighs' were just some of the insults. She was very hurt. As she pointed out, all the Spice Girls have been criticised about their weight. She explained that she had been eating junk food, drinking, enjoying life and as a result had put on a few pounds. For the moment she didn't reveal the real problems she was facing. She was suffering from depression, literally spending weeks at a time lying in bed in her flat.

Melanie took Prozac to help her through a ghastly time in her life – the 'dark cloud', as she called it. Six months later she explained, 'It's an illness and nothing to be ashamed of. I hope that I can dispel the stigma attached to this condition.' This was close to twenty years before the rest of the world caught up with the importance of talking about mental health issues.

She was at a low ebb when the Spice Girls' third album, *Forever* – named without a trace of irony – was finally released at the beginning of November 2000. It had seemed like ages since 'Goodbye' was number one – two years in which the Spice Girls had become Spice Women, all in their mid-twenties and dealing with the myriad problems and anxieties that life was throwing at them. Girl Power was nowhere to be seen.

The album, recorded in London and Miami, had been a long time coming. Although 'Goodbye' featured, the lead single was a double A-side, 'Holler' and 'Let Love Lead the Way', and gave the girls their ninth and final UK number one. This was an entirely different Spice Girls sound, produced mainly by R&B master Rodney Jerkins.

It hadn't started out that way, though, because the initial recordings featured Geri – they had been done that long ago. Almost all of these were scrapped. 'Goodbye' was kept but it was the only track co-written and produced by Matt and Biff. Eliot Kennedy kept a writing credit on 'Right Back At Ya', which was originally recorded at his studio in Sheffield. He was unimpressed by the finished remixed track, describing it as a boring piece of R&B.

Rodney was a very fashionable producer under the stage name of Darkchild. He was younger than any of the Girls but had established a formidable reputation working with female artists including Mary J Blige, Brandy, Jennifer Lopez and Whitney Houston. His collaboration with Destiny's Child was the most relevant for the new sound of the Spice Girls. He co-wrote and produced 'Say My Name', their US number one that won two Grammy Awards. One cannot imagine any of those artists featuring on the favourite playlist of Melanie Chisholm, unlike Emma, Victoria and Mel B, who were particular fans of R&B.

The Girls were contractually obliged to deliver a third album. Nobody said it but, transparently, their hearts weren't in it. There seemed to be more important things in life for all of them than the Spice Girls. Most days, Mel B and Victoria would bring the babies down to the Abbey Road or Whitfield Street Studios in Marylebone and the Girls would take it in turns to watch them. Melanie C observed, 'I think we've all just mellowed out a hell of a lot.'

Their more relaxed outlook was reflected in the music. Gone was the poppy exuberance of Matt and Biff, Eliot and Absolute. In its place was a series of Beyoncé-lite songs. Even the cover photograph of the new album suggested more mature listening, with both Emma and Melanie C sporting new blonde hairstyles. Collectively they looked as if they were on their way to an expensive club for the evening and not the Saturday night disco. Their linking of hands in the picture looked a little awkward and unnatural, too.

During the launch party for the album Melanie was seen downing vodkas at the fashionable Red Cube club in Leicester Square. The place was full of journalists, so perhaps it wasn't the best occasion on which to allegedly refer to Westlife as a 'talentless bunch of tossers' and condemn their music as 'hyped-up shit'. In the battle for number one album, Westlife's *Coast to Coast* outsold *Forever* three to one. The irony was that the critics liked this Spice Girls record more than their first two albums, probably because it sounded more current. Arguably, it hasn't lasted as well.

Every time Melanie was at something official, the alcohol police in the media seemed to be checking how much she was drinking. There was genuine concern, however, that she was indulging too much for a woman on strong anti-depressants. She summed it up, wistfully, 'I suppose I am the living proof that fame and wealth don't necessarily make you happy.'

She had almost been too indiscreet when she referred to the Spice Girls in the past tense in a television interview with Frank Skinner, forcing everyone to backtrack. It was true, of course. Just before Christmas 2000, the four Girls had a secret meeting at their modest offices in Bell Street, Marylebone, at which it was decided that they were not going to release another single from the album because that would mean continuing a promotional campaign that nobody wanted. Melanie and Victoria, in particular, were keen to call a halt. The Spice Girls were closed for business until further notice.

They decided not to tell the world, though, as moving forward that might adversely affect all commercial ventures. Victoria and Emma had their own albums to complete and promote. Mel B, with encouragement from Max Beesley, was intent on reigniting interest in her solo career. And Melanie was halfway through her seventy-three-date *Northern Star* world tour. She was looking forward to the North American leg. In Los Angeles, in April 2001, she told a reporter from Reuters that she didn't intend to do any more work with the Spice Girls. It was easy to see how far she had moved away from them musically. Emma was sweet about the gaffe. 'I don't think she meant to say it. She has been working very hard and was probably very tired.'

In the end, the album *Northern Star* sold four million copies worldwide, so the extensive touring was worth it commercially. *Forever* sold a similar number, which was a resounding endorsement of Melanie's solo career. Although that was a great success for Melanie, it was dismal for the Girls in comparison with their previous albums; *Spice* alone racked up sales of twenty-three million.

At the end of her tour, Melanie returned home to London, only to confront the same sort of celebrity issues that Victoria had faced – sick letters and death threats – which was not the sort of homecoming she wanted. She took decisive action, though. After making sure the police were involved, she went to stay with her mum on Merseyside. It was what the doctor ordered – three meals a day and lots of tender loving care.

# 18

# BABY LOVE

——————

If Melanie C wanted to catch up with any of the Girls for a coffee and a chat, she would simply knock on Emma's door. The block close to Hampstead Heath was a perfect location for Baby Spice. She had no desire to swap the North London neighbourhoods that she loved and knew so well for anonymous splendour in the sun. She was the one who appeared most normal and who had adjusted to life best after the madness of the world's most famous girl group.

It helped that she was in a settled relationship. Her boyfriend, Jade Jones, was the lead singer of R&B boy band Damage and understood the demands of the music business, although perhaps not the unfettered fame of Spice World. Although Emma had long ago ditched the cramped family flat in Barnet for a new home in Hertfordshire, as well as her London flat, the couple did their best to retain normality when Jade was staying over: they were quite happy to pop into their local McDonald's for a portion of fries in the evening. He explained, 'If you make yourself stand out, then you will get people coming up to you, but Emma is so down to earth that people only get excited about her from a distance.' When Emma nipped into Sainsbury's or Brent Cross Shopping Centre, she simply donned a baseball cap;

she wasn't wearing a pink mini dress with her blonde hair in bunches.

Jade, who sported a gold tooth like Melanie C, is three years younger than Emma and they were in no rush to settle down, despite media attempts to make them do so at every opportunity. In fact, they hadn't started living together when they were first rumoured to be man and wife. Emma picked up the paper one morning to discover that they had married the previous day at a hotel in Cockfosters. There was an alleged wedding photograph that showed Emma in leather trousers and a long coat. 'I'm not getting married in that,' she laughed. In fact, there had been a wedding that day – her mum Pauline had married her long-standing boyfriend.

Emma enjoyed a relationship where she could phone up her man and ask, 'What do you fancy doing tonight?' When he wasn't touring, Jade still lived with his mum Rita at her house in East London. Both his mother and his Jamaican-born father were social workers and had sons and daughters from previous relationships. As a result, Jade was one of eleven children, a large family that would be touched by more than one tragedy.

Like his girlfriend, Jade had a performing arts upbringing. From the age of eleven, he attended the Barbara Speake Stage School in Acton, which was founded in 1945 and was one of the best known in the country, that boasted a host of famous former students, including Phil Collins, Naomi Campbell and Michelle Gayle. While he was there, Jade met the two founder members of Damage – Noel Simpson and 'Ras' Bromfield. The pair recruited Jade for the band one lunchtime when they heard him hit the high note from 'If I Ever Fall in Love' by the American soul group, Shai, and realised he was a brilliant singer. It was like a scene out of *Fame*.

By coincidence, a fourth member of the band, Andrez Harriott, went to the Sylvia Young School, although he was a couple of years below Emma. He and Jade became friends when they appeared at the Old Vic together in the musical *Carmen Jones*. With his stage school training, Jade understood the importance of application and professionalism in the entertainment business – just as Emma did – and it gave them a common bond.

Damage battled away for three years as teenagers before they were noticed by Jay Kay of Jamiroquai, who paid for the recording that eventually led to a deal with Big Time Records. Bizarrely, their first album, released in 1997, was called *Forever*. Their biggest hit was a cover version of Eric Clapton's 'Wonderful Tonight'. Damage had the distinction of being the first black band to be featured on the cover of *Smash Hits*, an issue which became one of the magazine's biggest sellers. The boys were polished and professional and enjoyed a good reputation in the record industry, deftly overcoming any racial preconceptions. As an insider observed, 'They were polite and nice and never had anything mean to say about anyone.'

Jade met Emma the following year, backstage at a Spice Girls concert in Manchester's NYNEX Arena. He helped her sort out a problem with her mobile phone – always a classic ice-breaker for couples who liked the look of one another. Emma was attracted to Jade's easy-going nature and shared the same sense of humour. She observed, 'Jade's in a cool band but with me he drops his cool façade and is one of the silliest people.' She had been deeply hurt by the kiss-and-tell stories of her teenage boyfriends, so she was in no hurry to commit to something too intense. For the first year or two, their relationship was more relaxed than serious.

They enjoyed dating in a normal way – going out to the cinema with a pizza afterwards was a favourite way to spend an evening, or staying in with a pizza and watching *Big Brother* on the television. She could have been called Sociable Spice because she didn't want to retreat behind the walls of a massive country estate – although she valued her privacy. Jade felt the same way, criticising celebrities such as Geri Halliwell, who used their relationships to 'advance themselves', as he called it.

Emma was there to support Jade when his pregnant sister Annette died in a car crash. Jade was devastated and appreciated Emma's love during such a difficult time for him and his family. He confided, 'Emma is the kindest, most gentle girl in the world. She is my rock. I don't know where I'd be without her.' Jade's family had already had to deal with another tragedy before Emma and Jade started dating, when his elder brother John was stabbed to death outside a pub in Tower Hamlets in 1997. Jade appeared on *Crimewatch* seventeen years later to appeal for witnesses following a cold case review.

Emma was happy to babysit for the Spice Mums, too. Mel B had moved into a house nearby in Hampstead and would often drop Phoenix off at Emma's flat before heading to the gym. Emma would get the little girl ready for bed while Mel worked out. Some things hadn't changed since the earliest days of the group in Maidenhead; Emma still disliked the gym and would much rather slob out in pyjamas than work out in a tracksuit. She was in no rush to follow Mel B's and Victoria's example and become a young mother, either. When asked in interviews – and all female stars are asked this question frequently – whether she wanted children, she responded that she wasn't ready and wanted to wait until she was twenty-seven or twenty-eight. In the meantime, she had made a pact with Jade that they would never spend longer than a month away from each other – something that wasn't easy with such demanding schedules.

Emma was not resting on her laurels or counting her considerable fortune in luxurious surroundings. Nobody seemed quite sure how much the Girls were worth individually. Sometimes it was £10 million, sometimes it was £20 million. They had made so much money so quickly. They had their whole lives in front of them, however, and none of them were content to slip into obscurity.

At first, it seemed Emma was launching a new career as a TV personality. She presented a weekly programme on VH1 called simply *Emma*. The idea was not that inspiring – she would introduce pop videos and read out emails, although using artists in this manner is something music channels continue to do. After five episodes, Emma decided not to sign up for any more.

She hadn't joined the rush to record. She had reminded people that she was still active by releasing 'What I Am', a duet with the electronic duo Tin Tin Out in November 1999. The song had originally been a hit in the eighties for Texan singer-songwriter Edie Brickell, who married the legendary Paul Simon in 1992.

Emma's version just missed out on making number one. That would not be the case for her aptly titled single, 'What Took You So Long', which made it to the top of the charts in April 2001, a few months after the Spice Girls had quietly called it a day. Once again, Biff Stannard and Spike Stent were involved, but the co-producer was Julian Gallagher, who had written some of 5ive's biggest hits. In the small world of pop, he also co-wrote 'Lullaby' with Mel B. When Emma's single went to number one, it replaced 'Pure and Simple' by Hear'Say, who were the *Popstars* winners managed by Chris Herbert.

It didn't help that Emma was frequently asked about the future of the Spice Girls when she was trying to promote her album, *A Girl Like Me*, which came out a couple of weeks later. The

reviews were positive. AllMusic thought it contained 'unapolo-
getically catchy and well-constructed pop songs' and was 'better
than not bad'. Pleasingly, the *Birmingham Post* noted that there
wasn't a duff song and that she could definitely sing. It reached
number four in the charts, just as the débuts from Geri and
Melanie C had done. A second single, 'Take My Breath Away', a
love song inspired by Jade, also featured in the top ten.

Emma was determined to promote a clean-living image, and
while she was happy to talk a little about Jade, she seldom
mentioned her friendships with Rio Ferdinand, the England
footballer, or award-winning actor John Simm, then best known
for his starring role in the drama, *The Lakes*. She dated both men
when on a break from Jade in the early days of their relationship.
John led a double life with his group Magic Alex and first
bumped into Emma at a recording studio canteen. Intriguingly,
John thought Emma was just too famous, but he enjoyed their
brief flurry of dates: 'I didn't expect to like her at all but she was
the sweetest girl imaginable. She was very funny and charming:
And much cooler than I expected.' She did lose her cool, though,
when a film crew caught her smoking in Café de Paris in the
West End, complaining that she was a 'role model and that it set
a bad example if she was seen having a cigarette'.

Professionally, 'What Took You So Long' was not a stepping
stone to Spice Girls-style success for Emma. The chart performance of her singles became progressively worse until 'We're
Not Gonna Sleep Tonight' barely scraped into the top twenty.
Virgin had lost confidence and even suggested that she should
do a demo of some of the material for her next album. Emma,
who has an inner steel, was not having that. She decided to walk
away: 'We put so much into it and when they don't give you the
support any more, it's quite heart-breaking. I said, "Thank you
very much for the demo idea, but I want to take this where I

know people are going to be right behind me and work as hard as I do.'"

She took it back to Simon Fuller and asked if he would be her manager once more. His re-emergence into the world of the Spice Girls would prove highly significant in the future, but for now he set about raising Emma's profile and improving her prospects. His ever-expanding 19 Entertainment business empire was a formidable organisation to have in her corner, especially now it was raking in millions through the success of *American Idol*.

Emma was the only one of the Girls to perform at the concert in the garden of Buckingham Palace that celebrated the Queen's Golden Jubilee in June 2002. This was big news. Party at the Palace was watched by a television audience estimated at 200 million and was headlined by Paul McCartney, Rod Stewart and the legendary group, Queen.

Looking sensational in a black strapless mini dress, Emma sang the old Supremes' hit, 'Baby Love'. This was a perfect choice for two reasons: first, it suited her voice; secondly, the song reminded everyone that 'Baby' Spice was back. She returned to the stage to perform the iconic 'Good Vibrations' alongside Cliff Richard, Atomic Kitten and its composer Brian Wilson. She also took part in the free-for-all sing-along encore of 'All You Need is Love' and 'Hey Jude'.

Her appearance reminded everyone that there was life after the Spice Girls. A guest role in the comedy series *Absolutely Fabulous* did the same. She featured as herself in an episode called 'Cleaning', in which she was a new client of the main character, Eddie, played by her friend Jennifer Saunders. Emma didn't show a great desire to go up for more acting parts at the time, however, preferring to concentrate on her music.

The pop world was beginning to realise that Emma was a good singer. She may have lacked the power of Melanie C's vocals but she sang in tune and had Spice Girls charisma. Marti Pellow was very impressed when they sang a duet of 'Let's Stay Together' at a charity concert in aid of Teenage Cancer Trust, one of the many causes she supported, at the Royal Albert Hall. He described her as 'very radiant and wee'.

Victoria decided to follow Emma's lead and return to Simon, too – and she brought David and the Beckham brand with her. She had been the last of the Girls to launch a solo career, perhaps lacking the commitment to recording music that the others had. At first it looked promising; Dane Bowers, who had been a member of the boy band Another Level, approached Virgin and asked if Victoria would guest on his next single. He was collaborating with two DJs called True Steppers, who specialised in garage music. People assumed that Victoria was too busy shopping to take much interest in music but, according to Muff Fitzgerald, she had the most contemporary taste of any of the Girls. He recalled that she enjoyed 'good garage and quality soul music'.

Mel B came closest to sharing Victoria's musical preferences. The two Spice mums would never be best friends away from the confines of the group, but they met up from time to time with Phoenix and Brooklyn in tow to discuss being mothers. Mel was able to pass on first-hand the trials of being a single parent. Being rich did not necessarily make it easier, and Victoria was well aware of how lucky she was to have such a strong family unit. It would take an atomic explosion to break up the Beckhams.

The problem for Victoria was that 'True Steppers and Dane Bowers featuring Victoria Beckham' was very much seen as a solo attempt. That hadn't been the case with the other Girls' collaborations with Bryan Adams, Missy Elliott or Tin Tin Out.

The track 'Out of Your Mind' was quite cutting-edge at the time, although the vocoder effect made so popular by Cher and Madonna quickly became dated.

'Out of Your Mind' sold a very respectable 182,000 copies in its first week, but was pipped to number one by 'Groovejet (If This Ain't Love)' featuring the silky-smooth singing of Sophie Ellis-Bextor. Annoyingly, its sales would have placed it first the previous week when Melanie C topped the chart with 'I Turn to You'. Victoria had made a Herculean effort with publicity, giving everyone the superstar treatment, whether it was a dance club in Ibiza, a Radio 1 Roadshow in Paignton or a personal appearance at Woolworths in Oldham, to which 6,000 fans turned out. It still wasn't enough.

The record was deemed a failure by the media, which was unfair. Her solo album, however, was a genuine disappointment. Unusually for Victoria, perhaps the image was wrong. On the cover she wore a black mini dress, looking feline and sultry. It was more like a poster for the movie *Cat Woman* and perhaps did not reflect how the public saw her. She was a Spice Girl; *Elle* magazine's best-dressed female; the wife of the England football captain and all-round hero; and the mother of a charming little boy. She was not some sexy bit of stuff. The lead single, 'Not Such an Innocent Girl', continued the steamy theme but peaked at number six – swamped that week by the Kylie blockbuster 'Can't Get You Out of My Head'.

The album, unimaginatively titled *Victoria Beckham*, just made number ten before falling away. BBC Reviewer Jacqueline Hodges was unimpressed: 'A mish-mash affair of gushy sentiment and wishy-washy R&B.' The nearest thing to a controversial track was the one featuring Missy Elliott called 'Watcha Talkin' Bout', which seemed to accuse one of the Spice Girls of changing when fame came.

The public weren't aware that Victoria was the funniest of the Girls. She was perfectly prepared to work hard but she didn't take herself seriously. The star interviewer, Chrissy Iley, loves writing about her: 'She is hilariously self-deprecating – real laugh out loud. She is just wickedly funny and takes the piss out of herself. And any newspaper article that is written about her pout, she will out pout it.'

Victoria managed to have a laugh at the po-faced media's expense. In the run up to the album's 2001 release she appeared at the August Bank Holiday Party in the Park in Birmingham, sporting a ring through her bottom lip, which she claimed hurt like hell. For once she succeeded in taking the front page away from Geri, who was on the same bill. All sorts of 'experts' had their say about the pros and cons of such a fashion statement and the health risks if impressionable youngsters followed her example. It turned out to be a harmless accessory that she binned five minutes after coming off stage.

Victoria lost her deal with Virgin. The announcement in June 2002 that the contract had 'come to a natural end' was no surprise. In any case, she was expecting her second child shortly. Romeo James Beckham was born on 1 September at the Portland Hospital. Looking to her future career, she had just been voted the world's best-dressed woman by readers of *Prima* magazine. She had parted company with Nancy Phillips after a disagreement over press coverage, so it was the ideal time to move things forward with Simon – especially if she wanted her future to lie in fashion.

She could see how well he was doing with Emma, but the terms of a formal deal would take a year to finalise. In the mean-time, Victoria signed with independent record label Telstar, negotiating a healthy advance of £1.5 million with the help of her lawyer, Andrew Thompson, and her PR man, Alan Edwards, who had assumed some of the managerial responsibilities in the short term. She also linked up with the American producer and entrepreneur Damon Dash, who wanted her to publicise his Rocawear clothing line.

Brand Beckham was moving forward. David left Manchester United to join Real Madrid for £25 million in June 2003. Victoria recognised that the move was a huge commercial opportunity for the family brand and it was no coincidence that Simon was brought back on board the same month as her husband travelled to the Bernabéu Stadium. Announcing their arrangement, Simon predicted, 'With the Beckham name so renowned the world over for music, fashion and football, there are no boundaries to what we can achieve together.'

She had already made sure that David was by her side on a promotional tour – the Beckhams' first world tour – earlier in the summer. Anna Wintour, the hugely influential editor of *US Vogue*, hosted a welcome dinner in New York for the Beckhams, at which the couple were able to mix with other A-listers including David Bowie and Iman, Donna Karan and Calvin Klein. While the football-obsessed British media were focusing on David's move to Madrid, Victoria was looking at the bigger picture and saw a future in the US.

Madrid was just a stepping stone to bigger things, although it did produce some of the most unpleasant headlines of her life. The Girls had been for the most part free from kiss–and–tell stories since their split. Mel B and Geri had suffered the occasional revelation but Victoria had experienced none since those from her ex-fiancé Mark. A famous footballer like David, however, was entirely different and young women seemed to be queuing up to expose secret shenanigans. This was the first time such Spice stories involved a current relationship – and this was a marriage with children. Allegations had surfaced before they were even married but the most upsetting came from Rebecca Loos, David's personal assistant in Madrid.

Rebecca had lost her job when Simon assumed overall responsibility for David's management. She then hired the notorious Max Clifford to broker a deal with the *News of the World* for a reported £500,000. Her revelations did not break the marriage, though. Victoria and David posed for photographs in the snow during a hastily-arranged holiday at the fashionable resort of Courchevel in the French Alps. He gave her a piggy-back and they larked about and seemed completely at ease with one another, although it was pointed out that Victoria had a white baseball hat pulled down over her eyes so that it was impossible to see if she had been crying.

Star columnists lined up to blame Victoria for what had allegedly been going on behind her back. Julie Burchill told her 'to give up your so-called work, Madam, and stand by your man'. Tony Parsons observed, 'Victoria's casual attitude to her marriage is the reason this sad little episode has happened.' The TV presenter Fiona Phillips had a different view: 'She's funny, self-deprecating and appreciates the good fortune that's come her way. She's the one who's had to drag herself out in the snow with a broken heart and a beaming smile.'

Victoria gave an interview to *Marie Claire* magazine in which she said, 'I know for a fact David's been faithful to me and I know it in my heart.' She was given an ovation at a grand party at the Royal Albert Hall celebrating nineteen years of 19 Management. David was with her and gave a speech: 'I'm very proud to be part of the 19 party, but I'm even more proud of my beautiful and lovely wife, Victoria.'

The consequence of it all was that Victoria moved to Madrid. Her solo career would have to be put on hold for a couple of years while David saw out his contract. She and Simon were already planning her future in Los Angeles, where he had relocated.

In the short term, Victoria had to spend a lot of time catching planes between Gatwick and Madrid. On one trip she was seen in the airport VIP lounge by the writer and broadcaster Dr Miriam Stoppard. She walked in with Romeo in her arms. Miriam noticed he was quite a little lump for such a slight woman to carry and watched her while she sat down on a sofa. Victoria was by herself with no mother, nanny or minder in sight. She played with Romeo while she rang David on her mobile phone to tell him everything was OK. Miriam observed, 'She enquired about David in an affectionate way. She said she loved him and she was clearly sincere.'

19

# LOOK AT ME

---

After she left the band, Geri was prevented from releasing anything for at least three months by a legal agreement. In any case, she needed time to absorb what had happened, and new music was a low priority. Instead she went to stay with George Michael and his partner Kenny Goss at the superstar's villa, Chez Nobby, in the South of France.

Despite being a long-standing fan, it was only in early 1997, soon after his mother Lesley had died from cancer, that Geri had met George for the first time. Geri was deeply impressed that he could speak about his mum so openly in front of the guests at the Capital Radio Music Awards. 'I was floored by that,' she recalled. She waited for a moment to grab his attention and try a little flirting, because she still fancied him, but didn't get anywhere despite exchanging phone numbers. Eventually he called her: 'He dropped in the phrase "my boyfriend" and my jaw just dropped, I was so shocked.'

She barely saw him again until she so dramatically left the group and he rang, out of the blue, and invited her to relax for a couple of days at the villa overlooking the ocean near Saint-Tropez when he and Kenny were staying there. George was intensely private and not someone who would encourage open house to celebrities he barely knew. It meant something. She recalled fondly how sweet he was to her: 'I was supposed to go for a weekend and stayed three months. He was so kind and made me laugh.'

George became fond of Geri as well as expressing his admiration for her, which was a welcome boost to her fragile ego. He believed her contribution to the Spice Girls had been undervalued. He observed, 'Geri is one of the most remarkable people I have ever met. I really think she *was* the Spice Girls. No disrespect to the others. I met them and they are all great girls, but, let's be honest, who were you looking at when you watched a Spice Girls performance?'

George and Kenny, a handsome Texan with whom she forged a great friendship, did their best to restore her confidence. The three of them would go out for meals and laze about in the sun all day. George understood better than most her battles with poor body image, because he too had struggled with that. He always made sure she had a proper dinner when she was staying with him and Kenny. She took up yoga and did her best to lose weight without succumbing again to the bulimia that had so blighted her adult life. They popped over to London for George's thirty-fifth birthday party, which had a Cowboys and Angels theme after one of his best-known songs. George was a cowboy and Geri went as an angel.

Back in Saint-Tropez later that summer they dined with David and Victoria, who were staying nearby in Elton John's villa. The evening at the Le Girelier restaurant was very relaxed. Victoria and Geri chatted a little but didn't sit beside one another – the former was more interested in cuddling her boyfriend. George was not delighted when a photographer started taking pictures of their private meal. Later, Victoria complained that they had been set up – pointing the finger firmly at her former bandmate.

Geri hadn't rushed back into the spotlight. George had advised her to take her time, as he always tried to do. She signed up with leading PR Matthew Freud, in order to make the most of her fame. Symbolically, she sold her Spice Girls memorabilia at Sotheby's – not just her Union Jack dress but all her costumes and her old MGB Roadster. Her entire collection raised £147,000 for the Sargent Cancer Care for Children charity.

Lawyers, meanwhile, had to disentangle the Spice Girls' business interests, but Geri didn't need any money; she was working on her life story, *If Only*, and being filmed by documentary-maker Molly Dineen for a revealing look at her life after the Spice Girls. The result was a highly personal insight into a woman who was entirely different in private to the Spice Girl we saw in public. Geri herself said she was grieving for what she had lost. She confessed, 'How dare I, the luckiest girl in the world, have the luxury to be depressed?'

Geri described George as a 'mentor, father figure and friend' all rolled into one; he helped save the day when she needed a kind word to be able to move on with her life and career. He went with Kenny to her dressing room to wish her good luck before she went on stage at the Royal Albert Hall in London to sing 'Happy Birthday' to Prince Charles at his fiftieth birthday concert. 'You'll be wonderful,' said George.

Her song for Charles was a big deal, as it was the first time she would appear on stage without the other Girls. Dressed in a figure-hugging royal blue ballgown, designed by her friend and stylist Kenny Ho, she looked like a movie star as she crooned 'Happy Birthday' in the style of Marilyn Monroe. Nobody could match the Hollywood icon's famous version to President Kennedy in 1962, but Geri made no mistakes and Charles was delighted.

Her performance in front of the Prince of Wales made headlines a couple of weeks before he was guest of honour at the

Royal Command Performance at the Lyceum in London. This time the Spice Girls closed the show when they sang 'Goodbye', which would soon be their third consecutive Christmas number one, another feat not achieved since The Beatles in the sixties. Both Mel B and Victoria were now obviously pregnant and wore flowing evening gowns and all four remained seated for the song. Even Melanie C was wearing a tasteful dress. They couldn't jump around the stage, so they presented a more mature image to the audience.

While Geri couldn't compete with the Spice Girls' juggernaut, she did sign an estimated £2 million record deal with Chrysalis for her solo career. The label, then part of the EMI group, was already home to Robbie Williams, who was a good example for Geri to follow. The plan would be for a launch the following year. Geri would be twenty-six soon, and the time was also opportune to look at other career possibilities, including television presenting, which would be much less taxing than all that dancing. The best comment on her future came from her Spanish aunt, Maria, who summed it up: 'Geri has come out of nothing to be somebody. If she ends up being a nobody again, we will love her just the same.'

Geri had no intention of being a nobody. As well as casting off her old image she was pictured in the South of France – in what appeared to be a suspiciously stage-managed photograph – clutching a self-help book entitled *Further Along The Road Less Travelled*, by the American psychotherapist, Dr M. Scott Peck. She was trying to pull herself together after the break-up with the Spice Girls.

She was going through a period of rebranding as a more serious person, elegant rather than end of the pier. She ditched the ginger hair, the bright red lipstick and the low-cut dresses. She appeared on the BBC's breakfast programme in a crisp white blouse and sensible dark suit. She was photographed by Patrick Demarchelier for *Marie Claire* magazine with her now-blonde hair scraped back, dressed in the sort of black outfits that would have had Victoria purring. Patrick had taken the famous pictures of a barefoot, jeans-clad Princess Diana in 1995, a fact that would not have been lost on Geri.

Geri also stopped shouting Girl Power at every opportunity; that was for the Spice Girls. Instead, she told the magazine, 'Life is more about people's passion rather than their ability.' She advocated for breast cancer awareness, took part in a Comic Relief expedition to the Nile, and became a United Nations Goodwill Ambassador. These roles were useful to the UN because well-known celebrities could highlight causes that were genuinely important: Bianca Jagger, for instance, brought the mass rape of Bosnian women to public attention. Most famously, the film star Audrey Hepburn had worked tirelessly for UNICEF and as a Goodwill Ambassador for the UN.

Geri travelled to New York to meet the Secretary-General, Kofi Annan. She was given a role as part of the UK initiative of the UN Population Fund, an organisation whose mission, as well as promoting birth control and safe pregnancies, sought to reduce violence against women and promote equality – in some ways it was Girl Power for grown-ups. It's easy to take such celebrity postings for granted, but they were not given out lightly. She explained, 'All I'm doing is lending my fame to help raise awareness for important issues that we all care about.'

Her début solo single, 'Look At Me', was more Shirley Bassey than Spice Girls and described by *Billboard* as 'ballsy, brash and slightly bonkers'. Radio DJ, Jonathan Coleman, thought it 'sounded like a James Bond theme in that it's very melodramatic. It's not at all what I expected.' Fellow DJ Jo Whiley thought it a very good record and 'more mature than the Spice Girls' sound'. There were still Spice Girls connections, however. The video, shot in black and white in Prague, was made by Vaughan Arnell, who had directed 'Say You'll Be There'. More recently he had worked on 'Outside' for George Michael and directed most of Robbie Williams's memorable videos, including the famous 'Angels'. Geri's new sensible image took a slight knock when she was photographed between takes puffing on a cigarette, a habit none of the Spice Girls could seem to break.

Vaughan wasn't the only Spice Girls connection. The song was co-written and produced by the group's old Absolute partners, Paul Wilson and Andy Watkins. It just missed out on becoming number one, selling just 700 copies less than Boyzone's saccharine 'You Needed Me'. Media predictions that this failure would prove to be a quick ending to her musical ambitions were wide of the mark, especially as the track achieved total sales of 1.5 million worldwide.

Geri couldn't rely on the hospitality of George Michael forever. She needed her own home, so she spent an estimated £2 million on a 200-year-old former nunnery called St Paul's House, which was set in seventeen acres of parkland in the village of Middle Green, near Windsor. She intended to spend £500,000 turning it into a dream house, her personal *Gone with the Wind* mansion complete with indoor swimming pool, gym and tennis court and a huge wall around the property to safeguard her privacy – and that of her guests. She threw a big two-day party and invited all her old rave friends from Watford as well as celebrities including Dawn French, Elton John and George Michael, of course, but she never properly settled there – it was too isolated for a single woman. In her documentary, Molly showed Geri to be rather sad and lonely in the big house, an image that Geri was anxious to ditch in the future.

George went with her to Battersea Dogs Home to help her choose the right pet to share her new home and then comforted her when she burst into tears at the number of old, abandoned dogs that were living there. Eventually she chose a loveable Shih Tzu, who took a shine to George and wouldn't stop licking his face. Geri thought it was a shiatsu until he pointed out that was a massage and not a breed of dog. Harry, as she named the puppy, would be her constant companion for the next sixteen years. Not everyone was enamoured with little Harry – one of her entourage uncharitably referred to it as 'that frigging dog'. When she went to important meetings, Harry would always require his own chair.

Her début album, *Schizophonic*, met with mixed reviews – just as the output of the Spice Girls tended to do. *Rolling Stone* said her voice had 'a surprising, undeniable charm'. *BBC Music* commented, 'She's not going to change the face of world music with this offering, yet you can't help but admire her.' While it stalled at number four in the charts, worldwide sales were still a very healthy three million.

Melanie C, who took her music very seriously, was uncharacteristically blunt in Q magazine: 'For me, she's just cotton wool. She's not a talented musician and she's not a very strong singer. She's a great celebrity, but musically it doesn't come from the heart. It's just hollow.' The two women were both part of a 'Music for Life' charity concert at the MEN in Manchester, but they didn't share the stage. Melanie opened the event in aid of the specialist cancer unit at the Christie Hospital and had long since left the building when Geri, as the headliner, closed the show.

Surprisingly to some, Geri had the last laugh when the next three singles from her album all made number one. 'Mi Chico Latino' was her first chart-topper, followed by 'Lift Me Up' and

'Bag It Up'. Geri had the satisfaction of beating Emma's 'What I Am' in what was publicised as a battle between the two. A 'fling' with Chris Evans seemed to last the length of the promotional push. It had all the hallmarks of a celebrity faux romance, especially after it was pointed out they were both clients of Matthew Freud. Geri has always maintained it was real, even if it was brief.

Intriguingly she was already talking about a possible reunion, perhaps aware of the enormous commercial potential if the Spice Girls reunited. At the moment it was just idle speculation. She didn't join them at the Brits in 2000 when the Girls collected the Outstanding Contribution to Music Award and Mel B gave a gracious thank you to Geri: 'Without her we wouldn't have been able to have done this.'

Geri performed earlier in the evening. She didn't wear a Union Jack dress but she did collect the headlines, demonstrating all her familiar flair for getting attention. She suggestively straddled a pole between a pair of giant inflatable female legs as she sang 'Bag It Up' in a black push-up bra. The moral majority were suitably outraged – job done. Melanie C thought it 'quite vulgar'. Both she and Geri were nominated for Best British Female but lost out to Beth Orton, who was more critically acclaimed than commercially successful. Geri also missed out on Best New Pop Act, which was won, ironically, by Chris Herbert's boyband, 5ive.

After the Chris Evans fling Geri embarked on another friendship that was met with much cynicism. The whole world, it seemed, knew about Geri Halliwell and Robbie Williams. They saw a lot of one another. Their first holiday together in Saint-Tropez in August 2000 was paparazzi paradise. It did not escape the notice of cynics that Robbie's album *Sing When You're Winning* was about to be released and Geri's book *If Only* had just been published in paperback. The front page of the *Sun* declared,

'Robbie and Geri. It's love.' It was certainly good business, as 'Rock DJ' topped the charts.

They took different flights to Nice but rendezvoused at a villa down the coast – close to both George and Elton's homes – that Geri had rented for a couple of weeks. There were plenty of opportunities for the photographers, who fortunately were in prime position right from the start. Soon after arriving, Robbie joined Geri by the pool, she in a bikini that revealed her toned body, him wearing checked Bermuda shorts. They chatted, swam, dived and played with Harry the dog. Then they went off on a scooter tour of the area. Much was made of Geri wrapping her arms around his chest as a gesture of love, but it was more likely fear at being his pillion passenger. Geri's red bikini photographed beautifully when she went jet-skiing. The whole jaunt made an excellent photo spread in *OK!*, although her other guests at the villa stayed well away from the lens.

Geri and Robbie had time to have a row in a local restaurant, when Geri was allegedly upset at Robbie paying too much attention to Clare Staples, the glamorous fiancée of hypnotist Paul McKenna. Rob left early after he and Geri exchanged some witty repartee, which involved liberal use of the f-word. It may have been staged, although Geri was reported as ending the night being sick in the ladies' loo, which was a worrying development.

She held her twenty-eighth birthday party at the villa. George couldn't make it but Kenny flew in to join her.

The hysterical media coverage of Geri and Robbie's friend-ship did raise their profile at useful moments, but was it a real relationship? They did not *have* to go on holiday together on several occasions during the year. Nobody believed there was anything much to their friendship until she was spotted leaving his Notting Hill flat in the small hours. He would later tell

Graham Norton that he once smuggled her out in a sports bag that he slung over his shoulder. Geri has consistently denied that she and Robbie slept together, although not everyone believes that. A record company insider revealed, 'Geri and Robbie were brought together by the label but they were shagging.' Revealingly, perhaps, Robbie's best friend, Jonathan Wilkes, described Geri as their big sister.

Both Geri and Robbie retained a sense of humour about it. When Geri presented Robbie with Best British Male at the 2001 Brit Awards, she said, 'The winner is healthy, talented and according to press reports, giving me one. So it's about time I returned the favour and gave him one – the winner is Robbie Williams.'

Generally, if the media wrote about a relationship it probably wasn't serious. For instance, she had quietly been seeing million-aire businessman Bobby Hashemi, founder of the Coffee Republic chain and a keen polo player. They dated for three months and Geri never said a word about him.

Geri's finest hour as a solo performer came with the release of the lead single from her second album. 'It's Raining Men' was quintessential Geri Halliwell and her most successful release. Originally a hit for The Weather Girls in 1982, the song had become something of a gay anthem over the years. It turned out to be the last song recorded for the new album, which was all set to go until the producers of the film *Bridget Jones's Diary* asked her if she might like to record it. She jumped at the exposure. Her own video was shot in Greenwich and clearly inspired by *Fame*, with stage-school students dancing on cars in the street. Geri also took the opportunity to show off her new well-toned physique. The song became Geri's fourth consecutive number one, which was then a record for a female artist. Her management consultant at the time, Jon Fowler, recalled proudly, 'It was a great video. She was a force in those days.' Jon, an old friend of George Michael's, was also from Watford, and the two of them, both from working-class backgrounds, hit it off from the beginning. Other than her mum, Jon was only person who could get away with calling her Geraldine.

Geri was now a very different physical specimen from her Spice Girls days. Her slimmer, clearly defined shape was a result of yoga classes, running, gym sessions and a very careful diet. She ate small amounts, often and at specific times. Jon observed, 'Her regime was very strict. Her hair and make-up time might be 5 a.m. but her breakfast always had to be there. Then, mid-morning she needed some more food. If you missed it, she would be a grumpy girl. I've always said with talent, all they need is their money and their food and they are absolutely fine.'

On one occasion, she was travelling back from Paris after giving a speech for the UN and decided to get an earlier train, which was a calamity for Jon, who knew his life would be a misery for days if she missed a meal. The hotel venue wouldn't let him take food out but he spotted a chicken restaurant across the road. They plated up some grilled chicken, a few greens and potatoes. Jon was thrilled and sat opposite Geri on Eurostar waiting for her to ask for her food. She promptly fell asleep for the whole journey, so he had to sit there with Geraldine's dinner on his lap until they reached St Pancras.

She showed off her new shape for the troops at two training camps in Oman. With minimal fuss or fanfare, Geri flew out to the Middle East to entertain soldiers and Marines, who were training in the gruelling desert heat for important postings that included Iraq and Afghanistan. The concert was organised by CSE live events, which stood for Combined Services Entertainments. Geri was top of a bill that included the pop group Steps and Bobby Davro, who acted as compère and comic.

Geri's troupe consisted of about twenty dancers and singers. Most of the dancers were young teenage Italians, men and women recruited by Geri's go-to choreographer Luca Tommassini. The whole situation was becoming quite tense, with terrorist fears around the world – it was just a month after 9/11, and the troops expected to be deployed to the fighting at a moment's notice. Jon took Geri to one side and said, 'Look, it's not great.' Even he had to phone his own mum every hour to reassure her they were all OK.

They were staying at a hotel in Kuwait and Geri called everyone into her suite at 9 a.m. on the morning of the show and told the young dancers, 'If you want to go home, then absolutely your families must come first.' Jon recalled that Geri totally understood the worries and, as a result, they all decided to stay.

Members of the Royal Engineers constructed an earthworks known as 'Geri's Mound' ready for the erection of the stage. Geri was in fine form, marching on in her military uniform: 'Hello boys, how are you doing?' she asked in her best Marilyn Monroe voice, before launching into a version of 'Wannabe' that sounded more Glenn Miller than Spice. It was great fun and the soldiers loved it.

The shows proved to be a bittersweet occasion. As Jon observed, many of the young soldiers hadn't had a drink for months and there was no security. At one show, Bobby Davro shook up a can of lager that showered the first rows of soldiers. Jon remembered that the whole stage was deluged with bottles and he told the officer in charge that he wouldn't let Geri go on in these circumstances. Steps had to be escorted off when bottles started being thrown. The officer strode on to tell everyone to calm down and to take the occasion seriously.

Geri battled through, putting on an exhilarating performance of 'It's Raining Men' before Jon eventually had seen enough and took her off stage during one of her slow numbers. Afterwards, reports suggested that scores of soldiers had to be stretchered out of the show suffering from acute dehydration; there was no mention of alcohol or fighting. Geri, normally so amenable to being quoted, said nothing. Afterwards, the commanding officer sent her a special note thanking her for her efforts.

Privately, Geri wasn't doing so well. She was living in a large house close to George in Highgate. Both Emma and Melanie C lived just the other side of Hampstead Heath but they didn't socialise with her. George was often working on music so she would go out shopping with Kenny for the day. She saw more of him than her superstar friend. She shut up St Paul's, put the house on the market and took herself off to Los Angeles, ostensibly to work on the second volume of her autobiography – the first had sold more than a million copies and she gave her £500,000 advance to Breast Cancer Care.

Robbie was so worried about her plummeting weight loss that he encouraged her to go into rehab to deal with her recurring bulimia. She checked into the Cottonwood centre in Arizona. There, she took up with a handsome actor called Damian Warner, who was from Chicago and heir to a multi-million-pound fortune. They reportedly became secretly engaged, although Geri never confirmed that. He did show up in England when she was hired as a judge on the show *Popstars: The Rivals*, but they rowed publicly and he went back to the US.

*Popstars* found the next big girl group – Girls Aloud. In a twist on the old 'art imitating life', two of the original five were replaced – just as happened in the Spice Girls. Unfortunately for Geri, that was the last series of the show, which was replaced the following year by *The X Factor*. She had a taste of life away from being a pop star herself and returned to LA to see what else she could do after the Spice Girls.

Despite her determination to cast off her Spice Girls persona, she wasn't above using it if she had to. She was queuing with a small entourage outside the fashionable Blue Door restaurant on Miami Beach. Nobody recognised her, so it was going to be a long wait. Geri was exasperated, especially when she realised that Didier Drogba, the footballer, had no problem getting a table. 'Right,' she told Jon Fowler. 'Go and tell them it's Ginger Spice.' They were quickly ushered in.

# 20

# REASONABLE DOUBT

It was too soon to talk of reunions, but Victoria did invite all the Girls to a dinner party at Rowneybury in February 2003. This was the first time that Geri was welcomed back properly, although Mel B couldn't join them at the last minute. At least they were talking to their ex-bandmate now. Inevitably, when news of the gathering leaked out there was speculation that they would get back together. Simon Fuller was never keen for any return of the Spice Girls to happen before the tenth anniversary of 'Wannabe', which would have been in 2006 at the earliest. A music insider observed, 'Anything before then would have seemed desperate and quite frankly a missed business opportunity.' Keeping the possibility alive, however, with some tantalising gossip now and then made good sense. The evening itself went well and the Girls ended up having a dance to their old hits.

They were all concentrating on solo projects and new music was unlikely to recapture the wonderful days of the old songs. Melanie C was determined, though. Her follow-up to *Northern Star* had been recorded at a time when she was on anti-depressants and not at her best. Virgin seemed to be dithering about what tracks to include and in what order. Eventually *Reason* was released in the spring of 2003. The first week wasn't too bad and the album reached number five in the charts. It was all downhill from there and it dropped out of the charts completely after three weeks.

Melanie had signed up too as the first Spice Girl in a reality show, to help boost her profile and sales. Her participation in *The Games* in 2003 was a disaster. She badly hurt her knee during a judo bout with former Miss World, Azra Akin, and abruptly left the Channel 4 programme. She needed five days in hospital and keyhole surgery to repair the damage. As a result she was unable to properly promote any new releases from the album.

At least she had her family and now someone special to visit her. She had fallen in love with a rugged and wealthy builder she had met on holiday the previous New Year's Eve, which she celebrated in Barbados, a favourite destination for all the Girls. He was called Tom Starr, was a director of a construction company and had absolutely no connection with the music business.

From the very beginning Tom kept away from the limelight. Even on his thirty-sixth birthday he was happy to stay in the background, sipping a beer in her dressing room while Melanie went on stage at Middlesbrough Town Hall at the start of the *Reason* tour.

They had only known each other a few months but already she was happy to talk about being in love and wanting children. 'This is the real thing,' she said. She even dedicated the song 'Reason' to him during her performance. While the couple divided their time between Melanie's apartments in North London and Liverpool, they were keen to find somewhere completely away from the bustle of city life. They found it in the village of Catbrook in the Wye Valley, just over the border into Wales.

The six-bedroom house had spectacular views across the valley, the same landscape that had inspired Wordsworth's famous poem, 'Tintern Abbey'. She was determined to be part of the community and not just a big-time star who drifted in from time to time and annoyed everyone with parties and lack of consideration. She even switched on the Christmas lights in Tintern – slightly different from when the Girls did the same job in Oxford Street in 1996. She loved life in the country, having grown tired of the nightclubs and celebrity trimmings of London. She and Tom liked nothing better than heading down the M4 for the weekend. There, it would be long walks, big roast dinners and 'going to the pub and having a Guinness in front of the fire'. Melanie was happy with life.

She had been the last Girl to keep a deal with Virgin, the label that would always be part of Spice Girls history. Melanie had mixed feelings when she finally parted company with them at the beginning of 2004. In the modern music world, it was inevitable following the disappointment of *Reason*. She said, 'I knew they were starting to lose faith in me, so I was actually quite relieved to go.' She thought about what to do next and decided to start her own label. She formed Red Girl Records with the help of Nancy Phillips. She would now have total control over what she released.

Emma's second solo album, *Free Me*, was released on Simon's 19 label. Like Victoria, she opted for a grown-up, sexy image to show that she was now a more mature young woman of twenty-seven. She looked as toned as the other girls, even confessing to the odd trip to the gym but mostly achieving her slimmer shape through her beloved dancing. The title track was the lead single and a top ten hit but it was the next release, 'Maybe', that showed how much Emma had progressed as an artist. It had the feel of 1960s' sunshine, open-top cars, sharp fashions and bossa nova rhythms: Champs-Elysées meets Carnaby Street. The video, in which all the dancers wore black, had the retro look of Nancy Sinatra and the Bob Fosse musical *Sweet Charity*.

While 'Maybe' reached no higher than number seven in the charts, it's aged well. *Billboard* ranked it number one among all the solo recordings of the Girls: 'Emma looks and sounds like she's having the time of her life. No other solo Spice track exudes as much joy.' For good measure, another song from the album, 'What Took You So Long?', was ranked number three on the list, with only Melanie C's 'I Turn To You' spoiling a one-two for Emma. Looking back retrospectively at *Free Me* in 2019, Quentin Freeman, author of *Record Redux: Spice Girls*, called it 'timeless, defiantly breezy' and a 'masterpiece'. On a promotional trip to the US, Emma met Motown legend Smokey Robinson in Los Angeles and he told her he enjoyed the 'loveness' of it.

Geri had started writing songs for her third solo album, *Passion*, as long ago as 2001 but it was a hesitant project because she could not reach an agreement with EMI about the direction she should take. Instead, she spent most of her time in LA after *Scream If You Wanna Go Faster*, having decided that she was going to make a concerted effort to break into films and television across the Atlantic.

She stayed at George Michael's house in Beverly Hills, shopped with Kenny and took acting lessons, securing a cameo role in *Sex and the City*. She was also a judge on a talent series called *All American Girl*, which only lasted one series but did re-connect her with Simon Fuller, who was one of the figures behind the show. Sadly for Geri, she never succeeded in becoming a judge on the wildly successful *American Idol* that Simon had created a year earlier.

*Passion* was eventually released in 2005. The momentum of her early solo career had been completely lost. The album was originally called *Disco Sister* but many of the original tracks were discarded. One single, 'Ride It', reached the top ten but her old Spice Girls fans seemed unimpressed by her new sensual image. Sexy as a serious persona just didn't seem to work for any of the Girls. There was a world of difference between the approachable fun of attractive girls and the smouldering look of the more mature women. In the end, *Passion* didn't make the top forty and Geri parted company with her record label, just as the others had done.

Faced with a career lull, Geri had to contend with the usual media questions of when she might have children and there was even speculation that she was thinking of a celebrity sperm donor, with Kenny Goss nominated as her preferred choice. Instead, she started a relationship with a thirty-nine-year-old English journalist and writer called Sacha Gervasi, who had also moved to Los Angeles, hoping to break into films. Sacha, from St John's Wood in London, was well connected – he was an old boy of top public school Westminster and a graduate of King's College London, where he obtained a degree in modern history.

Sacha had struggled in Hollywood at first and his biggest claim to fame was that he was once in the band that became Bush. He battled away, though, taking a screenwriting course at UCLA (the University of California) and achieved his big break by writing the screenplay for the Tom Hanks film, *The Terminal*. He was a man on the up when he met Geri, and she became pregnant during their brief romance.

They didn't last as a couple – seemingly lacking much passion and splitting up over a coffee in Starbucks. Geri faced most of the pregnancy by herself. She came back to London to give birth at the Portland Hospital, as Mel B and Victoria had each done with their first child. The baby was born on 14 May 2006. Her mum and her sister, Natalie, were there to offer support. Geri had signed an exclusive deal with *Hello!* magazine for first photographs. She named her child Bluebell Madonna, explaining that in the last few weeks of pregnancy she kept seeing bluebells in the park.

Emma was also making major decisions in her personal life; she and Jade had been hoping for a baby as well but were not having much luck. They had finally moved in together. His band, Damage, had split in late 2001 and he had briefly formed a new group, Cherry Blackstone. Despite lots of rumours over the years, they only split once, when the pressure of their ridiculous work schedules briefly derailed their relationship. After this short break, which they both hated, Jade called her and asked if she wanted to get back together. 'I always knew the answer would be yes,' she recalled, romantically.

This new commitment spelled the end of silly stories linking her gratuitously with pop stars or actors. She was looking forward to becoming a Spice mum; however, her desire to start a family with Jade was put under strain when she discovered that she suffered from endometriosis, which could hinder her ability to have children. The condition had a far worse effect on her than the break-up of the Spice Girls. Emma, who appeared to be the Girl best adjusted to the pressures of fame, admitted, 'It nearly broke me.' The diagnosis had turned her world upside down: 'I knew I had the right partner. I knew I wanted to be a mum. I didn't give up hope but it wasn't happening.'

Emma would have to wait until she was appearing on the 2006 series of *Strictly Come Dancing* to receive the longed-for good news. She told the writer Louise Gannon that her doctor had been watching the show and noticed that Emma was standing with her hands over her stomach: 'She just had a feeling I was pregnant. I did a test straight away and I was.'

Emma likes to joke that *Strictly* got her pregnant, although it's true that all the exercise, training and dancing week after week might have helped. She didn't win the competition, though. Despite consistently being given the highest marks by the judges, the public eventually voted her and dancing partner Darren Bennett out at the semi-final stage. Perhaps she was considered too professional. Two sportsmen, Matt Dawson and eventual winner, cricketer Mark Ramprakash, contested the final. In 2014 the *Radio Times* conducted a readers' poll to find the best-ever celebrity dancer. Emma came first with twenty-three per cent of all votes.

The publicity generated by *Strictly* did not lead to a flurry of interest in her third solo album, *Life in Mono*. Again, the tracks had the retro feel of the sixties, none more so than her version of Petula Clark's timeless 'Downtown', which she released as a charity single for *BBC Children in Need*. Nobody seemed to want the album in their Christmas stocking that year, and it didn't even make the top forty, which was obviously a disappointment.

Emma's priority now was her pregnancy, so she opted out of full promotion and, disillusioned, she wouldn't record another album for nearly thirteen years. Her success on *Strictly Come Dancing* persuaded her that her future prospects were brighter in television and radio. For the moment, she and Jade, who had decided to train as a chef in North London, settled into a lavish new family home not far from the flat in Barnet she was brought up in and close enough to the Orange Tree pub for that to be a local favourite once more. Her mum and brother were only ten minutes away in the car, sharing the house Emma had bought for them.

Emma was always enthusiastic about a Spice Girls reunion, particularly if Simon was involved. Victoria was the first to sign up because it was part of the grand design for Brand Beckham. The initial plan to celebrate 'Wannabe' had to be postponed when Geri fell pregnant. The main stumbling block, however, was the initial reluctance of Melanie C. She did not want to revisit times that had caused her so much anguish. Her first solo album on her own label had been a much happier experience and she had renewed optimism for her own career. While sales in the UK of *Beautiful Intentions* were lukewarm, the album was a huge success in continental Europe, where she had a very strong and loyal fan base. The critics much preferred it to *Reason*: the *Evening Standard* thought it was 'really rather good' and could see Melanie becoming a British Sheryl Crow.

Melanie would sooner or later need to make a decision about the reunion. Although Victoria had the initial discussions with Simon, it was, as ever, Geri who was dynamic in driving the plan forward. Melanie C cheerfully recalled, 'I always dreaded the phone call about getting back together. I always knew the day would come. Geri called me – the Ginger one – ironically the one who bloody left.' The others were all on board but Melanie still needed persuading. She agreed to meet up to talk about it seriously, however, so that was a start.

# 21

# THE RETURN OF THE
# SPICE GIRLS

———

Mel B now considered Los Angeles home. She found the city a breath of fresh air, as it is for many British stars. There are so many famous people wandering around that nobody takes much notice. Robbie Williams, for instance, is seldom bothered in LA because he would not be considered at the top of the celebrity tree in the US. It was the same for Mel – and Phoenix loved California.

She saw little of the Girls. Emma and Melanie C both came to New York when she was appearing on Broadway in the play *Rent* but everyone was so busy and they no longer lived nearby. She and Geri didn't mix in the same circles in LA. They bumped into each other at a cinema but, just as it was at the gym back in England, this was no more than a passing hello. Their lives were totally different now to the times when they were like 'sisters' in the Spice Girls. Mel confided that it was awkward.

She went back to the UK on occasion, but these visits became less frequent when Phoenix started school. She sold the house in Little Marlow, which had never suited her, and bought a new house in the fashionable Los Feliz district of LA. Her mum, Andrea, moved over for six months to help her settle in, and ex-husband Jimmy also relocated, which meant Phoenix saw plenty of her dad. Mel graciously said, 'I have to thank him for the fact that we have a beautiful kid.'

Mel enjoyed being able to take Phoenix to the Wonderland Avenue Elementary School without having to look glamorous and worry about the prying lenses of paparazzi waiting across from the school gates. That just didn't happen in the US. She also liked the privacy regarding her personal affairs. She was able to enjoy a long-standing relationship with the film writer and director Christine Crokos without having to read any mock outrage or innuendo in the pages of the British tabloids.

Christine, the daughter of Greek immigrants, was quite new to Hollywood, having received some attention for a short film called *Heroine Helen*. She was executive producer, along with Will Smith and Jada Pinkett-Smith, of *The Seat Filler*, in which Mel played the best friend of the lead character. The musical comedy was a vehicle for future *X Factor* judge Kelly Rowland, from Destiny's Child. Kelly did all the singing and the movie failed to provide the Hollywood breakthrough for Mel. Christine then cast Mel as the lead in her short film *Love Thy Neighbor*, but it too failed to push Mel's acting career forward.

Eventually a photograph surfaced of them kissing passionately on a bench that rather let the world know they were involved. Mel was not happy when one report suggested this was experimentation. She told *Gay Star News*, 'I fell in love with a woman for five years. An experiment doesn't last five years.' Her preferences were not a secret. One of her friends in LA observed, 'She's been very open about her sexuality.' She added a very pertinent observation about Mel: 'She is just a really good person and she tells the truth.' In her most recent autobiography, *Brutally Honest*, Mel chose not to write about Christine, who remained a friend after their relationship fizzled out. Again, she told *Gay Star News*:

'I didn't think it was fair to name her or put that relationship out there.'

She was, however, prepared to devote many chapters to her next big romance, the one she has called the 'most beautiful, nurturing and loving relationship' of her life. Eddie Murphy had risen from working-class roots in Brooklyn, through stand-up and *Saturday Night Live*, to become one of Hollywood's biggest stars. In American terms, he was several divisions above Mel B. It was, she said, love at first sight when she went to his gated mansion in the Hollywood Hills for a dinner party. She was too nervous to speak to him properly.

Eddie already had seven children – five with his recently ex-wife Nicole Mitchell and two sons from earlier relationships. He readily accepted Phoenix and the relationship with Mel moved quickly from casual to very serious. They were inseparable for seven months. They had their signatures tattooed at the top of their thighs and, according to Mel, talked of marriage at a very early stage.

The first the world knew of their love affair was when they were pictured on holiday at the Four Seasons Resort in Maui, Hawaii. It was an entourage holiday: a big gang on vacation together. Eddie took all his children and some pals, including the world champion boxer Sugar Ray Leonard. Mel invited her good friends Nicola and Teena Collins. They were models turned filmmakers from the East End who lived near Mel in Los Feliz. The identical twins would often pop round to hang out at her spacious mansion.

The twins were guests at the dinner party when Eddie was introduced to Mel's father and where, according to Mel, he asked Martin for permission to marry his daughter. Eddie has not confirmed this account. Mel apparently became pregnant while they were on a romantic break in Mexico, three months after they met. This time it was just the two of them, without Eddie's friends and family.

During the pregnancy, Mel began to feel trapped in Eddie's world and wanted to maintain some independence, spending time with her friends and in her own house. They had rows. Matters came to a head when she rushed back to Leeds to get some space and see her family. Eddie thought she had left him and made a statement that went round the world.

He was on the red carpet at the première of his new film, *Dreamgirls*, in New York, when asked by a Dutch television reporter if he was a happy father-to-be, now that the former Spice Girl was pregnant with his child. He replied: 'You're being presumptuous because we're not together any more. And I don't know whose child it is until it comes out and has a blood test. You shouldn't jump to conclusions, sir.'

Mel was on a flight back to Los Angeles and landed to find that she, Eddie and her unborn baby were the story of the day. Eddie already had a new woman by his side on the red carpet, Tracy Edmonds, the ex-wife of R&B producer Kenneth 'Babyface' Edmonds; she would become his next partner. For Mel's part, it really was all over now. The Girls rallied round. Despite their differences over the past few years, all four of them – including Geri – were in touch to make sure she was all right. If ever Girl Power was needed, this was the moment.

Mel was magnificently defiant. She hosted a baby shower for thirty of her friends at the Beverly Hills Hotel on Sunset Boulevard. There were no publicity-seeking celebrities. By this time she was more than eight months pregnant but she needed two bodyguards to walk in with her because, as her former US manager Louisa Spring recalled, 'She was wearing all this fabulous jewellery. It was amazing. It was the most incredible baby shower ever!' In true Hollywood style, Mel had embraced the well-being powers of crystals; instead of the traditional baby bonnets and shawls, she asked for gifts from her favourite crystal shop on Melrose Avenue. As well as the obligatory champagne – lots of it – there was a cake in the shape of a woman's pregnant stomach clad in an edible leopard-print loincloth.

Her second daughter, Angel Iris, was born at Santa Monica Hospital on 3 April 2007. Bizarrely, it was also Eddie's forty-sixth birthday. She insisted that he took a paternity test, which conclusively proved that he was Angel's father. After eighteen months of legal wrangling, it was reported that Eddie had agreed to pay £35,000 a month until two-year-old Angel reached the age of eighteen. That amounted to £7 million over time. He has had little contact with his eighth child. He now has ten, including two more young children with his current partner, Australian actress Paige Butcher.

Mel embarked on a new relationship with a little-known film producer called Stephen Belafonte. It wasn't his real name and he was no relation to the famous singer and Hollywood star, Harry Belafonte. He was born Stephen Stansbury in Los Angeles, but aged twelve he moved with his mother Sheryl and six brothers and sisters to Point Pleasant in Ocean County, New Jersey. He moved back to LA to go to college at Loyola Marymount University on the west side of the city.

After a few years on the fringes of the film industry, he set up a company called Remag Productions and directed two documentaries about rappers entitled *Straight from the Projects*. The biggest film he had worked on, as an associate producer, prior to meeting Mel B was the satirical comedy *Thank You for Smoking* that starred Aaron Eckhart and featured an all-star cast including Rob Lowe and Katie Holmes.

Stephen is very handsome and charming, but not all Mel's friends were impressed. One confided, 'There is definitely like a dark streak in there when you meet him, to be honest. There is something a little desperate. But Mel would always go with her gut feeling, basically, rather than what people tell her. It's very hard when you have come out of a relationship with Eddie Murphy where he is questioning your child's paternity and then you've got someone who is there for you and is willing to take that on. Looking back on it, at her most vulnerable, he just swooped in.'

Nobody saw a Vegas wedding coming, however, just two months after Angel's birth. For the second time, she bought her own diamond engagement ring and both wedding rings. It wasn't until *Brutally Honest* that she acknowledged she had misgivings about the marriage from the start and almost had the marriage annulled the same day. But she didn't, and she had to live with the consequences.

The media did not take long to wake up. The papers soon discovered that Stephen had been married before in Vegas to a woman called Nancy Carmell. Apparently it lasted twelve weeks before she 'fled' back to Honolulu. The *Sunday Mirror* tracked her down. She told them, 'I have regretted that marriage ever since. I just want to forget Stephen. I have no wish to relive what happened between us.' The paper claimed that the charming man she had married had become emotionally abusive.

It was also reported that he was put on probation and ordered to attend a domestic violence programme after an incident involving his former girlfriend, Nicole Contreras, the mother of his little girl, Giselle. Mel defended his reputation in *Hello!*: 'They're trying to make him out to be this aggressive, violent woman batterer and he's not.'

Mel's mum Andrea was worried, believing her to be in the grip of post-natal depression: 'Melanie's not normally the sort to be taken in by anyone, but her hormones were all over the place after the baby. Maybe Stephen came along at just the right time and said all the right things.' As far as Stephen and his new wife were concerned, her mum was saying all the wrong things and now there was a rift between Melanie and her family back home that would last for ten years.

The newly-weds didn't move in the same circles as the Beckhams but they accepted an invitation to David and Victoria's Welcome to LA Party at the Museum of Contemporary Art. The extravagant evening was hosted by Tom Cruise and his then wife Katie Holmes, as well as Will Smith and his wife Jada Pinkett-Smith. The celebrity count was high, including Eva Longoria, a new close friend of Victoria, Demi Moore, Jim Carrey and Bruce Willis.

David had signed with soccer team LA Galaxy and Victoria was determined to use their relocation to maximum advantage. The 'official' pictures from the party revealed how snugly the Beckhams would fit into this glamorous A-list world. David looked born to Hollywood in a pristine white shirt perfectly complementing his movie star smile. Victoria preferred to pout beneath her now famous blonde 'pob' haircut. She did look a million dollars, though, in a trademark little black dress.

Victoria held centre stage, something that more and more people were observing; she generates an aura that eclipses others, including her husband. Alexandra Shulman, the then editor of British *Vogue*, observed, 'When they're in a room together, the one you notice – the one surrounded by a powerful force field – is Victoria.'

Posh Spice was more than ready for the reunion. The Girls had officially announced it at a press conference in June at the O2, London, a couple of weeks after Mel B's Vegas wedding. At last, the speculation was proved correct. The 'power of five' generated headlines around the world when they gave details of the tour. Tickets for the first concert at the O2 in London sold out in thirty-eight seconds, a triumph for modern technology.

Melanie C was also fully on board. She felt more comfortable about the tour when she talked it through with the others. One of the things that persuaded everyone was that it would be relatively short – 47 dates – and not the marathon 97-date *Spiceworld* extravaganza of ten years before.

They rehearsed together in Los Angeles, where Mel B's career had taken an unexpected upswing. In September, encouraged by Stephen, she appeared as a contestant on *Dancing with the Stars*, the US version of *Strictly Come Dancing*. Just like Emma Bunton in the UK, Mel was obviously the best dancer – probably more so than her ex-bandmate. During the run, she and her professional partner, Maksim Chmerkovskiy, received five perfect sets of ten (thirty points) from the three judges, including on her last dance of the competition. Bruno Tonioli, a judge on both sides of the Atlantic, gave her ten points eight times in the competition; Len Goodman awarded her a maximum six times – and she still didn't win. Just as it had been for Emma, she was defeated by a sportsman, Hélio Castroneves, a Brazilian racing driver.

Although it was small consolation, Len told her she was 'the most versatile dancer that we've ever had on *Dancing with the Stars*'. He added that she had been 'an absolute revelation' and described her mambo routine as 'incredible, fabulous'. The public preferred Hélio. All four of the Girls were in the audience and could only watch disconsolately as Mel struggled to hold back the tears when she realised she hadn't won.

The upside was that she had the tour to look forward to. The Girls warmed up for their return with an appearance at the Victoria's Secret Fashion Show. They wore military-style costumes designed by Roberto Cavalli to perform a joyful version of 'Stop Right Now'. They were under enormous pressure to look their best. They could never just pluck a smart blue suit and matching tie out of the wardrobe. New mum Emma was dieting like mad to get in shape. She had given birth to her son, Beau Lee Jones, at the Portland Hospital on 10 August 2007. Mel B had a personal trainer in LA and, thanks to all that dancing, had lost three stone since Angel's birth. Geri had gone on a relentless diet and exercise regime; Melanie C had put her problems behind her, was in a happy relationship and was in excellent shape. Even Victoria had enlisted the help of a personal trainer, although mums everywhere would testify that looking after three boys was enough of a daily workout. Her youngest, Cruz David Beckham, was now two. He had been born with little fuss on 20 February 2005 at the Ruber International Hospital in Madrid before the family moved to the US. Victoria was rumoured to be on a diet to put weight on.

David and the boys flew into a snowy Vancouver when the tour began, bringing diamond bracelets for each of the Girls, who had drilled themselves into a formidable fighting unit. Their performance was a triumph of exuberance and professionalism. Polly Hudson in the *Daily Mirror* described it as camp, ridiculous, super-enthusiastic, beyond over the top and absolutely amazing. 'If you don't love every second of it,' she continued, 'check your pulse please because I think you might actually be dead.'

In the end, even Melanie C loved the tour: 'I enjoyed it so much more than the first time round.' Part of that enjoyment came from the fact that they were 'older and wiser and a lot easier on one another'.

Victoria said she wanted to do it so that her three boys would really know that their mother was a pop star once upon a time. She was still Posh Spice, but as Victoria Beckham she was now by far the most famous of the five. Her persona was more approachable than before. When someone at the O2 threw some Y-fronts onto the stage in front of her, she good-naturedly picked them up and said, 'I hope these are clean! I will give them to David and we'll reuse them … even if it's as a shower cap. It's good to recycle.' She revealed an easy, natural quality that had been lacking in the old rigid image.

Perhaps because of her enduring fame, she received the biggest cheer, even though she didn't display the onstage energy of the others. The Girls all performed one solo number: Victoria went first but didn't sing. Instead she walked up and down a catwalk to the strains of RuPaul's 'Supermodel (You Better Work)', just to remind everyone that fashion was now her business. Mel B followed with a version of the Lenny Kravitz hit 'Are You Gonna Go My Way'. Emma chose 'Maybe', while Geri performed 'It's Raining Men'. Melanie C, still the strongest vocally, closed out the individual numbers with 'I Turn to You'.

They also performed a new song together, 'Headlines (Friendship Never Ends)', which was written with Matt and Biff but failed to recapture past triumphs. When it was released just before the tour began, it became the first Spice Girls' single not to reach the top ten, peaking at number eleven. It was one of their old-style mid-tempo tracks, suggesting musical tastes had moved on. Critics thought it 'drab'.

The song was really an extra promotional tool for the *Greatest Hits* album, which performed better than the single, reaching number two, but was beaten to the top by the Leona Lewis début, *Spirit*. As ever, reviews were mixed, but Nick Levine of *Digital Spy* online summed it up: 'As a document of late-nineties pop music, it's unbeatable.' It was a perfect accessory to the live concerts. An even better one was the Christmas advertisement for Tesco, which even the *NME* described as 'the most iconic advert of all time'. In it, the Girls, unbelievably, are shopping for each other's presents in the same Tesco store at the same time and trying to hide from one another. They each earned £1 million from it: 'Every little helps.'

At the O2, the girls hooked up with Chris Herbert, who had come along to see the show and went backstage to say hello. Victoria told him, 'You've got to come back on the Friday because it's our last night and you'll have to bring your little boy, Southan. Come down early and he can play with the boys and he can meet David.' Needless to say, meeting David Beckham made his son's year.

Chris and his family sat with Victoria's parents, and he chatted with Tony Adams. 'Her father said to me, "All these years I've never really known what to say to you. I feel really awkward about it but it's nice that we've finally sat down and had a conversation."' Chris was impressed with the way Victoria looked after everyone: 'I thought she was incredibly down to earth; it was like back in the day really. We had a really good laugh.'

Towards the end of the show, they brought most of their children on for 'Mama' – a sentimental moment that would have been cheesy in any other hands.

Their long-time friend and spokesman, Alan Edwards, said the 2007 reunion tour was the biggest he had been involved in. It was made particularly appealing because all the original Spice Girls were taking part. They played twenty dates in the UK, including seventeen at the O2 watched by 20,000 a night. Alan estimated that they generated £16 million in the process. He also thought worldwide they generated £200 million in ticket and merchandise sales.

Melanie observed refreshingly, 'Being completely open, honest and candid, you make money by doing it.'

## 22

# OLYMPIC GOLD

---

The triumph of the *Return of the Spice Girls* tour achieved some-thing just as important as swelling their already healthy bank balances; it gave the Girls an opportunity to progress their indi-vidual careers. They had different plans for the future, but they were linked by a common thread – a desire for success.

Only Melanie C was intent on continuing as a recording artist. For her, the money earned from the reunion tour meant she had pocketed a lottery win that would finance her solo career for life. More immediately, she had to catch a plane to Canada. With the applause of the fans still ringing in her ears, she honoured a commitment for a short, nine-date spring tour promoting her fourth studio album, *This Time*. It had been released more than six months before the tour but had been relatively unnoticed in the UK, failing to reach the top fifty. The fifth single from the album, 'Understand', was also low-key but, for once, Melanie had a new priority in her life and it wasn't music. She was now in her mid-thirties and she wanted to start a family. When the Girls sang 'Mama' during the concerts, they had brought their children on stage. It was a reminder for Melanie that she was the only one who was not a mum.

Melanie was very settled with Tom. He warned her that it might not be so simple when they discussed trying for a baby

– but it turned out that it was. Unlike Emma, who had to wait years, she became pregnant almost immediately. She acknowledges happily that her life changed forever when she slipped into the Portland Hospital and saw the first scan of her unborn baby: 'I knew that I'd always love the child, no matter what.'

She had dinner with Victoria, Emma and Geri to be given the benefit of their experience as mothers. Better than anyone else among her friends, they understood what it would be like trying to cope with motherhood when you were so famous. Only Mel B wasn't free to join them, but at least she kept in touch by phone. The others had no idea of the difficulties she was facing and would continue to confront in her marriage.

Melanie C gave birth to a baby girl, Scarlet Starr, on 22 February 2009. She had just turned thirty-five. She was concerned that her history of mental health problems might make her more liable to be affected by post-natal depression (PND), but that was not the case. She did have to cope with getting up throughout the night to spend hours trying to settle her crying baby: 'You can feel like the worst mum in the world because you think everyone is doing better than you.'

Tom rallied round and her mum Joan came to stay, but there were times when she was by herself that it all became too much. On one such day the doorbell rang and it was Emma and Jade popping round for a surprise visit. Melanie opened the front door and burst into tears. The two women are genuinely very close and not just showbiz-friendly. Emma quickly appraised the situation, handed Scarlet to Jade, who was an expert at soothing a crying baby, while she put her arms around her sobbing friend to reassure her that all mums have days like this.

Melanie was in no hurry to return to work, but when she did she enjoyed one of her greatest career triumphs. Ironically, she received the best reviews she had ever had, but not for an album, this time for her role as Mrs Johnstone in a revival of Willy Russell's *Blood Brothers* at the Phoenix Theatre in London.

All those years ago at school, she had dreamed of playing the part. The story of the Liverpool mum is so well known – the show had run for twenty-one consecutive years – that it's difficult to put your own stamp on it. Melanie succeeded so completely that she received an Olivier Award nomination – the annual British theatre version of the Tonys. She retained a good sense of humour about her success, however. When praised for being nominated for her first professional acting role, she responded in her best luvvie accent, 'I think you'll find darling that my first professional role was in Spice Girls the movie.'

Melanie had suffered some rough rides over her solo singing career but this time the whole cliché about rave reviews was justified. On the opening night she received a standing ovation … from the critics. The *Mail on Sunday* observed, 'Beleaguered but bearing up, she fills Russell's forlorn melodies and hopeful ballads with heart and soul.' The *Daily Telegraph* said that Melanie 'gives one of those performances that grips with its emotional truth from the start and never loosens its grip'.

All the Girls came to see the show and support her. The advantage of a West End run was that she could stay at home in North London and watch Disney films with Scarlet every day – although she found the whole process of musical theatre much more demanding than she expected. She was the hottest ticket in town but she was in no mood to rush into another production. She committed to one more outing as Mrs Johnstone when *Blood Brothers* went 'home' that autumn for a two-week run at the Liverpool Empire. She was understandably nervous about going back but, again, it proved an enormous hit, and in a poll conducted by the *Liverpool Echo* she was named as the city's 'favourite hero'.

She was still fiercely ambitious musically and was hard at work on her next album, although life and other projects were getting in the way. Her fifth solo studio album, *The Sea*, was released on her own label in the UK in September 2011, four years after *This Time*. It blended many styles, from acoustic ballads to dance and rock. While it only just scraped into the top fifty, the critics were kind. The *Daily Express* were still impressed with her vocals, noting that the album gave her voice a real workout. Her records remained more popular throughout Europe than at home.

Melanie was finally living up to her persona as Sporty Spice. Backflips may have been a distant memory but she was training regularly to compete in triathlons – a combination of swimming, cycling and running – and raised £11,000 for the children's medical charity, Sparks, when she competed in her first event.

Making the next Olympics was not her goal, but the Spice Girls were always in the conversation when discussing possible acts for the opening or closing ceremonies. Simon Fuller was thinking ahead to the massive worldwide audience. Part of the marketing strategy for such occasions is to keep the public guessing; it builds interest. Simon was a master of this. If you say that the Spice Girls are definitely re-forming for London 2012 – a done deal – then it's one story. If it's a maybe, a 'Melanie C isn't sure' sort of thing, then it can run and run. And that is exactly what happened, right up until the Games started.

While she had been so immersed in music, Melanie had avoided joining the judging circuit on TV talent shows, but they were invaluable for exposure. The judges reaped just as much benefit as the contestants in terms of exposure. She agreed to be part of Andrew Lloyd Webber's new search for a musical star. She was able to tell him that her whole career might have been different if she had had won a part in *Cats* after she left stage school. On this occasion Andrew was looking for a newcomer to star in a touring production of *Jesus Christ Superstar*. As well as acting as a judge, Melanie had signed up to play Mary Magdalene, her second classic role. In musical theatre, she had started at the top.

Emma was an old hand at television judging but she was moving more into grown-up presenting. She co-hosted *Richard and Judy* when Judy Finnegan was recovering from an injured knee, and she also appeared several times on the panel of *Loose Women*. She filled in impressively for Lorraine Kelly on her show when the morning host was on holiday. She admitted it was nerve-racking covering for such a famous personality. Memorably, it was the first time she had worked on TV with Jade. He joined her as guest chef, preparing meals in the *GMTV* kitchen for other guests, including singers Craig David and Gabriella Cilmi.

In the eyes of the public, it was as if Emma had turned on a switch when she became a mother and passed thirty. That was clear when she was such a popular judge on *Dancing on Ice*. She admitted, 'I'm usually shouting at the telly when I'm watching it so I might as well be in the studio giving my tuppence-worth instead.' She instinctively knew what it was like to be a performer and battle on regardless. She explained, 'It's all about confidence. Even if things aren't going well, as long as you're smiling and people are enjoying it, then it doesn't matter.' She had perfected the art of niceness.

Inevitably, Emma was offered her own talent show, but it did not prove to be as successful as she had hoped. *Don't Stop Believing* on Channel 5 was billed as *Glee* meets the *The X Factor*. The problem with bringing out something new in 2010 was that it was such a crowded marketplace, even if this show concentrated solely on groups. Emma was suitably rude about the shows that milk 'sob stories' from the contestants. She stressed, 'It's not that kind of show!'

The competition was won by an amateur female choir from Derbyshire called DaleDiva – a fitting example of Girl Power success. Ratings for the show, however, were poor. The big winner was the theme tune, one of the great eighties' songs by rock group Journey that had enjoyed a big revival thanks to performances by contestants on the *The X Factor* and Emma's show. It had also been one of the most popular recordings from the original television series of *Glee*.

Emma was always a popular choice as a guest presenter. She had already moved into radio for the first time when she filled in on the breakfast show on Heart when Harriet Scott was away. It was the start of a long and successful alliance with the station. She took over the Saturday afternoon drive-time slot. Radio was ideal – even more so than television – because the broadcast was pre-recorded and she didn't have to change out of her trackie bottoms to present it.

Radio and television had many advantages for Emma – they kept her in the public eye and she was good at it. Perhaps most importantly, she didn't have to travel far from home so she could enjoy being a mum, too. The *Return of the Spice Girls* had happened so soon after the birth of Beau that she barely had time to draw breath, having to learn all the new routines and get in shape. Now, she could relax. She said, 'I didn't realise you feel a lot more settled when you reach thirty. I had my little boy, obviously – it's been fab.' Her mum still lived nearby and the two women had grown even closer since Pauline had become a grandmother. 'You can talk about lots more,' said Emma.

They could, for instance, chat about Emma's second pregnancy, which she announced on Twitter. She also used social media to reveal that she and Jade were engaged. She posted at the end of January 2011: 'Yahooooo I'm engaged! Love you Jade! I'm a very happy lady (sic)!' She also put up a picture of her engagement ring, which boasted a large diamond. Jade had proposed at home on her thirty-fifth birthday when they had a house full of friends and family and Beau was sat on her lap. They had been together for thirteen years and had no need to dash off to Vegas. In fact, they had no wedding plans at all other than waiting for their children to grow up a bit so that they too could enjoy the day. Four months later, on 6 May 2011, they welcomed a second son into the world, Tate Lee Jones. Both their boys had names that sounded as if they were born to be rock stars.

While she had no ambition to be a fashion mogul like Victoria, she did start her own children's clothing line in conjunction with Argos called Baby & Beau. Her eldest son, now four, was signed up to model some items from the ninety-nine-piece collection and would feature in the catalogue, just as Emma had done as a child. She laughed, 'It's great to make a return appearance.'

She posed happily with Beau for an article in British *Vogue*. She wasn't on the cover, but then fashion was only a useful sideline. It was, however, the principal focus for Victoria, and she was making a great success of it. She had made the magazine's cover and followed that by being on the front of *Vogue*'s Russian, German, Indian and Turkish editions. She had become international in this world.

The *Return of the Spice Girls* had led to Victoria's dVb fashion brand being sold in 'some of the coolest stores', including Harvey Nichols in London and Fred Segal in Los Angeles. 'I've spent years banging these bloody doors down,' she exclaimed. Everything was meticulously planned with Simon Fuller's guidance. Leading designer Marc Jacobs chose her as the face of his spring/summer collection in 2008. His patronage was a huge deal in the insular and protected world of fashion. Marc noted that they were similar in that they both took chances and were willing to 'push the envelope and refuse to be categorised by what people think'. As well as Marc's support, she was mentored by her friend, the French fashion designer, Roland Mouret, who was also backed by Simon. They had formed a company called 19 RM, which allowed Simon to pick his way through the business world of fashion, something that was going to be of great benefit to Victoria moving forward.

Victoria brought the legendary Spice Girls determination to her new career. Her own eponymous line of dresses – The Dress Collection – was launched during New York fashion week, which was not exactly a small gig. Imagine if the Girls had skipped the showcase at Nomis and gone straight to the O2? She didn't go over the top straight away, though, showing just ten dresses with retail prices starting at £650. They were luxury, ready-to-wear limited-edition lines. The reviews were excellent and she had the last laugh on experts who predicted a rapid failure. Harriet Quick of *Vogue* was impressed and called the designs 'school mistress meets Audrey Hepburn'. Only four hundred dresses were made and the demand was instant. Selfridges in London took seventeen dresses and had only three left by lunchtime on the first day of sale.

Her second collection was even better received the following year, with fashion writers appreciating its more youthful bias. She introduced each design herself, demonstrating complete professionalism. Laura Craik called the collection 'astonishingly accomplished'. She added, 'If Victoria had only wasted less time singing, who knows what virtuosity she could have reached by now, for clearly this is where her heart lies.'

Victoria has always understood the importance of promotion and proper marketing, right from her earliest days at stage school. The Girls helped when they could: Melanie C wore an exquisite black Victoria dress to the Olivier Awards while Emma modelled a stunning creation at the première of *Sex and the City 2*.

With Simon's encouragement, Victoria continued to make TV appearances to remind people that she was still a very famous Spice Girl as well as a fashion designer. She was a guest judge, for instance, on a couple of episodes of *American Idol*, but she seemed to be appearing less as the years went by. She never topped her cameo role in the hit show *Ugly Betty*, when she sent herself up in an episode entitled, 'A Nice Day for a Posh Wedding'.

But fashion was her passion. As well as designing, she liked collecting. She owned more than one hundred Hermès Birkin bags, worth a million pounds in total. For the moment Los Angeles was the family base and Victoria even described it as their 'spiritual home'. David was still playing football with LA Galaxy and the boys were safe and secure and went to the Curtis School on Mulholland Drive. There was always a villa in the South of France or another one in Dubai for the holidays. She was proud that her sons had good manners. At home they had a punishment chair – when you had done something naughty you were supposed to sit down on it and think about your behaviour. Apparently it worked a treat.

Beckingham Palace was put up for sale. Rowneybury had been perfect when they needed a family home away from Manchester, but time had moved on and both David and Victoria agreed that a townhouse in London would suit them better. One ingredient was still missing from Victoria's near-perfect life: she longed for a daughter. There was just 'too much testosterone' at home. She needed someone, she confided, with whom she could share her handbag collection – she was now including them in her own brand – and who she could sit with and watch the kickabouts in the back garden. She was thrilled to be told, therefore, that the fourth child she was expecting would be a girl.

Her last public appearance before giving birth was at Simon Fuller's Hollywood Walk of Fame ceremony. They had both come a long way since Posh Spice had bounced into his office all those years ago. She and Brooklyn stood next to her now-legendary manager as he proudly unveiled his star on Hollywood Boulevard. None of the other Girls were there. Emma would certainly have made it if she could, but she had given birth only two weeks before. Just under two months later, on 10 July 2011, Harper Seven Beckham was born in the Cedars-Sinai Medical Center in Los Angeles.

All those years ago when she was expecting Brooklyn, Victoria had been pregnant at the same time as Mel B. Now, it had happened again – and Emma's news meant that the Girls had the hat trick. Mel had also dabbled in fashion – as the new face and body of Ultimo lingerie and with her own fashion line, Catty Couture, which did not do well. She was the first and so far only Spice Girl to star in Vegas, too, with a four-month run in the burlesque production *Peepshow* at the Planet Hollywood Resort and Casino. Mel described it as 'very sexy, very spicy and it's all about empowering women'.

According to a report in the *Las Vegas Review-Journal* published in 2017, 'there were frequent complaints from the hotel staff about Belafonte's abrasive personality and rough treatment of the staff'. Apparently Mel proved too expensive to keep in the production after the original run. She moved on to a project called 7 *Days on the Breadline*, in which celebrities gave up their pampered lives for a week to live like poor people who were really struggling to survive in the modern world. Mel went back to Leeds to look after five children aged six to eighteen on a budget of £264 for a week. She didn't tell her family she was there.

Back in Los Angeles, Mel starred in a reality show about her own life in an attempt to emulate the success of *The Osbournes*.

Called *Mel B: It's a Scary World*, it was shown on the Style Network and was meant to be an amusing look at life with Stephen, her two daughters and his little girl. Eddie Murphy made a guest appearance in the first episode (only in Hollywood). Relations with Eddie had improved since he invited them all to the première of *Shrek Forever After* and threw a birthday party for Angel. During the promotional interviews for the series, the *Daily Mail* asked Mel directly if she and Geri had ever had an affair. She neatly deflected the question, 'I've had affairs with all the Spice Girls as far as I'm concerned.'

The public didn't take to the show and it didn't come back for a second season. In the tenth and last episode Mel is concerned that she might be pregnant again. That turned out to be true. She gave birth to another baby girl, Madison Brown Belafonte, at Cedars-Sinai on 2 September 2011. She announced it on Twitter and Emma replied, 'Well done Mummy.' The only dampener was that she was no longer speaking to her family back home in the UK. Her sister Danielle followed her on Twitter, so she knew she was an aunt again but hadn't been able to tell Mel that she too had become a mother. Her dad Martin said, 'I just want to speak to her, so I know those children are happy. If she wants this strange relationship, that's her choice. She's my daughter and I love her to bits.'

After several false starts, her TV career started to pick up again when she was chosen as a judge on *The X Factor Australia*. It might not have had the prestige of the British equivalent but her natural flair for the format was not lost on Simon Cowell.

Meanwhile, Geri's attempts to become the female face of Saturday night talent shows in the UK was not going well. She was unlucky that *Popstars: The Rivals* didn't open more doors, but disappointingly a spell covering for Dannii Minogue's maternity leave on *The X Factor* did not lead to anything more permanent. She may have seen herself as 'Nasty Geri', much in the manner that Nasty Nigel Lythgoe and Simon 'I don't mean to be rude' Cowell had made their own, but it didn't seem to work so well for Geri, who was roundly booed by the audience during the live auditions.

Geri was never going to be daunted by one setback. She was still a force of nature. Her entry into the lucrative children's fiction market proved to be a great success. She had signed a six-book deal for a series of novels involving the nine-year-old heroine Ugenia Lavender, who was inspired by Geri herself. She generated publicity for the project by revealing that some of the characters were based on famous people, including George Michael, Gordon Ramsay and Wayne Rooney. She used the success of the reunion to generate interest in the books, which she said were a 'rebirth of girl power'.

Sceptics noted that children's author Jonny Zucker received a small thank you on the back flyleaf, but Geri and her publishers, Macmillan, were adamant that they were all her own work and Jonny simply gave advice when she asked him about writing the books.

Geri had launched her own swimwear collection under the Next banner and had told the photographer at the catalogue shoot that she was now proud of her imperfections and they should not be photoshopped – a massive change in attitude to the insecurity of fifteen years before when the Spice Girls were just getting going. The change had been brought about partly by a settled relationship with Old Harrovian Henry Beckwith, heir to a £330 million fortune. Henry, who was seven years younger than his famous girlfriend, had a reputation as a playboy, which may have contributed to their break-up after two years together. More importantly, she was thriving as a mother to Bluebell and didn't rule out the possibility of another child if she could find the right partner.

As usual, Geri was brimming with ideas. She rang the producer Judy Craymer, the woman behind the phenomenally successful Abba musical, *Mamma Mia!*, to suggest making a show about the Spice Girls. It was a good thought, although it was not something that was going to happen in a week. Gradually it took shape over a couple of years. Jennifer Saunders, who had become good friends with the Girls, and Emma in particular, came on board as the writer.

Eventually, in June 2012, all five of the Girls gathered for a press conference to announce *Viva Forever*, a musical based on their songs that would be opening in London in November. Fittingly, they held it at the Renaissance Hotel where they had shot their first video for 'Wannabe'. They didn't confirm their appearance at the Olympics, preferring to keep the guessing game going as long as possible. In reality, they were rehearsing furiously. It became apparent on the night of the closing ceremony that this was not a case of rolling up, joining hands and singing a hit or two.

The Girls arrived at the Olympic Stadium, each in the back of a black cab, one of the great symbols of the capital. They launched into 'Wannabe' before being helped onto the roofs of their individual cabs to sing 'Spice Up Your Life' and do a lap of honour in front of a cheering crowd of 80,000. Their exuberance and joie de vivre owned the night. As ever, they were the story the next day – pictures of the Girls lighting up the papers as much as they had the night sky above London. A peak viewing figure of more than twenty-six million watched the scene unfold on television; the audience worldwide was estimated at 750 million.

It was spectacular. It was epic. And then they were gone into the night.

## 23

# SPICE WORLD AGAIN

Victoria made it quite clear that she considered their Olympic triumph to be the last hurrah of the Spice Girls. She had absolutely no desire to perform again and she never wavered from that decision, despite intense speculation about future reunions. The closing ceremony of London 2012 was the last time all five Girls sang on stage together.

That did not mean she stopped being a Spice Girl, though. She joined the others for the opening night of *Viva Forever* a few months later. A huge crowd had gathered outside the Piccadilly Theatre and cheered wildly when Emma, Geri and the two Melanies arrived. Victoria wasn't with them. She turned up fashionably late, escorted by a smiling David and her boys. They had been held up in traffic.

Inside all went well, with some of the enthusiastic audience getting up to have a little dance just as thousands had done over the years to the sounds of Abba in *Mamma Mia!*. Victoria hadn't sat with them, but after the show she joined everyone on stage – the cast, Judy Craymer and Jennifer Saunders. The applause was deafening and Mel B summed it up, 'That was fucking great.'

The critics didn't think so. The show received the worst reviews imaginable. The *Daily Telegraph* did not hold back: 'This show is not just bad, it is definitively, monumentally and histor-ically bad.' The *Daily Mail* thought the jukebox musical had all the makings of a notable West End flop: 'It's almost as if it had a death wish.'

Much of the hostility centred around Jennifer Saunders's plot, which focused on a teenager called Viva who was in a girl group trying their luck on a TV talent show, obviously based on *The X Factor*. Perhaps there was nothing new to say about this world of overnight celebrity and the sob stories they encouraged.

It had all seemed so promising when they had been kicking ideas around Geri's kitchen table. Emma and Melanie C had a little cry when the Girls first saw the production take shape at special workshop days fully a year before its première. Mel B was impressed and declared, 'They sing better than us.' Emma and Geri were particularly involved, turning up to watch the numbers being rehearsed whenever they could. Even Simon Fuller was optimistic. In real life, he linked both worlds – the Spice Girls and television talent shows. He told Judy, 'You have succeeded in putting your arms around twenty-five years of pop culture.'

The first hint that all was not well came when Jennifer revealed there had been last-minute changes to the script just two weeks before the big night. She explained, 'A massive amount is changing. Entire scenes are being cut and the order is being changed.' That hinted at panic.

It's impossible to know if the negative reviews changed things. Geri did her best, coming back to see the show more than once and adding glamour when she did. But she couldn't will success by determination alone, and 'with heavy heart' Judy announced it was closing. *Viva Forever* lasted six months.

They had tried to make the show brighter, lighter and funnier but they just couldn't get it to work. Judy signed off: 'We set out to create a contemporary story that truly reflects our time; to take a satirical look at the underbelly of a TV talent show and the chaos that ensues for a mother, her daughter and their friends, a theatrical event to embrace all generations both on and offstage.'

The suspicion remained that TV talent shows, while still enjoying great ratings, were not ageing as well as the Girls themselves. All five, as well as Simon and Judy, had put money into the production. Losses were reported to be as high as £5 million. *Viva Forever* was probably the biggest disappointment of the Spice Girls' story. With hindsight, perhaps the project's principal flaw was that they weren't in it. Before it opened, Emma said, 'It's weird hearing other people sing our songs.' Maybe only they themselves could sing them.

Melanie C and Emma loyally went along to the last night on 28 June 2013. They were still the best of friends and had worked together professionally once more on Melanie's album *Stages*, a collection of some of the best-loved songs from musicals. They duetted on 'I Know Him So Well', the emotional ballad from the musical *Chess*. Melanie confided that they found it hard recording together because normally, 'We just like to get cocktails.' They performed the song, which had been a number one for Elaine Paige and Barbara Dickson, on that year's BBC Children in Need appeal.

Melanie also included 'Tell Me It's Not True' from *Blood Brothers* and 'I Don't Know How to Love Him' from *Jesus Christ Superstar*. The album was a big departure for her but the timing was perfect because of the publicity she was receiving as Mary Magdalene on the arena tour – the 'rock experience' – of Andrew Lloyd Webber's musical. She played venues she had previously visited as part of the Spice Girls, including the O2. Quietly, she had split up from Tom, so she was now a single mum. It was her decision to end the relationship, calling it 'the most catastrophic thing I experienced'. Mainly, she kept her feelings to herself as she always tended to do. 'It's all too raw,' was all she would say.

'Being a mother comes first,' she declared, trying to sort out childcare. Her mum Joan was standing by.

Fortunately, relations with Tom settled down and he played his part in looking after Scarlet, but Melanie acknowledged that it was tougher being a single mum. She was loving being a mother, though, declaring, 'She's brought so much joy into my life.' Melanie's efforts as a single mother were noticed, and she was named Celebrity Mum of the Year at the Tesco Awards at the Savoy Hotel in March 2013. There was nothing sporty about the elegant woman who confidently posed for pictures on the red carpet in a chic cream dress. Fittingly, Joan went with her.

Coincidentally, Emma was named Celebrity Mum of the Year in a different poll the following month. Hers was run by Foxy Bingo, the online bingo site. She said all the right things: 'This award is extra special because this is the most important thing – being a mummy.'

Emma seemed to have the balance between celebrity and motherhood just right. She was an active supporter of UNICEF, eventually becoming an ambassador for the organisation and visiting Africa as part of the ongoing fight against child malnutrition and the need for proper vaccination. Her radio career was blossoming and she became the full-time host of the breakfast show on Heart alongside Jamie Theakston at the start of 2013. She enjoyed the intimacy of radio, chatting easily to listeners without having to put on a performance for the cameras.

The daily routine suited her, even if it meant arriving at the studio before the larks were up: 'I can come in, have a laugh and a fry-up with Jamie and finish work in time to pick the boys up from nursery.' Some mornings she would do her make-up in the car and sometimes she wouldn't bother. She would go running with Melanie on Hampstead Heath when time allowed but would usually end up gasping for breath while the triathlete forged ahead.

They could run over to Geri's house if they needed a stop and a catch-up. Like Melanie, she was a single mum. She continued to have little luck with men. She was involved with online betting consultant Anton Kaszubowski, but he turned out to be still married to a Russian model. Geri had once admitted, 'I think we all know that relationships haven't been my strong point.'

That changed when she became involved with Christian Horner, the millionaire boss of the Formula One Red Bull team. Geri had always loved cars – even her faithful old Fiat Uno – ever since her beloved dad took her to car auctions and local banger racing in Watford. Ironically, she had a reputation – at least in the old days – of being a terrible driver. She had several friends in the Grand Prix world, including Bernie Ecclestone and Eddie Jordan. She had first met Christian as far back as 2009 but at the time he had a long-term partner, Beverley Allen, with whom he had a daughter, Olivia, in October 2013. Six months later he was with Geri, but she was adamant he was single again by then.

While not exactly a whirlwind romance in the manner of Mel B and Stephen Belafonte, things moved faster during an idyllic summer. He chartered a yacht to take her sailing around Portofino and the Italian Riviera to celebrate her forty-second birthday. Christian was very well connected – his brother Guy was married to the daughter of the Earl and Countess of Clarendon. After leaving Warwick School, Christian opted for a career in motor sport, becoming a professional driver with Arden International Motorsport, which he founded with his father, Garry. He gave up driving aged twenty-five and went full-time into the business side of the sport.

He became the youngest team principal in Formula One when he was appointed head of Red Bull Racing at the start of 2005. This was big business. He became responsible for a work-force of 550 and budgets running into hundreds of millions of pounds. In 2010, when lead driver Sebastian Vettel became world champion and the team won the constructor's title, each employee was handed a £10,000 bonus. In 2013 Christian was given an OBE in the Queen's birthday honours for services to motorsport.

He and Geri announced their engagement the old-fashioned way in the *Times*. This was a new Geri – or Geraldine as she was styled in the paper – opting for tradition rather than the modern method of telling the world your life story on social media. They were married at St Mary's Church, Woburn, in Bedfordshire on 15 May 2015, the day after her daughter Bluebell's ninth birthday; there were no fireworks or razzamatazz but Geri described it as 'truly, the happiest day of my life'. She wore a classic white bridal dress, designed by Phillipa Lepley, and he, a traditional morning suit. Bluebell was a bridesmaid, sister Natalie was maid of honour and her mum, Ana Marie, walked her down the aisle. Christian's parents didn't attend, reportedly upset at their son's break with Beverley.

The wedding wasn't a Spice Girls reunion. Melanie C was filming in Malaysia; Victoria was in Singapore for her fashion show, but she sent a dress for the honeymoon and posted a sweet note on Twitter: 'Sending u love and happiness. I'm so sad I couldn't be with you on your special day. X I love you X'; Mel B apparently pulled out at the last minute, but Emma was there with Jade. She was a constant presence in the lives of her bandmates, seemingly regarding them as an extension of her family. She seemed no nearer to naming a day when she too would marry, although she posted an amusing picture of Jade at the reception in Woburn Abbey, clutching a bunch of flowers with the caption, 'Jade caught the bouquet! Uh oh!'

While everyone was wondering about another Spice Girls return, it was Jade who had a musical comeback. His old group

Damage took part in a series called *The Big Reunion*, in which bands would get back together for the TV cameras. The man behind it was none other than Chris Herbert, who never seemed short of a good idea. In the first series he had encouraged 5ive to reunite and now he was doing the same with Jade's band, as well as with Eternal and Girl Thing, who were Simon Cowell's attempt to emulate the success of the Spice Girls in the late nineties.

Emma would show up to support Jade whenever she could. Chris observed, 'Jade is a really nice guy and Emma is beautiful both inside and out. She's just lovely. I can see why he and Emma get on so well. They were like an old married couple.'

Geri was now actually married and embracing life as Mrs Horner. She didn't see taking Christian's name at the outset as any rejection of Girl Power. She explained to the writer Louise Gannon, 'I believe in equality but I'm also proud to be his wife and this is me saying I believe completely in the union of marriage and everything that goes with it.'

She hadn't lost her personal ambition, though, and over the coming months she put the finishing touches to an album of solo material that would show off a new, improved vocal style. She had released one single, 'Half of Me', in Australia a couple of years before but it sold an embarrassing 393 copies.

She gave interviews about the unnamed album, but so far it has never been released. She soon had other priorities; she was expecting her second child. She had wanted another baby and had unsuccessfully tried IVF before conceiving naturally. Her pregnancy postponed any plans for a Spice Girls reunion marking the twentieth anniversary of 'Wannabe'. That would just have to wait. She gave birth to Montague George Hector Horner on 21 January 2017. She had decided on his second name as a tribute to her dear friend George Michael who had died tragically at Christmas. Monty, as they called the newborn, is the twelfth Spice baby – a round dozen for the group photo in years to come.

Melanie C was tied up in the Far East, filming her first series of *Asia's Got Talent*. She was finally content to occupy the calmer waters of television and followed both Geri and Mel B into the 'Got Talent' world. Her programme was recorded at the Pinewood studio complex in Johor, Malaysia. This was much lower-profile than the UK. She didn't want to be in the papers every day. She turned down *Strictly Come Dancing* for the same reason.

Away from the spotlight, Melanie could work quietly on a new solo album. *Version of Me* was released towards the end of 2016 – nearly ten years after her last original album, *This Time*. Some of the songs were about Tom, but she tried to look forward rather than back. It helped that she had found a new boyfriend, Joe Marshall, another man who was not a celebrity and didn't court publicity. They shared a love of keeping fit and she appointed him her manager after splitting with Nancy Phillips. They were seldom seen out together, preferring to stay at home with their children. He had two, who were a couple of years older than Scarlet. She was spotted, however, teaching him to drive near their North London home.

The timing of Geri's wedding – clashing with Singapore Fashion Week – was especially unfortunate in that Victoria and David had moved back to England after his contract ended in Los Angeles, buying a Grade II-listed townhouse in Holland Park, west London, for a reported £31 million. They spent a further £8 million on improvements and decoration. It's a cliché, but really, no expense was spared. Victoria posted pictures on Instagram of their luxurious décor to ensure the whole world was thoroughly jealous. One drawback was that the garden was too small for an outdoor swimming pool. While the house was being redone, they rented one across the road.

Victoria brought her Beverly Hills lifestyle home with her. She was up at 6 a.m. five days a week for a personal training session before downing a juice concoction specially prepared by their cook. The only time she varied her routine was when she was too hungover after her fortieth birthday party to get out of bed. After 'breakfast' it was the school run before starting the day's business, trying to tick off entries in her crowded diary. She had many staff to help, including a full-time security guard, a personal assistant and a PR. Often, her days would involve a trip to the airport to catch a plane.

Fashion was a global business and she treated it seriously. Victoria Beckham Ltd employed a hundred people. In the past she had two personas: funny, self-deprecating Victoria and unsmiling, poised Posh Spice. Now she was still the former but the second had been replaced by Victoria Beckham, fashion designer. She still didn't smile much in public, though. The branding that had worked so well for the Spice Girls worked in exactly the same way for her fashion house. People had a personal investment in her life and her style.

She probably had less time to herself than when she was a Spice Girl. She opened a store under her name in Dover Street, Mayfair, a sure sign that you had arrived as a designer. She had offices in New York and London and her collection was available in 400 stockists in fifty different countries – no wonder she spent a lot of time on a plane. One particular trip she made was not in the name of fashion, though, but to the HIV clinics of South Africa as an International Goodwill Ambassador for the UNAIDS programme.

The Spice Girls always had the royal seal of approval but Victoria had it officially when she received an OBE from Prince

William in April 2017 for services to the fashion industry and for her charity work, although she breached protocol by telling everyone the good news before the official announcement.

The only cloud on her sunny outlook was the news that her fashion label was running at a considerable loss. At the end of 2018, NEO Investment Partners put in £30 million to help the business expand. The remodelling of its finances did not impinge on the Beckhams' personal wealth, which the *Sunday Times* Rich List of 2019 put at £355 million.

The Spice Girl who was not enjoying life was Mel B. To the outside world it appeared she was thriving – at least professionally. She was now an integral part of the Simon Cowell family. He thought she was 'fantastic' as a guest judge on the 2012 UK series of *The X Factor*. She began a six-year stint as a judge on *America's Got Talent* the following year; and back in Britain she took the place of Nicole Scherzinger on *The X Factor* in 2014. Simon Cowell was back leading the panel himself and Mel impressed throughout the series – striking just the right note between being forthright and fair. She declared confidently, 'Honesty is the best policy.'

Relations with her family in Leeds had not improved and she did not attend the funeral of her grandmother, Mary, who was Andrea's mother. She had cut off all ties. Despite that, all seemed well until it was announced she was ill and would have to miss *The X Factor* final. There were whispers that she had been hospitalised due to taking too much cocaine. Officially she'd been crying out with stomach pains. She had missed a press conference and rehearsals on the Thursday and the big night on the Saturday.

To the surprise of everyone, she somewhat shakily appeared the following evening for the grand finale and the announcement of the winner, Ben Haenow. She wasn't wearing a wedding ring. She kept the true sadness of what had happened to herself for three years. She had tried to take her own life through swallowing pills for the second time. She revealed the harrowing details of the day in *Brutally Honest*. She wrote that she was 'emotionally battered, estranged from my family'.

The finger of blame was firmly pointed at Stephen: 'I felt ugly and detested by the very man who once promised to love and protect me, my husband and manager Stephen.' It was explosive stuff. Saddest of all was the admission she had written notes to Phoenix telling her to get her younger sisters to Leeds so that they could be looked after by Andrea. When she awoke in hospital suffering from liver and kidney damage, Phoenix was by her bedside.

Mel was reunited finally with her family in unhappy circumstances. She made a mercy dash from Los Angeles to Leeds in March 2017 when she learned that her father Martin had only days to live. He had been battling multiple myeloma cancer for five years. She had last spoken to him in 2013 when they had a furious row. They made their peace on his death bed, even though he could no longer talk. Her sister Danielle, mum Andrea and Phoenix were with her when he died, aged sixty-three.

In her memoir, she would write how his death gave her the strength to divorce Stephen. She did not attend the funeral, but instead flew back to LA, moved out of the family home, rented a house, took out a restraining order against Stephen and filed for divorce – just as she had promised her dad.

The divorce was exceptionally messy even by Hollywood standards, with lurid allegations of threesomes, sex tapes, drug taking and domestic abuse. There were also claims that she had little left of her vast Spice Girls' fortune. When the divorce was finally agreed she was ordered to pay Stephen's legal bill of

£270,000 as well as £32,000 a month in child and spousal support. They had to sell their £6-million home and set aside £850,000 to pay back taxes. Stephen agreed not to make the sex tapes public. Her legal bill was estimated at £750,000. Although she still had her television work, Mel was understandably keen to rebuild her fortune and her life by rekindling interest in the next Spice Girls reunion.

Victoria would not be persuaded but the others were on board. Melanie C had gone cold on the project when she was immersed in *Version of Me* but, in the end, thought it too good an opportunity to turn down and wanted to help Mel get back on her feet. Geri also wanted that for Mel and hoped the tour would help her heal. Geri was now a member of the country set since she had moved into Christian's vast Cotswolds estate near Banbury, where if she popped next door it was to visit her 'adorable' neighbour, Lady Jane Wellesley.

Emma was always enthusiastic about reunions and decided to take a break from the breakfast show on Heart to spend 2019 concentrating on the tour and releasing another solo album, *My Happy Place*. The highlight was a duet with Jade on the Ashford and Simpson classic, 'You're All I Need to Get By'. Emma had been named as Radio Presenter of the Year at the 2017 Television and Radio Industries Club Awards (TRIC) and had nothing more to prove, although she kept a Sunday evening programme. The album was released in April 2019, a month before the *Spice World – 2019* tour began in Dublin on 24 May.

Mel B had guaranteed maximum publicity for the concerts in advance by appearing on *Piers Morgan's Life Stories*. Melanie C was in the audience, sat beside Andrea, Danielle and Phoenix. She talked at length about her emotional abuse from Stephen. Piers was careful to stress that her ex-husband had denied all allegations.

Her candour did not make the headlines. Instead, it was the revelation that she had a lesbian fling with Geri. It was news because she had never admitted it before, but it was not much of a surprise. She said it was just the once. The media over-reacted in typical style – it was like being back in the *News of the World* nineties, which was rather timely considering the interest in the reunion of the biggest group of that era. A spokesman for Geri said, 'She would like you to know that what has been reported recently is simply not true and has been very hurtful to her family.'

The revelation was obviously a big talking point in coffee shop queues the next morning. But the media had made the same mistake they had made with all the steamy kiss-and-tell stories back in the day: the Spice Girls were fun and sexy but they were never sexual. They belonged to a more innocent age and were alarmed that their own children were bombarded with grown-up images. Melanie C, for instance, was concerned that Scarlet was a fan of Rihanna, whose videos she thought too sexual for young girls. She wouldn't let her daughter watch them. Far from empowering women, she believed they were objectifying. In Los Angeles, Mel B had restricted her teenage daughter's internet use. She didn't want Phoenix getting old before her time. Geri wouldn't allow Bluebell to have an Instagram account and policed her online activity.

Melanie C explained that inevitably they had all changed as they grew older: 'We'd become mothers but were still those girls who wanted to rule the world, and did.' During the 2019 tour the Girls played thirteen stadium dates around the UK in front of nearly 700,000 people, grossing £64 million. The three nights at Wembley were a special thrill for Geri, who had always regretted missing out twenty years before. She had predicted that the tour would be a joyful experience. It was – just as loving the Spice Girls always had been.

# LAST THOUGHTS

———

We can all dream a little …
*Spice World*, Wembley Stadium, 13 June 2019.

It's like a giant themed party. Entry is only for those wearing something that Mel B might have put on during the golden days of the Spice Girls. Looking around the sea of fans – all 80,000 of them – many had made the effort to dust off their leopard-print party dresses and accessories, wearing their hair in Scary space buns or Baby double buns.

Geri's iconic Union Jack costume was not as popular as I expected it to be. I did see quite a few hairy-chested men sporting it, though. More significantly, everyone seemed to be wearing a smile. There's nothing more joyous than nostalgia, reconnecting with a past life that was simpler and more innocent.

Men are in short supply tonight. That reminds me that the original idea for an all-girl group was one that would appeal equally to young men and women. That was abandoned when it became apparent that the great majority of fans were pre-teen; they weren't thirteen- to seventeen-year-old schoolgirls latching on to the latest fashionable pop stars or bands of the moment.

I remember asking journalist Chrissy Iley about it. She interviewed all the girls back in the nineties and many times since then. Her view was that when the Spice Girls burst on the scene it was the first time that little girls had their own pop star adventure – a Disney ride all of their own. The Spice Girls had harnessed a gap in the market that was enormously powerful.

Two mums in the row in front of me have brought their daughters of seven or eight, which was probably the age at which their mothers became lifelong fans. They were all happily giggling as they took photos that were being posted immediately on Instagram.

Mel B used her Instagram account to post pictures of herself travelling to Wembley on the Jubilee line. She was doing her make-up and nobody seemed to recognise her. That didn't surprise me because she wasn't wearing leopard print. It reminded me of the time that I was in the Gadget Shop in Brent Cross shopping centre and Emma Bunton walked in with Alan Carr. Nobody reacted because, although she was just about recognisable, she didn't look at all like Baby Spice.

Packing up abruptly at the height of their fame meant that the images so carefully constructed by the Spice Girls remain ingrained in our minds. We haven't witnessed their personas grow older – only watched the young women themselves mature as they have got on with their lives post Spice Girls.

Mel B will always be Scary, but privately she isn't like that. In LA, Louisa Spring told me that she was outspoken – very much so – but not in an aggressive way: 'She is just a very good person and she tells the truth. She is very warm, very open and very fair. She is not such a fireball as everyone says. She is a bit more measured than that, but fun.'

Superficially, Mel came across as the strongest of the Spice Girls. She is a proper diva – and that is not meant in any sort of derogatory way – but in the long term she has been the most vulnerable. Chrissy Iley explained it to me: 'In the past, the big divas like Dusty Springfield, Judy Garland and Whitney Houston, for instance, have all been hugely vulnerable. It's that juxtaposition in terms of strong woman meets vulnerable woman. We all want to be strong but we are all vulnerable and that's where the identification thing kicks in and why you become a fan. We think, "She feels it like me." If they were all just singing and dancing superstars, there would be no connection.'

Melanie C has become more 'sporty' as she has grown older, competing in triathlons, but I'm not convinced she was a tomboy character or the least bit plain back in the day. She is warm and feminine and would much rather have been called Singing Spice. She was always very pretty but diligently played her part as the trackie-wearing gym lover who could do a backflip on demand.

Despite being the youngest and being called Baby, Emma was arguably always the most measured and grown-up. Perhaps that's because she started in showbusiness so young. She could play her character with consummate professionalism – and still does. I think it's easy to underestimate her actual talent because she is so proficient at everything she does, a legacy of her stage school training. One of the most pleasant surprises for me has been discovering her solo music – perfect for a summer drive in the car or an hour or two on the garden sun lounger.

I'm not sure the Spice Girls would have made it without the publicity flair of Geri Halliwell. She had such a huge effect that it's easy to forget she was part of the group for little more than four years. As George Michael said, the eye was always drawn to Geri. Ginger wasn't much of a nickname; she only had to change her hair colour to cast it off. At the time she might have liked to be called 'Sexy Spice', but that too would have been an image she wanted to lose a year or two later. She has been refreshingly frank about her problems – as all the Girls have been – reinforcing the point that vulnerability is very relatable. I'm sure that her honesty about her eating disorder has helped other young women address those issues.

These days she is Geri Horner and happily married to a multi-millionaire, living the life of a horse-riding lady of the manor, and she seems finally to be very content indeed. The drug of fame is a difficult one to abandon, though, which perhaps explains why she became the central figure of the Saturday night peak-time talent show, *All Together Now*. It's not been re-commissioned but I wouldn't bet against her returning in something else.

As the crowd waits for the grand entrance of the four remaining Spice Girls, I wonder if we are going to miss Victoria. The last time I saw the Spice Girls live was in 2007 when she paraded around like a catwalk model and received by far the biggest cheer. Then, she brought a star quality to the stage that perhaps she didn't display in the nineties.

Victoria was the luckiest of the Spice Girls with her nickname. Posh is brilliant for headlines and it doesn't age. She can be Posh Spice at seventy without a trace of irony or nostalgia. Friends have told me she is intelligent and purposeful and able to make the best of a situation. She probably should have been called Witty Spice but she has done very well as Posh – becoming the richest and most famous of the Girls. Some argue that she owes much of it to David Beckham, but would he have become a modern icon without her fame and drive?

The Spice Girls were always greater together than as individuals, so I don't expect her absence to be too noticeable tonight. We're about to find out. It's time to see if the famous Spice Girl images are still relevant today. On the dot of 8.30 p.m., the persistent drum beat lets us know it's starting. The giant screens introduce us to the Girls in turn, starting with Sporty, then Baby, Scary and finally Ginger. Each is greeted with an enormous cheer.

And then they are here – Emma, in pink with matching hair; Geri, petite in a curious Union Jack ballgown that a designer-conscious Elizabeth I might have worn; and the two Melanies. Mel C is in fantastic shape, like the superfit heroine of a Marvel comic; Mel B is squeezed into a leopard-print catsuit that makes it hard to believe she celebrated her forty-fourth birthday two weeks earlier. All the Girls have remained youthful-looking.

'I knew they'd start with this,' shouted the young woman on my left as the band belted out the opening bars of 'Spice Up Your Life'. It's a theme tune. Everyone in the audience that I could see seems so happy and they've only been going a minute.

'If You Can't Dance' proved that the Girls still could. Funny to think that is the career role they might have had themselves if the Spice Girls had never happened. Scary and Sporty are still a class above, but Emma and Geri are not far behind.

The audience haven't forgotten the moves, and those hours spent in front of a mirror practising being their favourite Spice Girl seem never to have left anyone. And it's not just the exuberant dancing; it's the lyrics as well. No help is required as everyone knows the words to each song: for 'Who Do You Think You Are' the noise of the sing-along is deafening. Everyone is happy to 'Swing it, shake it, move it, make it.' In the run-up to the tour, the *Guardian* ranked this as number one among all Spice songs.

The Girls pause for breath and a little chat. Geri welcomes everyone to *Spice World* and reminds us that this is where the Spice Girls started. I'm not quite sure what she means because they really began in a drab semi in Maidenhead.

It's a bit confusing that this tour is called *Spice World* and the original one was called *Spiceworld*. Four of the first five numbers are the same as they were back then in 1998. No doubt many of tonight's audience were there. 'Do It' introduces us to the 'Spice Boys', the male dancers who are young and superfit. The Spice Girls keep up, though. The song may sound as if it's going to be a sexy invitation but 'Do It' is not that at all. The lyric is encouraging women to make something of their lives and do what they want to do: 'Make your own rules to live by.'

'Do It' ends with the famous Girl Power salute – one arm stretched defiantly upwards. Geri announces, 'We are all in our forties but we have got better with age.' I could have sworn Mel B had a tear in her eye but perhaps it was a trick of the light. Next up, 'Something Kinda Funny' is one of the first Spice Girls songs and as fluffy as candyfloss; while very nineties, it's another song that seems to have aged well.

Girl Power is the slogan that's never far away. The anthem of 'Sound Off' rings throughout the stadium – a rare song that manages to get Girl Power and Wonderbra into the same lyrics. The famous advertisement poster that featured supermodel Eva Herzigová in a black Wonderbra declaring 'Hello Boys' was first launched in 1994, so it is celebrating the same anniversary as the Spice Girls.

The first costume change and they are back in black, looking like the stars of an *X-Men* movie, to perform 'Holler' and reprise 'Sound Off' as a chant with crowd involvement. 'Holler' has more sexual overtones than most Spice Girls' songs – a declaration of the power that women could hold over men: 'I wanna make you holler.' But there's something rather harmless about the sexual content of the Spice Girls. They are as quintessentially British as a seaside special or a *Carry On* film, despite media attempts to sexualise them. Tonight's experience is reassuringly innocent – even if there's a fair amount of post-teen drinking going on.

Geri, of course, had left by the time 'Holler' was number one, but she seamlessly performs the bits that Posh would have done – no adjustment required. The *X-Men* costumes only lasted one number. They return in pink and blue. I wouldn't blame the Girls if they had slipped into some thermal underwear; it's absolutely freezing for June and everyone is putting their coats back on.

The early dates on this reunion tour were troubled by sound issues and there's some evidence of lingering problems on the slow segment. That's a pity because Mel C is putting everything into 'Viva Forever' and 'Let Love Lead the Way', pretty songs but slightly lost thanks to the distorted bass. There are lots of kisses and cuddles on stage, even more when they sing 'Goodbye'. For me, it's the best song yet, poignant and sentimental and wearing well. Geri, who is holding hands with Mel B, seems a little subdued at this point.

Mel B probably has the best costumes on the night and returns from another change in silver hot pants and gold thigh boots. Emma, though, looks amazing in a sparkling silver mini dress that definitely had Baby Spice's name on it. Imagine if all the costumes got muddled backstage and she came on wearing one of Sporty's designer gym outfits? Throughout their career, clothes have been a vital part of creating the individual persona of each girl.

The entire audience has been given recyclable white wristbands that glow when you rip off a tab. As everyone waves them towards the sky, it's as if thousands of fireflies have descended on Wembley. The effect is stunning and a vast improvement on the old hazardous cigarette lighters or irritating mobile phones.

After 'Never Give Up on the Good Times', the Girls tackle the only cover of the night – 'We Are Family', the Sister Sledge disco classic, a song that perfectly suits the nostalgic mood. I remember them performing it at their last reunion. They did quite a few non-Spice songs then, including some solo numbers. The woman on my right wants them to perform 'It's Raining Men', Geri's finest hour, but there's no time for that as they belt out 'Love Thing' from the first album, *Spice*.

'The Lady is a Vamp' is not everyone's favourite Spice Girls' song, but, for me, it helps to define the stage-school influence that was evident in everything they did. The track wouldn't be out of place in any West End musical and illustrates perfectly the Hollywood show element of the Girls – a tribute to the great names that have shaped our popular culture: Jackie O, Marilyn Monroe, Twiggy and Elvis are among the many that get a name check. If a group like Little Mix performed the song now, they could write a verse about the Spice Girls themselves. I've no idea what the line, 'She's a da da da da da da da,' means, but it doesn't matter.

From this point on, it's one blockbuster hit after another. First, there's 'Too Much', their second Christmas number one. The song was the opening track in the film *Spice World* and is another that features stand-out soaring vocals from Mel C. As this reunion concert progresses, it becomes more apparent that Melanie Chisholm is the one Spice Girl the others cannot do without. She was low-key when the group began and the media and publicity focused on the more obvious charms of Geri and Emma, but the sporty look is arguably now the most fashionable. And the others, whose voices are perfect for harmonies, could not replicate her very individual vocal style, which is so much a part of the Spice sound. That's also evident on 'Say You'll Be There' when she sings 'This I swear!' It's probably the biggest sing-along of the night. '2 Become 1' closes the main set. The song is the Spice Girls at their sweetest.

While we wait for the encore, the Girls appear on the big screens once more to let us know what it all means to them. Girl

Power is about 'women supporting other women', says Geri. 'We're sisters,' says Emma. 'I'm always going to be a Spice Girl,' says Melanie Brown.

The first number of the encore is 'Stop', my personal favourite among all their songs. Perhaps best described as a homage to sixties' Motown, but with an edge. Diana Ross and The Supremes had a hit with a track called 'Stop in the Name of Love', which was a plaintive plea not to 'break my heart'. The Spice Girls do not sing about broken hearts; instead they want to have fun and not get tied down by a boyfriend moving too fast.

One last ballad is 'Mama', a tribute to mothers everywhere who are suffering the ups and downs of a relationship with their teenage daughters. And so to 'Wannabe', of course – a musical signpost for a generation of young girls and another of their songs that doesn't age. Fireworks light up the night sky for a glorious finale. And then they were gone – finishing on the dot of 10.30 just as they were supposed to do, like the true professionals they have always been. They hadn't overstayed their welcome.

I don't expect to see Mel B on the tube on the way home! Instead there are many smiling and contented faces from those who had experienced one of the great nights. If you loved the Spice Girls twenty or so years ago, you still have a place for them in your heart. The Girls themselves lived the dream and all their fans could dream with them. Emma once said that they would be like the Rolling Stones, touring as crinkly Spice on their Zimmer frames, still singing 'If you wannabe my lover'.

Let's hope so.

# SPICE STARS

## Geri Halliwell

Geri's chart is stamped with the marks of leadership. The Sun, symbol of vitality and future direction, links tightly to both assertive, competitive Mars and rational, clever Mercury. This planetary cluster is in the courageous, recognition-loving sign of Leo – a first and forceful indicator of a desire to successfully engage passionately, expressively and joyfully in being somebody. This central cluster also links to ambitious, authoritative Saturn and disruptor Uranus – planets connected to the collective, the bigger picture – suggesting a drive to be seen on the main stage in life, to be heard, celebrated and remembered. These planetary gifts – the intelligence, the boldness, the celebratory drive befit a performer but are only the start of a more complex image presented by the chart.

Geri will be able to sense the mood and trends of the future and be able to give them substance. The positive link between innovative, rebellious Uranus and disciplined, structuring Saturn means she will be able to project and carry reform, to accelerate change. It should be noted that Saturn, planet of status, strength and mastery, is strong in this chart, forming many positive links, a promise of longevity and accomplishments which will grow steadily over time.

These planetary placements are fortunate and have helped Geri shine, but there are other, harder aspects revealing the anxieties which force growth in a life. Venus, planet of love and money, in the cautious, protective sign of Cancer hints that she can be wary of real trust and will find it hard to forget hurt. Venus forms a harsh link to intense, controlling Pluto – possessiveness, compulsive attractions, horror of rejection, jealousy, manipulation, sabotage should all feature somewhere, at some point, in relationship mixes whether professional, familial or personal. From the earliest age Geri's antennae were sensitively attuned to the humiliation and threat of failure and instinctively she would have fought hard to survive in what can be a very harsh world.

Geri has huge drive, daring and charm. She knows instinctively how to please and it is this ability to beguile which reveals her real power – it is the traditional seductive female power, projecting sexuality and kindness, which used effectively will deliver the goods.

And thus she embodies a conundrum. On the one hand she IS the modern woman – independent, gifted, strong, her own master, brave, forthright, intelligent, adventurous, successful. On the other, she has openly and proudly used the oldest means in the book – her allure – to accomplish her goals. Perhaps this should be seen as less of a problem and more the solution. Venus has played its part but alongside the well-placed outer planets – future focused, rebellious Uranus and ambitious, prudent traditional Saturn. This is one woman's approach to getting that power.

Looking ahead: The early part of 2020 looks dynamic for Geri. On 1 February karmic Saturn joins the North Node in her chart, suggesting meetings with those who can really take her forward. The North Node, placed in Capricorn, is a point which indicates where one needs to go in this life. For her it is very much about assuming greater responsibility in wielding her expertise and wisdom. This first contact with Saturn suggests a facing up to necessary growth, a gaining of status and authority which will carry weight. Then in April there is another triggering of this important chart point by beneficent Jupiter and heavyweight Pluto bringing up the rear. It is a major turning point, a time when she can expect life to take a dramatic turn for the better. Whatever starts at this time will intensify in January 2021, promising exciting times!

## Melanie Chisholm

At first glance Melanie's chart suggests her ability to live with dignity and great success in the modern world. A second glance illuminates a powerful desire to connect with and deliver something more – there is here a sense of mission, a need to be useful and a yearning for suitable legacy.

Both of the planetary 'lights' – the Sun and Moon – are in 'earthy' signs of Capricorn and Virgo – a hint here that Melanie has her feet on the ground and will know instinctively how to approach the goals of living well, of flourishing and getting to the top. Her Sun, in ambitious Capricorn, will thrive on hard, demanding work and linked tightly to messenger Mercury points to her communicative skills.

Similarly, Melanie's Moon in discerning, perfectionist Virgo will have its needs met through diligence, productivity and aiming to serve others. Melanie will be happy getting on independently with things, and a tendency to worry, to feel unequal to whatever tasks arise, will drive her to greater accomplishment.

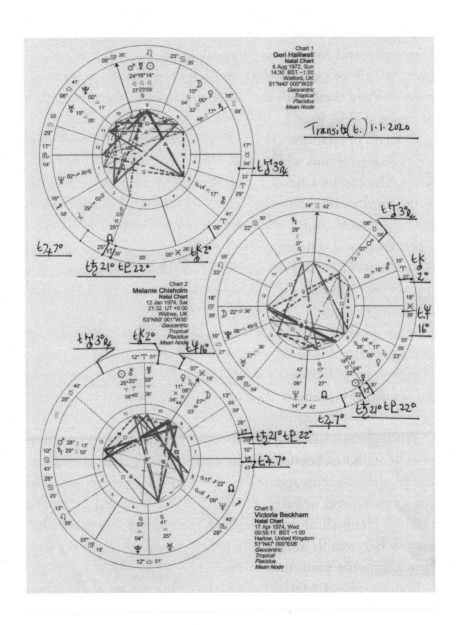

But there is within her a hunger to give. Neptune, planet of compassion and creativity, links positively to Venus, symbol of femininity and love in the sign of unconventional Aquarius. Melanie will be proud of her original ideas and vision and will want to share these with the collective. This will be her gift and what she will be keen to hand on.

In terms of relationships and how she acts as a role model, she will need space and will be unselfish in letting others be themselves. She can be over-critical of herself and others, will resent restrictions and fight for her rights. A difficult aspect between passionate Mars and a cool Venus hints at stormy relationships when there is a difference of opinion – getting the flow right between assertion and compliance may take time but Melanie's over-riding belief in equality and fair play is deep rooted and will mark her out.

With egoless Neptune linked positively to regenerative, healing Pluto, Melanie will have a strong sense of intuitive connectivity with those close to her, her audience and, in particular, her followers. She will be inspirational, loyal and supportive to the group – an example of a modern feminine etiquette.

Through modelling responsibility, dedication to developing her talent, independence of mind and spirit, generosity, support and loyalty to group and collective ideals, Melanie has used her power to redress imbalance. Like her fellow group members, through channelling her creativity into something which has earned her wealth and public recognition, she is successfully challenging the status quo.

Looking ahead: Melanie is well into a period of great creative and ambitious output. Throughout 2019 she will have experienced the need to put every vital ounce of being and energy into her work as relentless Pluto transited her Sun. This planet ruthlessly strips away anything superficial, directing the individual to greater personal autonomy and power, promoting the deepest growth. It cannot have been an easy time, but with generous success bringing Jupiter hastening to join her Sun in March 2020, it will all seem worth it. Pluto has not yet completed its regenerative visit. From March 2020 until November 2021 it will move backwards and forwards over communicative Mercury, altering her ideas, changing her style, deepening her creative output. It is a gift to a musician, but hard work. Melanie must take breaks and get a bit of distance from the process sometimes to avoid an implosion or steam coming out of her ears.

## Victoria Beckham

Victoria has the wonderful gift of innovative leadership marked clearly in her birth chart, but achieving the recognition she desires may take her in different directions.

With her courageous Aries Sun joined to maverick Chiron and opposite unpredictable Uranus, there is wounding around her identity – perhaps that strong need to be first will require her to go out on her own and make the most of her pioneering spirit. Forceful, domineering Pluto opposite Mercury, the planet associated with siblings, may have sometimes made her feel less visible within a group – she needed to head up something that is hers alone.

Chiron facilitates healing in others and the manner in which Victoria leads her public life will allow many to learn from her. Issues Victoria may raise, in a world which seems focused on appearances, could revolve around diet and regenerative procedures. There is enormous pressure on young women to conform to beauty stereotypes and she could use her honesty and power, her awareness of body dysmorphia, to be an inspiring role model.

Victoria may well struggle with a fear of change, but resistance to the inevitable can be debilitating and may ultimately undermine her.

Victoria's feisty Aries Sun, linked to a combination of enterprising Mars and strategic Saturn, will provide the ability to think long term and plan with entrepreneurial talent. These planets of discipline and drive are linked to future-orientated, wealth-generating Jupiter and Venus, the planets associated with attractiveness. She has the ability to intuitively tap into future trends, instinctively knowing what can bring people together – this is a great advantage for anyone valuing commercial success and something not possible to teach.

Victoria will find much validation and creative fulfilment through her fashion career – a leading light in an industry which helps define social tribes, uplifts and gives joy and pleasure to millions. She has shown courage and the willingness to persevere in the search for success. She has embraced tradition in establishing her family but managed famously to build a powerful commercial career. She has achieved perhaps the most conventional societal status on her own terms, a different model again of the successful woman.

Looking ahead: Testing links between taskmaster Saturn and Victoria's Sun during 2020 (exact February, August and November) suggest she may meet obstacles in her goals and will be pushing herself hard this year. She will need to prioritise carefully and remember that with Saturn thoroughness, integrity and patience always pay off a little further down the line. She has great resources of courage and resilience and in early June these will benefit her greatly when a lovely link from Uranus to lucky Jupiter brings encouragement and unexpected positive outcomes.

## Melanie Brown

This chart delivers clear evidence of a powerful communicator, someone who can speak out about the truth and illuminate things society often prefers to ignore. With the Sun, planet of self-expression in communicative, curious Gemini, linked positively to intense Pluto and courageous Mars, Melanie will need to understand power, exercise power and challenge misuse of it in others. She is magnetic and extrovert, mentally agile and will be brilliant at helping others in the transformations of life – those points where one acknowledges a need for change, however threatening and dangerous it may seem.

Melanie will have had her own inner conflicts to resolve – with warrior Mars linked harshly to ruthless Pluto there is an instinct to win at any cost, a trait which will get you far in a competitive world but then can rebound; if personal ambitions are achieved through the power and advantages given by others there needs to be a giving back both at an individual level and to the collective. She may also meet this ruthlessness in others and will learn that the monster shrivels when held up to the light of the public.

Pluto in adaptable Libra and Mars, strong in impulsive, direct Aries, the sign it rules, are both planets connected to sex and regeneration. Melanie will be at home in her skin, able to embrace sexuality in a way which will inform her creativity and set others free to acknowledge and celebrate their own physical vitality.

In Melanie's chart the Moon, significator of her emotional nature and needs, is linked harshly to disruptive Uranus. She may have had to grow up quickly and could find it hard to ask for support and nurturance in all relationships – setting the bar too low. Her moods may change quickly and there will be times when she is unable to provide the sympathy others require. Positively, change will excite her as the unpredictable can make her feel vibrant and alive.

An opposition between unworldly egoless Neptune and Melanie's Sun, planet of identity and being, hints at a delicacy of life force – her body can be sensitive and there will be periods when she will need to learn how to re-engage with goals and pick up on the challenges of existence. Fortunately spiritual Neptune links also to Jupiter, planet of possibilities – Melanie has such ability to help others understand their lives through providing purpose and meaning that empowering others should always reawaken her trust in the future and what it can bring. This level and depth of experience – a life lived truthfully acknowledging darkness and light – gives Melanie the status of authoritative expert.

Looking ahead: For a year or so from April 2020 wise Chiron joins feisty Mars, planet of assertive action, in Melanie's chart. This is a classic sign of a shift into a mentoring/teaching role. Whilst such activity is usual to careers in entertainment it seems this development will be something bigger than the norm, something which will cement her identity as a powerful and influential communicator or campaigner covering issues of physical wellbeing and use and control of power. During this period she may well be focused on sorting many of her own issues, too, but the traditional way Chiron operates is by finding solutions for and healing others. This will bring her acclaim. Drawing a line under Melanie's personal agitations and trials is more likely to occur around August 2021 when the progressed position of the Sun reaches Venus in her chart – a lucky period for relationships and general good fortune.

## Emma Bunton

Emma's Aquarian Sun, planet of identity, is linked to Mercury, the planet which often represents youth and young people, so arguably there may be something about her nickname of 'Baby' which fits. However, this interpretation is stretched and really overridden completely by a tight link between her Sun and sober Saturn – Emma has never been young. She was born serious with her soul and mind set from the word go on very grown-up issues – responsibility, accountability, hard work. The Saturn link suggests she will accomplish a great deal in life but partly that is because she will generally feel – at least in early years – that others will not accept her as she really is. To gain that approval, she will need to earn it.

This issue with identity is marked out by another harsh link between her Sun and rebellious Uranus contributing to a feeling of not fitting in, of being in some way an outsider, of facing rejection. This link can contribute to feelings of restlessness, a desire for independence, a need for freedom from social restrictions, the adoption of a fairly anti-authority stance. There needed to be some way of directing this discomfort into something constructive if Emma's high levels of ambition and resolution were to come good.

The motivation for change was there and the way out obvious – with positive links between fortunate Jupiter and creative Neptune, a real show biz combination – a Great Escape into the bright lights beckoned.

Thank goodness also for a wonderful link between creative, regenerative Pluto and feisty Mars.

Firstly, this provides Emma with courage – she will stand up for herself and her beliefs all of her life. Secondly, whilst not picking fights, she will never back off if someone else does and she will battle fairly – for herself and any others treated unjustly. There is a hint here of self-reliance hard won and therefore not much sympathy for those who will not work for things. She expects others to make an effort, will be honest about this and, positively, this tough approach will trigger results.

That said, Emma is genuinely altruistic, as evidenced by the Jupiter links to compassionate Neptune and sociable Venus, both planets in philosophical Sagittarius. Emma is warm hearted, highly sociable and conscious in the best way that what might benefit others can also benefit her – she is the sort who will frequently set up those win–win moments and is a solutions finder. She has much integrity, setting high standards in relationships with an inherent sense of values and morality and is open about emotion. Emma is also willing to take risks if the goal is right. She will always benefit both from the realism and discipline Saturn linked to her Sun imparts and an expansive optimism and faith in life gifted by the Jupiter-Venus-Neptune contacts.

Emma provides the inspiring role model of success gained through hard work, faith, courage and a strong moral code – a powerful and healing message to project into the world.

Looking ahead: A number of planetary movements known as the 'mid-life transits' will mark 2020 out as significant for Emma. In March and April the great taskmaster Saturn will be opposite natal Saturn and then join her Sun. She will take stock and almost inevitably feel that some elements in her life have failed and need to go. She is also likely to experience success in many goals, and whilst the burden of responsibility can feel heavy, change will ultimately be invigorating. Uranus, planet of restlessness and change opposing her natal Uranus (first exact 2 May), will bring an urgency to address what no longer works for her and she will make sound changes – the sort which going forward will allow her to live more truly in line with her purpose. The other months when these energies peak are June, July and December 2020 and January 2021. There will be those she meets this year who will support Emma's creative, imaginative and spiritual instincts, allowing her to embark in new directions.

## The Group Chart

This chart combines the birth data of all five members and is symbolic of what the group values, its aims, impact, function and purpose.

With wounded healer Chiron joined tightly to the Sun in masculine Aries, it is inevitable that the fundamental issues the group will embody, explore and project will be those of female assertion and gender roles. Messenger Mercury, also in this cluster, signifies the drive to disseminate ideas. What is of interest to remember is that Chiron was the centaur that could heal others but not himself, so here we have an image of women (inevitably but appropriately in terms of self-denial, called 'Girls') providing something much needed and hugely healing for the collective which has come from their own hurt and injury and struggle to deal with it.

Immediately opposite this cluster, and so drawn tightly into the profile, is rebellious disruptive Uranus – it suggests the group will be driven to challenge male values and power, to be outriders for justice. Uranus is in Libra, a sign associated with redressing the balance, and is ruled by feminine Venus. It is a neat astrological image of female confrontation. Uranus deals in honesty – it is challenging the 'spicy' image of the Aries Sun – the 'girls' will flaunt their charms, knowing much of their power will have come from using their sexuality – that's the name of the game – but there is defiance too in the way in which they are

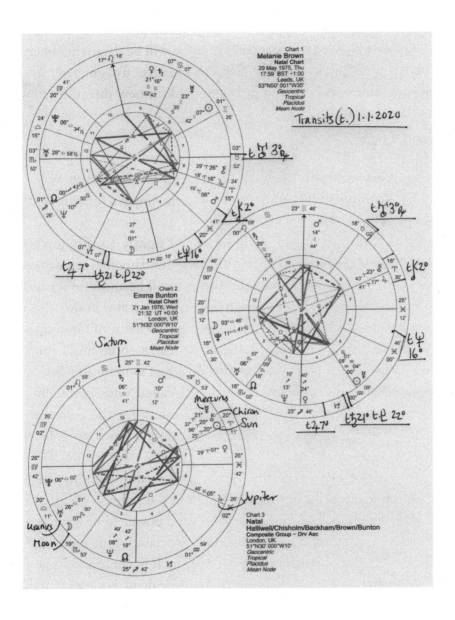

Chart 1
**Melanie Brown**
Natal Chart
29 May 1975, Thu
17:59 BST −1:00
Leeds, UK
53°N50' 001°W35'
*Geocentric*
*Tropical*
*Placidus*
*Mean Node*

Transits (t.) 1.1.2020

Chart 2
**Emma Bunton**
Natal Chart
21 Jan 1976, Wed
21:32 UT +0:00
London, UK
51°N30' 000°W10'
*Geocentric*
*Tropical*
*Placidus*
*Mean Node*

Chart 3
**Natal**
Halliwell/Chisholm/Beckham/Brown/Bunton
Composite Group – Drv Asc
London, UK
51°N30' 000°W10'
*Geocentric*
*Tropical*
*Placidus*
*Mean Node*

determined to win on competitive male terms, to come out on top.

Of note also are flowing links between three planets – Moon, Saturn and Jupiter. Briefly this ensures popularity, longevity, world-wide status and significance. The group is about the beauty and excitement of song (note the strong, positive link between creative Neptune and happy Venus in fire signs) while also providing a liberating, powerful contribution to the forever-everywhere-eternal debate about polarity, gender and power.

Of final interest is the present position of Uranus – much of the group identity is derived from its position in Venus-ruled Libra. Uranus has now completed a half cycle of forty-five years and entered (significantly) the Venus-ruled sign of Taurus. Again, the great disruptor is shaking up the world of entertainment and the feminine agenda, challenging the way power works – but this time in a sign which is dogged, obstinate and thorough. Whilst the period before (Uranus in airy Libra) was about seeding an idea ('girl power'), this time (Uranus in earthy Taurus) it is about consolidation and growth, and the changes may stick.

Madeleine Moore
September 2019

# ACKNOWLEDGEMENTS

One of the most enjoyable aspects of writing about the amazing Spice Girls has been discovering the number of fans still out there. They are everywhere. I know that's obvious from the hundreds of thousands who went to the stadium concerts in 2019 but, twenty years after their golden days, it's easy to forget what a phenomenon they actually were.

I was chatting about the book to my very cool hairdresser, Ivy, when she announced that she still had all her old Spice Girls' dolls in their original boxes. I was joined for one of the group's shows at Wembley by my chief researcher, Emily-Jane Swanson, who came along complete with leopard-print accessories and a comprehensive knowledge of the songs and dance moves. As always, many thanks to EJ for doing a wonderful job researching all things Spice.

At HarperCollins, I am grateful to my editor, Zoe Berville, who first suggested that I should write about the Spice Girls. She turned out to be a fan as well – so no pressure! Thanks also to Georgina Atsiaris for project editing; Claire Ward for her striking cover design; Sarah Burke in charge of production; Fiona Greenaway and Liane Payne for their patient picture research; and Laura Lees and Jasmine Gordon for looking after publicity and marketing.

Organising the lives of the Spice Girls was challenging enough for me, so I can only marvel at the terrific job the astrologer

Madeleine Moore has done with the star charts of five very different women. She has produced a series of portraits that are fascinating. She has crystallised these amazing characters both individually and as a group. Madeleine has contributed to many of my books and one thing always remains the same – we never discuss the subject in advance. She doesn't want to be influenced in any way by my opinions. That's why I love reading what she has to say – it's all new to me.

Thanks to my long-standing agent, Gordon Wise, for guiding me through another year. His assistant at Curtis Brown, Niall Harman, has once again been a huge help. Thank you to Jo Westaway for her help with the manuscript and her online expertise; to copy editors Hazel Orme and Helena Caldon for their superb work; and to Jen Westaway for transcribing my interviews so expertly even when they have been conducted in the noisiest restaurants imaginable.

I love getting out and chatting to people. I've travelled all over the country for my books, including many times to Liverpool and Yorkshire, but I had never been to Watford, where Geri Horner grew up as Geraldine Halliwell. I enjoyed wandering around the streets, coffee bars and pubs that were her old stamping ground. I am grateful to everyone who shared their thoughts and memories of the Spice Girls as they made their eventful journey through life. Some wished to remain anonymous because of the very small world of the music business and the rich and powerful circles that now surround the Girls. I have respected their wishes and I hope they enjoy the book. Thanks also to Neil Davies, Jon Fowler, Chrissy Iley, Kevin O'Sullivan, Rick Sky, Louisa Spring and, in particular, Chris Herbert; without his original vision, the Spice Girls would probably never have found each other.

You can read more about my books at seansmithceleb.com or follow me on Twitter and Facebook @seansmithceleb.

# SELECT BIBLIOGRAPHY

Beckham, Victoria, *Learning to Fly*, Michael Joseph 2003

Brown, Melanie, *Brutally Honest*, Quadrille 2018

Fitzgerald, Muff, *Spiced Up*, Hodder & Stoughton 1998

Halliwell, Geri, *If Only*, Bantam 1999

Halliwell, Geri, *Just for the Record*, Ebury Press 2003

Melanie B, *Catch a Fire*, Headline 2002

Sinclair, David, *Spice Girls Revisited*, Omnibus Press 2007

Spice Girls, *Real Life – Real Spice*, Zone/VCI 1997

# PICTURE CREDITS

# INDEX

# INDEX

# INDEX